Christian Perspectives
On Law Reform

Christian Perspectives On Law Reform

EDITED BY
Paul R. Beaumont
With a foreword by
Lord Mackay of Clashfern

paternoster
press

First published in 1998 by Paternoster Press

04 03 02 01 00 99 98   7 6 5 4 3 2 1

Paternoster Press is an imprint of Paternoster Publishing
P.O. Box 300, Carlisle, Cumbria CA3 0QS

British Library Cataloguing in Publication Data

A catalogue record for this book is available from the British Library.

ISBN 0-85364-852-2

This book is printed using Suffolk New Book paper which is 100% acid free.

Typeset by WestKey Ltd, Falmouth
Printed in Great Britain by Clays Ltd, St Ives House, London

For Catherine Beaumont

Contents

Contributors

Paul Beaumont, Professor of European Union and Private International Law, University of Aberdeen

Stephen Copp, Solicitor, Research Fellow and Director of the Centre for Taxation Research, Bournemouth University

David Harte, Barrister, Senior Lecturer in Law, University of Newcastle-Upon-Tyne

Lord Mackay of Clashfern, former Lord Chancellor, President of the Lawyers' Christian Fellowship

John Warwick Montgomery, Barrister, Emeritus Professor of Law and Humanities and Director of the Human Rights Centre, University of Luton, Professor of Apologetics and Law and Vice-President of Trinity College and Theological Seminary

Julian Rivers, Lecturer in Law, University of Bristol

Teresa Sutton, Solicitor, Senior Lecturer in Law, University of Westminster

Foreword

Right Honourable
The Lord MacKay of Clashfern

Secular law making and Christianity are not the most obvious companions. On a superficial level, the New Testament appears to reject legalism and to favour a personal morality based on grace and forgiveness.

The chapters of this book, which were originally talks given by their authors at a conference of the Lawyers' Christian Fellowship in September 1996, show how shallow that understanding is. Not only can the process of law reform in a modern secular democracy be informed by biblical perspectives, but there is also a great deal to be gained by considering our laws in this light.

I believe that our understanding of Christianity can also benefit from a rigorous consideration of the real problems faced by those who have to legislate for the circumstances in which we presently find ourselves. Sadly perhaps, the civil legislator cannot ignore the realities of the human condition, however far from the ideal it may be. The New Testament ethic of forgiveness, compassion and self-sacrificing love does not give any excuse to ignore current realities. On the contrary, it should be a very strong antidote to complacency and self-righteousness, and a reminder of how much the grace of which the New Testament speaks is required in our public life.

This book, then, represents an important contribution to the necessary dialogue between Christians and those concerned with law reform. Most of its contributors have a foot in each camp, as did I. To be in this situation can occasionally feel like being a 'house divided against itself', but I believe it to be a position from which the creative tension can be clearly observed. I congratulate Professor Beaumont and the University of Aberdeen on the production of this volume.

Introduction

Paul Beaumont

This book emerged from an idea I had a few years ago to try and get academic lawyers who shared a Christian faith to come together to discuss how their faith and work interrelate. At first I made a few tentative enquiries amongst some colleagues in the United Kingdom known to me. Although I received some constructive replies no clear pattern emerged as to how we might proceed. After leaving the matter dormant for some time I was prompted by some colleagues to attempt to organize a day conference and see what emerged. So with relatively little faith I decided to get the backing of the other members of the national committee of the Lawyers' Christian Fellowship (LCF), and organized a conference for the Friday of the LCF Annual Weekend Conference. So the first conference was arranged to be held at London Bible College on Friday 13 September 1996. To my surprise and encouragement I had more offers of papers for the conference than could be sensibly scheduled in the time available. This led me to think positively about making the conference an annual event and this was confirmed by those who attended the inaugural conference. Hence the second conference is scheduled for Friday 12 September 1997 at the University of Bristol.

The papers in this book all, bar one, began life as much shorter papers delivered at the Conference on 13th September 1996. The one exception is the chapter by Professor Montgomery which is the only paper previously published elsewhere, in an American journal which is not widely available in the UK, though it has been updated and amended for incorporation in this book. His paper replaces one given by Jean McHale, Lecturer in Law, University of Manchester, on 'The Decision to Withdraw Treatment — A Christian Perspective'. The other conference paper which does not appear in this volume was that given by Claire Archbold, Lecturer in Law, Queen's University, Belfast, entitled 'What God has joined together . . . ? Christian responses to the "new family" '. Unfortunately Jean and Claire were not in a position to be able to turn their conference papers into chapters in this book. Hopefully, the reader will find what remains to be sufficiently stimulating and challenging to justify the faith of the publisher in backing this endeavour.

Paternoster enthusiastically welcomed this book project, in particular their Publishing Manager, Jeremy Mudditt. The editor and chapter

writers are delighted that Lord Mackay of Clashfern has given his backing
to the project by writing the foreword to this book. He himself must be
categorized as a late twentieth-century Christian law reformer. He has
made many important changes during his tenure as Lord Chancellor,
including opening up rights of audience in the higher courts to solicitors
and radically reforming the divorce laws in England and Wales. He has
done this while making his own deep personal faith in the Lord Jesus
Christ widely known. He is respected within the legal profession as a
very able lawyer and a man of the highest integrity. Anyone who has had
the privilege of meeting him also knows him to be a man of humility.

All the contributors to this book have agreed that their royalties should
be paid to the Lawyers' Christian Fellowship. It is a diverse body of
around 1400 Christian lawyers in the United Kingdom of which nearly
half are solicitors, one fifth are law students, just under a tenth are
barristers/advocates, a twelfth are trainee solicitors, and the remainder are
judges, academics, legal executives, retired persons and others. The
organization was founded in 1852 and membership is open to everybody
involved in the practice, administration, teaching or study of the law who
accepts 'the principles of the Christian faith as taught in the Scriptures,
particularly faith in Jesus Christ as Saviour and Lord'. Therefore membership is open to Christians from all denominations. LCF has three main
objects:

1. To promote fellowship among Christians engaged in the legal
   profession.
2. To extend the kingdom of God, particularly in the legal profession.
3. To uphold Christian principles in the administration of the law.

The membership of LCF has grown significantly in recent years and its
capacity to fulfil its objects has been greatly strengthened by the administrative work of its secretary and treasurer in Glasgow, Alan and Joyce Holloway,
both Scottish solicitors, and by the various student and young lawyers
co-ordinators (SYLCs) it has appointed, currently an English barrister called
James Wakefield who is based in Nottingham. If as a result of reading this
book you wish to know more about the LCF then please contact:

Alan and Joyce Holloway
LCF Treasurer and Secretary
20 Waterside Drive
Mearns Park
Newton Mearns
Glasgow G77 6TL
Tel. 0141 616 0522

It must be stressed that the views of the writers of this book are purely
personal and in no way purport to be LCF policy. In relation to several
of these papers different positions are consistent with Christian belief, for
example on whether or not a bill of rights is desirable for the United
Kingdom.

This book is designed to help us develop a Christian mind rather than to prescribe specific solutions to complex problems as being necessarily the only Christian answer. John Stott regards the development of a Christian mind as a central part of the activity of preaching. He defines it as follows:

> The Christian mind (an expression popularized by Harry Blamires in his book of that title) is not a mind which is thinking about specifically Christian or even religious topics, but a mind which is thinking about everything, however apparently 'secular', and doing so 'Christianly' or within a Christian frame of reference. It is not a mind stuffed full with pat answers to every question, all neatly filed as in the memory bank of a computer; it is rather a mind which has absorbed biblical truths and Christian presuppositions so thoroughly that it is able to view every issue from a Christian perspective and so reach a Christian judgment about it.[1]

The development of a Christian mind among lawyers should include the consideration of the whole range of social and political issues encompassed within the framework of the law. If LCF members are to seriously try and 'uphold Christian principles in the administration of the law' they must think seriously about what the law ought to be and endeavour to influence the processes by which law is created and changed. It is not enough to be a good lawyer in the traditional sense, that is one who knows in great detail exactly what the law is, though we are unlikely to make much impact as law reformers if we fail to show we have an accurate appreciation of the current law. Inevitably Christians will not always agree on what the law ought to be but this should not deter us from trying to ascertain the relevant biblical principles and to apply them to our contemporary situation. John Stott has said:

> Although it is hardly the responsibility of a church or denomination as such to engage in direct political action, yet Christian individuals and Christian groups should be doing so, and should be encouraged from the pulpit to do so. For Christians should avoid the two opposite mistakes of laissez faire (making no Christian contribution to the nation's well-being) and imposition (trying to force a minority view on an unwilling majority, as with the American liquor laws during the Period of Prohibition).[2]

Christians need to bring the whole counsel of God to bear on their thinking and actions. It is very easy for Christians to have 'ethical blind spots'. Professor Montgomery points to examples of Christian people being involved in the extinction of the quagga and the passenger pigeon in the nineteenth century owing to a lack of thought about diversity of species and the need to be responsible stewards of God-given natural resources.[3]

[1] *I Believe in Preaching*, J. Stott (London, 1982) 170.
[2] *Ibid.*, 166.

The papers in this book reveal a number of reasons for arguing for a Christian perspective to be considered in making the law. The first two objects of the LCF can be fulfilled in doing so as well as the more obvious carrying out of the third one. We see in the example of William Wilberforce and his colleagues in the Clapham Sect as well as a number of the other 'team' law reformers mentioned in Chapter 1 the enhanced opportunity for fellowship that working together on a cause can bring. Would modern-day Christian lawyers (and indeed Christians in other walks of life) be in a more meaningful partnership together if they were engaged in concerted efforts to bring greater justice to the law? The kingdom of God can be extended by proclaiming the good news that man can be reconciled with God through the death of Jesus Christ on the cross. Any biblically-based proposals for law reform will explain the nature of the fall, man's rebellion against God, and the need for a new relationship with God to be established. The present mind-set of personal autonomy will have to be challenged. This can be seen in every chapter in this book. All of them appeal to biblical authority to derive the principles upon which their arguments are based. Chapter 3 stresses the opportunity to witness to the Christian faith in promoting environmental law reform; Chapter 1 highlights the fact that Christians who collaborate with non-Christians on law reform projects have an opportunity to share their faith with them; Chapters 2 and 4 both emphasize that individuals are not autonomous and Chapter 5 argues that good relationships should be at the heart of corporate governance.

Fundamentally Christians have a duty to look after the environment as stewards of God's creation and a duty to our fellow beings by modelling right relationships (as seen in the relationship between Christ and his heavenly father) in our relationships with God and other men and women. This affects our personal behaviour but should also impinge on the solutions we propose to the problems facing our society.

Apart from challenging Christian lawyers to engage in efforts to achieve law reform or preserve just laws it is hoped that the book will challenge non-Christian lawyers to think of the relevance and value of Christian principles to contemporary law. The book is designed to be helpful to Christians who are not lawyers but are concerned with the issues addressed in this book, the history of social reform, a bill of rights, the environment, euthanasia and the way companies are structured and managed. Other target audiences for the book include politicians and other policy-makers, academics and students (not just of the law but also of social history, environmental studies, medical ethics, constitutional reform and business/management studies).

3   Montgomery, J.W., 'Evangelical social responsibility in theological perspectives' in *Christians in the Public Square: Law, Gospel and Public Policy*, C.E.B. Cranfield, D. Kilgour and J.W. Montgomery, pp. 27, 32, 33 (Edmonton, 1996).

The editorial policy for this book was to submit each paper to an independent, anonymous, expert academic referee. The papers were subsequently amended in the light of the comments from the referee and myself as editor. In addition, the papers had already been read and commented on by other academics. I am very grateful to all who have commented on these papers in whatever capacity. The chapters were completed between September 1996 and May 1997 but it was possible for some minor amendments to be made at proof stage in September 1997.

It would be remiss of me not to thank two of my colleagues in the Faculty of Law, University of Aberdeen, Keith Wotherspoon and Dr. Roddy Paisley, for the assistance they provided in organizing the LCF academic conference at London Bible College and for continuing to assist me in managing the ongoing arrangements for future conferences; and the secretaries in the Faculty, Maureen Mercer and Amanda Walton, who have helped a great deal in the preparations for the conference and in the process of turning diverse scripts from five authors into a coherent format to be sent to the publisher.

The book is dedicated to my mother, Catherine Beaumont, who taught me to love the Lord Jesus when I was young and has never failed to provide a role model of real Christian service. I hope it will also be a source of encouragement and challenge to my nieces in the Law, Emma, Kirsten and Sarah. My thanks go to my wife Marion and my two children David and Anna for continuing to provide me with love and security.

Finally, the LCF text seems like a good place to end this introduction and begin the book: 'What does the Lord require of you, but to do justice, to love kindness, and to walk humbly with your God' (Micah 6:8).

1

Christians as Law Reformers in the Nineteenth and Twentieth Centuries

Teresa Sutton

I. INTRODUCTION

Interest in substantive law reform on the part of Christians is by no means a recent phenomenon. This chapter focuses on the nineteenth and twentieth centuries. It is plain that Christians have been involved in seeking justice through reform on both an individual and collective basis throughout this period. Historical analysis of some examples of such work has a contribution to make to any discussion about the ways in which Christians might wish to continue and develop such efforts in the twenty-first century. This chapter seeks to consider some examples of the strengths and the weaknesses of some past contributions. It will present participation in law reform as a type of Christian service and consider how the achievements and frustrations of past Christian law reformers may both inform and encourage today.

The following pages include a variety of law reforms and reformers. In each generation there are lawyers and judges whose faith is clearly the strength for their work. This chapter seeks to go beyond the development of legal principles and procedures and consider law reform in its widest possible context, including both changes to contemporary laws and calls for the introduction of new laws to deal with perceived injustices. In doing so it focuses on work towards social reform necessitating changes to the law. Sometimes particular reforms have been advocated by one or more of the Christian churches as a body. More often efforts have been driven by individuals or groups of individuals who profess a Christian faith. In the examples used commitment to Christianity and Christian, rather than mere moral, values have been cited as a driving force for the work.

II. THE BIBLICAL CALL FOR JUSTICE

The Bible is concerned with justice and justification on a number of levels. Isaiah 30:18 proclaims that the 'Lord is a God of justice'.[1] In Deuteronomy his justice is made plain:

[1] All quotations are from the New International Version of the Bible unless otherwise stated.

I will proclaim the name of the Lord.
   Oh, praise the greatness of our God!
He is the Rock, his words are perfect,
   and his ways are just.
A faithful God who does no wrong,
   upright and just is he. (Deuteronomy 32:3, 4)

Jesus, as God's chosen servant, came to fulfil the words spoken through Isaiah:

I will put my Spirit on him,
   and he will proclaim justice to the nations.
He will not quarrel or cry out;
   no-one will hear his voice in the streets.
A bruised reed he will not break,
   and a smouldering wick he will not snuff out,
till he leads justice to victory. (Matthew 12:18–21, Isaiah 42:1–4)

In turn the death of Jesus on the cross is described in terms of justification: 'He was delivered over to death for our sins and was raised to life for our justification' (Romans 4:25), ultimately offering salvation: '. . . having been justified by his grace, we might become heirs having the hope of eternal life' (Titus 3:7).

   The Bible also calls for justice in this world. In the Old Testament this includes demands for justice to be provided by rulers:

Woe to those who make unjust laws,
   to those who issue oppressive decrees,
to deprive the poor of their rights
   and withhold justice from the oppressed of my people. (Isaiah 10:1, 2a).

It also includes calls for justice on a more general level such as in the Psalms: 'For the Lord is righteous, he loves justice' (Psalms 11:7); 'Blessed are they who maintain justice, who constantly do what is right' (Psalms 106:3) and Proverbs: 'The righteous care about justice for the poor, but the wicked have no such concern' (Proverbs 29:7). Hearers are told to look for justice:

Stop doing wrong, learn to do right!
   Seek justice, encourage the oppressed. (Isaiah 1:16, 17)

Hate evil, love good;
   maintain justice in the courts. (Amos 5:15)

This is what the Lord Almighty says: 'Administer true justice; show mercy and compassion to one another.' (Zechariah 7:8, 9)

In the New Testament there is a continued concern with justice but this is expressed in different ways. We are told: 'Blessed are those who hunger and thirst for righteousness, for they will be filled' (Matthew 5:6). We see the Pharisees being reprimanded for their lack of interest in justice: 'But you have neglected the more important matters of the law — justice, mercy and faithfulness' (Matthew 23:23, Luke 11:42). However, the main emphasis is upon justice in terms of loving a neighbour. On ten occasions we are told to love our neighbour and the supreme importance of this commandment is emphasized. The rule to 'love your neighbour as yourself' is described as a summary of the other commandments (Romans 13:9, 10). It is envisaged that the rule will be applied on a personal level:

'The entire law is summed up in a single command: "Love your neighbour as yourself." If you keep on biting and devouring each other, watch out or you will be destroyed by each other' (Galatians 5:14, 15).

III. APPLICATION OF THE BIBLICAL CALL FOR JUSTICE

The Bible may be said to call us to recognize and love God as a just God, and flowing from that to seek justice and to love other people on a personal level as a result of our faith. Some would go further and suggest that a duty to love others can extend to acts directed towards seeking corporate change and that the call is to be seeking righteousness at both a personal level and a wider level. Bishop David Sheppard has suggested that the Gospel is concerned with changing 'social structures' as well as the hearts of people.[2] Writing about recent reforms to family law, Lord Mackay has observed that those with a faith cannot fence off their religion from other areas of life, including politics.[3] For some Christians this may include seeking substantive law reform.

Some Christians have viewed the late twentieth century as experiencing a revival of Christian interest in social and economic issues, both on a practical level and in terms of seeking fundamental change. The lobbying activities of the Churches Commission for Racial Justice, the Evangelical Alliance (and its member societies such as Care and Jubilee) and the Movement for Christian Democracy are but three examples of important and relevant efforts. One aspect of the work of the Churches Commission for Racial Justice has been to challenge perceived injustices in immigration law over the last thirty years. This has been through a variety of means including practical advice and assistance, high profile lobbying, publicity about those facing deportation and specific proposals for reform such as the amnesty proposal in 1993/4 intended for those who had been in Britain for more than five years with a child over two

[2] Bishop David Sheppard, foreword to D. Haslam, *Race for the Millennium*, (London, 1996), xi.

[3] The Rt. Hon. Lord Mackay of Clashfern, 'Family Law Reform', *Law and Justice*, 128/129 (1996), 5.

born and brought up here.[4] The work of the Evangelical Alliance includes lobbying Parliament on appropriate law reform issues, providing information for Christians on current debates and putting forward an evangelical viewpoint to the press.[5] Recent work on the part of the Movement for Christian Democracy has included conducting a survey of parliamentary candidates' views on a range of law reform issues including constitutional reform, abortion, euthanasia and world debt.[6]

Whilst evangelical Christians have been particularly conscious of a renewal of interest in seeking justice and of the need to develop such work further[7] they have not been alone in their concerns. It has been suggested that the 1985 report by a Commission on Urban Priority Areas, *Faith in the City*, set up by the then Archbishop of Canterbury, could be seen as a recent product of Christian socialism. As well as calling for practical change in the inner cities, it also observed the need for contributions from Christians at a national and local level on relevant contemporary issues.[8] More recently *The Common Good* paper published by the Roman Catholic Bishops' Conference has challenged Christians to reconsider how they are applying their faith in practice. There has been enormous interest in the paper.[9] In the introduction to *The Common Good*, Cardinal Basil Hume observes that:

> Discipleship involves seeking God in this world, as well as preparing to meet Him in the next. The Gospel imperative to love our neighbour entails not only that we should help those in need, but also address the causes of destitution and poverty. The deepening of the spiritual life must go hand-in-hand with practical concern for our neighbour, and thus with social action.

The paper urges Christians to 'claim whatever rights and opportunities are available' to 'exercise an influence on behalf of whatever we believe to be true and good' and in particular on behalf of the disadvantaged. It is suggested that evangelization, the 'spreading' of the 'message of salvation', includes both 'transformation of an unjust social order' and the denouncing of injustices.[10] This could quite conceivably include promoting law reform where necessary. Further contemporary com-

---

[4] Haslam, *Race for the Millennium*.

[5] *Called to One Hope, 150 Years of the Evangelical Alliance*, (London, 1996), 7.

[6] *The Christian Democrat*, February 1997, 4.

[7] On this area generally: P. Dixon, *Out of the Ghetto and Into the City, A Radical Call to Social Action*, (Esher, 1995), J. Wolffe (ed.), *Evangelical Faith and Public Zeal, Evangelicals and Society in Britain 1780–1980*, (London, 1995).

[8] B.G. Worrall, *The Making of the Modern Church. Christianity in England Since 1800*, 2nd ed. (London, 1993), 320, 321.

[9] *Christian Democrat*, February 1997, 8, reports that more than 45,000 copies have been sold.

[10] *The Common Good and the Catholic Church's Social Teaching. A Statement by the Catholic Bishop's Conference of England and Wales*, (London, 1996), 1, 7, 11.

ment is provided in the Church of England's paper 'The Churches' Enquiry into Unemployment and the Future of Work' published early in 1997.

Unfortunately renewed interest on the part of Christians in influencing reform has sometimes led to implied criticism of perceived inactivity in the past. Such suggestions can be misleading. Commenting in the particular context of the Anglican Church, Norman has observed the tendency of new generations of Christians to appear to believe that they are the first to formulate proper social policies.[11] *The Common Good* is at pains to emphasize the continuity of interest within the Roman Catholic Church on the issue of social justice. In fact individuals from all denominations can be seen to have had a continuing interest in social justice and through that in law reform throughout the nineteenth and twentieth centuries.[12]

The Free Churches and the Roman Catholic Church had some familiarity with nineteenth century law reform through their efforts to secure equal religious freedoms.[13] What has varied is how that interest has been applied in practice. Differing responses have been dictated by a number of factors, the most important of which have been choices made about priority and means. Law reform can appear low on a list of Christian priorities.

One of the key issues that seems to have dictated the amount of time Christians have devoted to substantive reform appears to be how they have personally or as part of a church reconciled the need to spread the word of the Gospel and the need to serve others. For some the priority has always been to spread the word of the Gospel with a belief that an individual's circumstances would change as a result of personal conversion.[14] Even where Christians have recognized actual law reform as a priority, there have been further difficulties over the appropriate means by which to bring such changes about. For some the directions on authority from the Bible, for example that 'Everyone must submit himself to the governing authorities, for there is no other authority except that which God has established' (Romans 13:1) and 'Give to Caesar what is Caesar's, and to God what is God's' (Matthew 22:21) have been a

---

[11] E.R. Norman, *Church and Society in England 1770–1970*, (Oxford, 1976), 4.

[12] Norman, *Church and Society 1770–1950* is an account of the Church of England and social and economic teaching. Others texts provide accounts for other denominations for example, K.S. Inglis, 'English Nonconformity and Social Reform, 1880–1900', (1958) 13, *Past and Present*, 73–86.

[13] Worrall, *The Making of the Modern Church*, chapters 8 and 9. Edward Miall's work to promote disestablishment and the Liberation Society is a particular example, Worrall, *The Making of the Modern Church*, 145.

[14] Worrall, *The Making of the Modern Church*, 41. Also more generally, D. Bebbington, 'The Decline and Resurgence of Evangelical Social Concern', in Wollfe (ed.), *Evangelical Faith and Public Zeal*, 175–197.

difficulty.[15] For others the delicate relationship between the Established Church and the State has brought about a reticence to be seen to be involved in law reform that might be interpreted as a political statement. The very recent debate over *The Common Good* and the previous debate over *Faith in the City* are but two examples of the manner in which a Christian contribution to debate which is relevant to law reform can be interpreted adversely as unmerited church involvement in politics (or in the words of the headline of *The Independent*: 'What gives bishops the right to tell us how to vote?').[16]

In practice Christians who have believed themselves called to work towards law reform have found a variety of practical methods to facilitate their efforts in seeking justice. As the following sections review some nineteenth- and early twentieth-century examples of Christian law reformers a range of models will be observed including open political campaigning in parliament; campaign work within pressure groups; individual research which has educated the churches and the public and charitable work which has brought injustices into view. Just as Paul observes that the church itself is to be made up of many parts, each called to a different function,[17] so we can expect God to use a variety of people in a range of different ways to work within a particular area such as law reform. In the same way the biblical pattern of God using unlikely people and equipping them for his service; of God using combinations of people over time to achieve his ends and of God working in his own time and not in ours, will be seen to be just as relevant to work in the context of law reform as in any other area of Christian service.

The areas chosen for discussion below are by no means exhaustive — a comprehensive analysis covering all Christian input into law reform in this period would be beyond the scope of this chapter — and are of course in addition to the continual reforming work which has been carried out by lawyers and judges within the legal system on a day-to-day basis. By choice the examples focus on law reform concerning social issues, particularly those concerning human dignity. Inevitably they generally focus on the examples of work of some individuals who have been open about their Christianity and who have been comfortable in publicly discussing their work in such terms. Most of the older literature about such individuals is unashamedly biased in promoting their achievements. It is particularly so where it has been written by other Christians or, as was often the case, by subsequent members of the individual's family. In

---

15   For discussion see D. Harte, 'How Christian is the Law?' in J. Cundy (ed.), *Law: Some Christian Perspectives*, (Leicester, 1988), 16–19. Harte also observes that secular law is inevitably defective because of the sinful state of man which it is trying to deal with.

16   'What gives bishops the right to tell us how to vote?' *The Independent*, 21.10.96.

17   Romans 12:4–6.

recent years historians have moved away from a heroic approach when considering these periods, preferring instead to look at reforms in a much wider context including social, economic and political factors. As this chapter is an analysis of some instances where Christians have chosen to be involved in law reform as Christian service, it appears appropriate to retain a focus upon individuals. Ultimately Christianity is about a personal response to the Gospel, and choices and conviction about Christian service are personal matters too. A consideration of responses to the call for justice cannot ignore individual interpretations of the past.

Wilberforce and the abolition of slavery

If one name is synonymous with Christian law reform and justice it is that of Wilberforce. Those writing of a revival of interest in social issues in the late twentieth century have often harked back to his efforts and those of the Earl of Shaftesbury in the nineteenth century. Wilberforce's anti-slavery campaign began in the late 1780s but it was only in 1807 that legislation was passed abolishing the British slave trades and the emancipation of slaves in the British Empire did not occur until the 1830s.[18] Like many of the other Christians who have found themselves called to seek justice through law reform, Wilberforce was an unlikely candidate for his particular cause. He was born into a wealthy merchant family in Hull in 1759 and from this background was able to achieve election to parliament at an early age in 1780. His character and his connections, including his friendship with Pitt, suggested a very different path to that of slavery abolitionist. It seems that Wilberforce did have some sort of Christian belief or interest at stages in his childhood, but it was at the age of twenty-six that he was converted. In time he found himself at home within the evangelical tradition of the Anglican Church.

Some writers (particularly ones writing from a Christian perspective) have been very kind to Wilberforce: 'Wilberforce lived that higher statesmanship which consists in serving not his own interest but his God's. His obedience to what he believed to be the Will of God brought freedom to millions.'[19] Others have been, perhaps unreasonably, far less complimentary about Wilberforce and the Clapham Sect as a whole, condemning them for their lack of interest in law reform concerning the oppressed at home. Whatever the subsequent analysis of their work, it is plain that Wilberforce and his colleagues had a clear Christian commitment and that this was the foundation for their work. On Sunday 28th October 1787 Wilberforce wrote in his diary that God had given him the task of surpressing the slave trade.[20] The suppression of the slave trade was by

---

[18] Abolition of the Slave Trade 1807 47 Geo III sess. i., c. 36. Slavery Abolition Act 1833 3, 4 Will IV c. 73. Whilst Wilberforce's work was begun in the eighteenth century it seems reasonable to include him in this chapter as little was achieved prior to the nineteenth century.

[19] G. Lean, *God's Politician, William Wilberforce's Struggle*, (London, 1980), 172.

[20] J. Pollock, *William Wilberforce*, (London, 1977), 69.

no means a new objective for Christian reformers. There had been challenges to the trade since at least the late seventeenth century from both Anglicans and Nonconformists. Pressure for abolition had mounted during the later eighteenth century and the Quakers had been particularly active in promoting reform. The 1772 court victory concerning slavery in Britain,[21] the Quaker committee for the relief and liberation of slaves and for the discouragement of the slave trade and Thomas Clarkson's research endeavours were all major factors.[22] By the late eighteenth century the need was for a parliamentary figurehead to introduce and promote abolitionist legislation in the House of Commons. Howse has described it as a need for a person who would both impress the House and compel it into action.[23] It was for this role that Wilberforce found himself called and equipped.

It appears that Wilberforce expected imminent success on a national or an international level fairly soon after he took up the cause. In January 1788 he wrote to William Eden: 'Assure yourself that there is no doubt of our success.'[24] However, such quick progress was not to be. A combination of political, social and economic factors (including the French Revolution) conspired to postpone progress for nearly twenty years. Wilberforce's concerted efforts during this period were at great personal cost. His health, which was already poor, suffered and it seems he developed a dependence upon the opium he was given for medicinal purposes. His clear conviction about the work he was supposed to accomplish sometimes brought him guilt about his lack of progress rather than comfort about what could be expected in the future. Wilberforce had to be patient and persistent. In the 1820s he was forced to hand on the work of the cause to another member of parliament, Thomas Fowell Buxton, who coincidentally had been born at the time that Wilberforce had originally taken up the crusade.[25] Finally, in 1833 the Abolition of Slavery Bill was passed by the House of Commons shortly before Wilberforce's death.

Whilst it is Wilberforce's name that will be linked with the abolition of slavery for evermore, it is important to acknowledge that recent research has demonstrated that Wilberforce's work should be regarded as just one factor in the movement that brought about the eventual law reform. Whilst Wilberforce was an important 'figurehead', he received much help and assistance from his Christian group of friends and colleagues, the so-called 'Clapham Sect'. There is no doubt that the group as a whole made a significant contribution to the abolition movement.

[21] *R. v. Knowles, ex parte, Somerset* (1772) 20 State. Tr 1.
[22] Lean, *God's Politician*, 8.
[23] E.M. Howse, *Saints in Politics, the Clapham Sect and the Growth of Freedom*, (Toronto, 1952), 11.
[24] Pollock, *William Wilberforce*, 75.
[25] Howse, *Saints in Politics*, 19.

Much more importantly, on a wider level and divorced from any religious commitment or motivation, a host of other people supported the reforms as a political issue. Public opinion was galvanized. Recent historical research on the subject of the movement has emphasized the need to consider the abolition in the 'wider world of contemporary and radical politics'.[26] Perhaps Wilberforce's experiences suggest that law reformers driven by conviction should expect to see their work accomplished in God's time and not necessarily in their own, and that in the achievement of their ultimate goal they may need to expect to work with others who seek the same result but for differing motives.

Shaftesbury and working conditions

Wilberforce's faith and achievements are often compared to those of Anthony Ashley-Cooper, Seventh Earl of Shaftesbury.[27] Shaftesbury may also be described as a legal reformer in the sense that he was a parliamentary representative for a variety of causes. Once again he has been showered with praise from some quarters: 'An awakened public conscience, if it is not to spend itself in futile emotion, must find a channel of expression. Shaftesbury taught it to speak with the voice of law . . .'[28] There are many similarities between the examples of Wilberforce and Shaftesbury as Christian law reformers. Shaftesbury was also born into a wealthy family, albeit a landed aristocratic family in 1801. His family's wealth and status also enabled him to be elected to parliament at a young age. If such matters can be judged, Shaftesbury's childhood experience of Christianity appears to have been stronger than that of Wilberforce, but again his faith was to deepen later in life and again he was to find himself comfortable within the evangelical tradition of the Anglican Church. As with Wilberforce, in his early years in parliament Shaftesbury appeared destined for an ambitious political career. Instead of achieving high office he became associated with and represented a whole range of reforming causes in the pursuance of justice including those calling for changes to working hours and conditions, measures protecting the mentally ill and public health issues. In terms of his own commitment to law reform, Shaftesbury seems to have viewed his time and abilities in terms of Christian stewardship.

[26] D. Eltis and J. Walvin (eds.), *The Abolition of the Atlantic Slave Trade*, (Madison, 1981), D. Hempton, 'Evangelicalism and Reform, c. 1780–1832', in Wolffe (ed.), *Evangelical Faith and Public Zeal*.

[27] Factual biographical material about Shaftesbury is drawn mainly from; G. Battiscombe, *Shaftesbury a Biography of the Seventh Earl 1801–1885*, (London, 1974), J. Pollock, *The Poor Man's Earl, Shaftesbury*, (London, 1985) and C. Smith, 'Anthony Ashley Cooper, Seventh Earl of Shaftesbury (1801–85), in H. Martin (ed.), *Christian Social Reformers of the Nineteenth Century*, 2nd ed., (Rochester, 1933).

[28] Smith, 'Anthony Ashley Cooper', 107.

On the priority issue Shaftesbury's key objective was evangelism but he saw certain social reforms as a prerequisite, believing that circumstances and hardship could impair a person finding faith. In some ways this explains the variety of causes with which he identified. It has also been suggested that Shaftesbury's belief in the imminence of the Second Coming, limiting the time available to save souls was an additional impetus for his work.[29] As with Wilberforce, Shaftesbury was an unlikely candidate to be a major law reformer. He has been described as 'a highly-strung introvert whose precarious balance of mind hung upon a thread' with an inclination towards manic-depression.[30] Christian writers making every effort to praise his achievements have acknowledged significant weaknesses: 'Ashley had very little insight and no tact; and he was not a leader, except of forlorn hopes which had a curious way of being successful at last.'[31] His diaries reveal that he too struggled mentally and physically with the burdens of the work he undertook and his struggles impacted upon his faith. One biographer quotes a line from his diary for March 1842 which asks: 'Where is the faith which can move mountains? I have a whole range before me.'[32]

As with Wilberforce, some of Shaftesbury's mountains did take a long time to move. His work with the Ten Hours Movement is a good example of this. Shaftesbury was first approached on the matter of working hours for factory children in 1833.[33] The Movement calling for a reduction of the working hours to ten (which would in practice result in a reduction in hours for all workers) was already well under way led by two conservative evangelicals, Richard Oastler and Michael Sadler. It has been suggested that there were three types of 'wickedness' which stirred evangelicals into political action in the nineteenth century. The Ten Hours Movement and the anti-slavery movement have been described as falling into the first category, that of 'obstacles' to the spread of the Gospel, preventing people from having the opportunity to hear the Christian message.[34] In 1832 Sadler lost his seat in parliament and the movement needed a new parliamentary figurehead or voice. Shaftesbury was approached and asked to take on the role. There is some dispute about how far up the list of possible candidates he was, but whether he was asked first or last what does appear plain is that he only ended up

---

[29] Battiscombe, *Shaftesbury*, 102.

[30] Battiscombe, *Shaftesbury*, 94.

[31] Smith, 'Anthony Ashley Cooper', 83.

[32] Battiscombe, *Shaftesbury*, 74.

[33] For a general account of the progress of the factory legislation: W.R. Cornish and G. de N. Clark, *Law and Society in England 1750–1950*, (London, 1989), 301–308.

[34] D.W. Bebbington, *Evangelicalism in Modern Britain, A History from the 1730s to the 1980s*, (London, 1989), 132–135. The other two categories were sins and matters perceived as substitutes for the Gospel.

with the role because of a lack of other suitable candidates. He did not have a particular interest in the issue and he had never had reason to visit such factories. Like Wilberforce he proved willing to adopt a potentially unrewarding and unpopular cause. In 1833 Shaftesbury introduced a new version of the bill that Sadler had been promoting. The matter was referred to a Royal Commission. The Commission did agree on the need for legislation, which was a step forward, but not on the detail of Shaftesbury's suggestions. The resulting Act[35] was a disappointment to both the Ten Hours Movement and the factory owners. The new controls were limited to a fairly narrow range of industries. They prohibited children under nine from working at all. Children between nine and thirteen were restricted to nine hours per day and a week of forty-eight hours and those between thirteen and eighteen to a day of twelve hours and a week of sixty-nine hours. In practice this permitted the continuance of a 'relay' system of working within the factories. Manufacturers questioned the practicality of the measures and a series of disputes about the enforcement of the Act began.

Shaftesbury worked on patiently, trying without much success to extend the unsatisfactory Act to other industries beyond textiles and highlighting the plight of other employees such as women and children working in the mines. Shaftesbury made other attempts to introduce a ten hours bill but it was only after he had resigned his seat (over the issue of the Corn Laws), and temporarily handed over responsibility for the cause in parliament to John Fielden that a ten hours measure for young people and women was finally passed in 1847.[36] Shaftesbury had worked towards this end for a number of years but the final achievement was not to be his. However, he was returned to the House as a member for Bath in time to be fully involved in the controversy over the application of the Act in practice and the necessary statutory amendments. Manufacturers took advantage of the wording of the statute to circumvent the true intention of the Act, for example by using 'false relays' making workers take breaks at the employers' convenience.[37] Shaftesbury and the remainder of the Ten Hours Movement were dismayed but their instincts as to how to deal with the situation differed and led to severe rifts between them. In 1850 Shaftesbury advised acceptance of and supported a compromise which permitted extension of hours to ten and a half in return for other concessions, including the abolition of relays.

The Ten Hours Movement broke with him, bitterly condemned him and found a new parliamentary voice. The situation was made worse by the fact that in practice these 'compromise' provisions were ultimately restricted to women and young persons. As there was no application to children, it was still possible to use relays of working children to enable

---

[35] Factories Act 1833 3 & 4 Will IV, c.103.

[36] Factories Act 1847 10 & 11 Vict c.29.

[37] *Ryder v Mills* (1850) 3 Ex. 853.

adult males to work much longer hours.[38] In time this defect was remedied by others. The progress of factory regulation continued and Shaftesbury lived to see further substantial steps forward in the 1860s and 1870s, but on a personal level he had made his contribution.

Shaftesbury's involvement in factory regulation is another example of the patience and persistence needed by Christians seeking law reform and of the need to work with others. Progress of any law reform can be tedious. Whilst his work in this particular area of factory regulation was at the very least frustrating, in other areas Shaftesbury did experience much swifter success. Battiscombe has observed that whilst it took fourteen years for a ten hours bill to become law, the Mines Bill took merely as many weeks to pass through parliament.[39] Shaftesbury's experience is also interesting in demonstrating that Christians will not always be in agreement on the means for reform or indeed on occasions with the actual need for particular reforms. One of Shaftesbury's contemporaries, John Bright, appears to have been a sincere and committed Christian devoted to promoting a whole range of reforms through parliament which he believed to be necessary. Nevertheless, he and Shaftesbury found their views to be incompatible. To take one example, the repeal of the Corn Laws, some of Bright's arguments for the repeal were expressed on a biblical basis. Briggs records Bright's comment: 'You find it in Holy Writ that the Earth is the Lord's, and the fullness thereof. We have put Holy Writ into an Act of Parliament.'[40] Whilst Shaftesbury saw the factory acts as addressing prevalent needs, Bright opposed them and promoted free trade as an alternative answer. The personal circumstances and background of the two individuals has been used as an explanation of the different approaches.[41] However, the troubling fact remains that they both categorically but genuinely believed they were called to obtain opposite results.

Whilst Wilberforce and Shaftesbury were called to serve in unlikely causes they were originally 'establishment' figures. They were the type of people who might have been expected to have been involved in parliamentary matters at that time. However, as the discussion of the biblical call to justice earlier in the chapter has shown the call is addressed to all Christians although it may be interpreted in different ways. A privileged background has not been a requirement for Christian involvement in law reform. William Booth, founder of the Salvation Army, had firsthand experience of some of the practical problems in society which needed addressing. Owing to difficult family circumstances he had been forced to leave school at the age of thirteen and was apprenticed to a

---

[38]   Factories Act 1850 13 & 14 Vict c.54.

[39]   Battiscombe, *Shaftesbury*, 148.

[40]   A. Briggs, *Victorian People. A Reassessment of Persons and Themes 1851–67*, (Middlesex, 1965), 211.

[41]   Battiscombe, *Shaftesbury*, 155–158.

pawnbroker prior to his conversion in 1844.[42] Keir Hardie's background was far removed from the wealth of Wilberforce and Shaftesbury and his political outlook was completely different, yet he too claimed that Christianity was the driving force for his work. This work included the promoting of employment law reform and women's suffrage in addition to his pivotal role within Christian Socialism.[43]

Elizabeth Fry and prison reform

One woman who found herself in a situation where her charitable work drew her into seeking more substantive legal reform was Elizabeth Fry. Fry's charitable work was extensive and varied, but it was her involvement in prison visiting which drew her into the arena of law reformers early in the nineteenth century. Fry was born into a wealthy Quaker family in 1780 and remained a member of the Society of Friends all her life. Once again her faith appears to have been the driving force for her work. She believed that she was spreading the Gospel through her work in a practical way which gave people the opportunity to respond on a personal level. Fry was not without other commitments, including obligations to her family of eleven children and to her family's business interests. Nevertheless, her prison visiting began at Newgate in 1813 and she continued to work on behalf of prisoners, particularly female prisoners, for nearly forty years. In time, in addition to the actual visiting, Fry and her co-workers called for a variety of reforms including improved supervision of female prisoners, better religious instruction, activities and occupations for prisoners, improved inspection, classification of prisoners and more organized provision for transportation. Their interference was not always welcomed. In 1821 one sheriff expressed his views about the boundaries of their work which included them doing 'nothing to unsure existing laws'.[44] Fry did not work alone. Her efforts were part of a wider movement, including the British Ladies' Society for Promoting the Reformation of Female Prisoners, which she formed in 1821.[45] The movement contributed to discussion of law reform in this area in the early nineteenth century and Fry was the first woman ever to give evidence to a parliamentary committee.[46]

Some of Fry's objectives were accomplished. Peel's Gaols Act of 1823 made provision, inter alia, for classification of prisoners, for improvements

---

[42] Worrall, *The Making of the Modern Church*, 237.

[43] C. Bryant, *Possible Dreams, A Personal History of the British Christian Socialists*, (London, 1996), 122–128.

[44] A. Summers, ' "In a few years we shall none of us that now take care of them be here": Philanthropy and the State in the Thinking of Elizabeth Fry', (1994) 67 *Institute of Historical Research Bulletin*, No. 163, 138.

[45] The movement included women from all Protestant churches.

[46] H. McLeod, *Religion and Society in England, 1850–1914*, (London, 1996), 164.

in occupations and for supervision of prisoners. In 1835 a further statute appointed Home Office Inspectors of Prisons. Ultimately all prisons were placed under the authority of the Home Office's representative commissioners.[47] Once again the campaigning was not without controversy. Some of Fry's practical work in prisons was criticized in the first Report of the Inspectors of Prisons for the Home District in 1836 as being inappropriate.[48] Fry's beliefs about the purpose of imprisonment and the changes in character that imprisonment was supposed to bring about sometimes brought conflict, including disagreements in approaches with other Christian reformers.[49]

Aside from these conflicts, Fry's work is also a useful illustration of God using a series of people to carry out reforms in a particular area. Her prison reform work may be seen as a continuation of work begun by reformers such as John Howard and was in turn continued by individuals and organizations such as the Howard Association (now the Howard League).[50] In addition the achievements of women such as Elizabeth Fry proved to be an encouragement for other women to become involved in law reform work.[51]

Whilst Wilberforce and Shaftesbury might be said to have been primarily 'figurehead' law reformers and Fry was primarily a charitable worker drawn into law reform, there have also existed some Christian law reformers who were primarily campaigners for justice through research. They have introduced accurate information about perceived injustices into the public arena thereby providing the impetus for reform. In the late twentieth century such a role may be all the more important bearing in mind the complexity of some of the contemporary issues that are being dealt with both in the courts and in parliament. Some of William Booth's practical work and his book *In Darkest England and the Way Out*, published in 1890 with W.T. Stead, might be viewed as publicizing the need for reform. Two other individuals who might be said to have worked in this way and may therefore be labelled law reformers are Benjamin Seebohm Rowntree, son of Joseph Rowntree, and Eric Roy Calvert.[52]

[47]   Gaols Act 1823 4 Geo IV c.64, Prisons Act 1835 5, 6 Will IV c.38, Cornish and Clark, *Law and Society in England 1750–1950*, 578–585, A.H. Manchester, *Modern Legal History*, (London, 1980), 254, 355.

[48]   Summers, 'Philanthropy and the State in the Thinking of Elizabeth Fry', 138.

[49]   Cornish and Clark, *Law and Society in England 1750–1950*, 580–585.

[50]   Heasman, *Evangelicals in Action*, Chapter Five.

[51]   For example in the 1870s and 1880s Josephine Butler was involved in leading the campaign for the repeal of the Contagious Diseases Acts; H. McLeod, *Religion and Society in England, 1850–1914*, 134–136. Worrall, *The Making of the Modern Church*, 148 discusses the influence of the 'Nonconformist conscience' on this work.

[52]   Further similar examples are easily identifiable such as Hugh Price Hughes, founder of the *Methodist Times*, McLeod, *Religion and Society in England*, 136.

Seebohm Rowntree and poverty

Rowntree was basically a very successful Quaker businessman whose main concerns were in the fields of commerce, social organization and the relationship of Christianity to industrial relations. He showed a particular concern for the problems of low wages and security of employment. It appears that his own Christian commitment informed and directed his work. Speaking about his book *Poverty, A Study of Town Life*[53] in 1901, Rowntree's opinion was that 'our duty as a church is not to enact social legislation — *or as a church* to ally ourselves with any political party — but . . . to strive to inspire our members with a *love* so real and so deep that it cannot rest while so much sorrow and injustice and misery remain in our midst.'[54]

Further confirmation of the strong connection between Rowntree's faith and his work is to be found in the series of tributes published after his death. These include observations on his work and his faith: 'He had a faith; and he believed that this faith should show itself in works. He had high ideals; but he seemed almost a little afraid . . . that idealism might run to seed, unless linked with practical social purpose.'[55]

The 'practical social purpose' which is most relevant for a consideration of law reform is to be found in the aforementioned book *Poverty, A Study of Town Life*. The book may be seen as an example of information and research contributing to substantive law reform. *Poverty* included the results and analysis of the finances of some eleven and a half thousand families in York from 1899. The research methods used were stringent and the book's value was in providing accurate factual information. In particular, new ground was broken by distinguishing between 'primary' poverty and 'secondary' poverty. Rowntree showed that nearly 10 per cent of families in York were living in primary poverty. This meant that the income reaching the family was not enough to pay for the 'bare necessities of physical efficiency', however carefully expenditure was planned. Another 18 per cent were in secondary poverty. They were in severe financial difficulties but their circumstances might be brought above Rowntree's modest poverty line by different patterns of spending.[56] Rowntree argued that the conclusions of the study pointed towards the need for new agencies to relieve existing poverty and for changes to existing laws to enable poverty to be tackled. Rowntree's provision of indisputable factual information can be seen to be a force which changed attitudes to poverty. Briggs observes that this included changes to the

---

[53] B.S. Rowntree, *Poverty, A Study of Town Life*, (1901).

[54] Lecture Notes of 24.12.01, as cited by A. Briggs, *Social Thought and Social Action: A Study of the Work of Seebohm Rowntree, 1871–1954*, (London, 1961), 78.

[55] Rowntree and Co, *B. Seebohm Rowntree 1871–1954, A Tribute to the Life and Work of B. Seebohm Rowntree*, (York, 1954), 13.

[56] Briggs, *Social Thought and Social Action*, 33, 34.

attitudes of 'religious reformers', some of whom had held unrealistic perceptions of the reality and causes of poverty.[57] On a wider scale, Rowntree's research ultimately fed into the movement seeking major new forms of poor relief and new welfare measures. Rowntree's contribution to the reforms which introduced the beginnings of the welfare state may have been overstated by some[58] or might have been viewed too optimistically,[59] but it was certainly of significance in highlighting the need for reform. His contribution should be viewed in the context of the wider contribution made by the Free Churches to the early welfare state through involvement in politics. Key legislation such as the Old Age Pensions Act (1908) and the National Insurance Act (1911) were passed at the time when Free Church representation in parliament was at its height.[60]

Calvert and the abolition of capital punishment

The lengthy movement for the reduction and abolition of capital punishment has been well documented.[61] Christians have participated in the debate on both sides and of all the areas discussed in this chapter it is probably the best example of disagreement on the need for reform. Christians have felt drawn both to oppose capital punishment and to support it in the name of justice. Recent research has argued that the church's role in the movement for the abolition of the death penalty was ambiguous, reflecting the division of Christian opinion on the subject. It has been suggested that the death penalty would not have survived for as long as it did without some religious endorsement; that the church decided to follow rather than direct public opinion on the matter and that ultimately abolition was a result of ongoing campaigning by individuals rather than through any efforts by the churches. Amongst the many who contributed to the abolition, one example of a Christian seeking law reform by changing attitudes through information is Calvert.[62] Again with Calvert, as with the previous examples, it would be correct to view his efforts towards law reform as part of a much bigger picture. As with Rowntree, it might be suggested that Calvert's real

---

57   Briggs, *Social Thought and Social Action*, 39, 40, 30.
58   Rowntree and Co, *B. Seebohm Rowntree*, 10.
59   Rowntree and Co, *B. Seebohm Rowntree*, 31.
60   Worrall, *The Making of the Modern Church*, 154.
61   For example: H. Potter, *Hanging in Judgment. Religion and the Death Penalty in England from the Bloody Code to Abolition*, (London, 1993), J.B. Christoph, *Capital Punishment and British Politics, The British Movement to Abolish the Death Penalty 1945–57*, (London, 1962), E.O. Tuttle, *The Crusade Against Capital Punishment in Great Britain*, (London, 1961).
62   There appears to be limited information about Calvert apart from in the context of his work.

contribution was in terms of providing accurate and persuasive information about the reform being sought.[63]

In the 1920s the abolitionists needed to encourage parliament to re-examine the issue of capital punishment again through publicity and lobbying. A central body which could represent all those involved in the campaign was needed to raise public awareness of the death penalty and thereby bring pressure to bear for reform.[64] Calvert became the secretary of the newly formed National Council for the Abolition of the Death Penalty and he wrote a key book *Capital Punishment in the Twentieth Century*.[65] Basically he worked to increase consciousness of the arguments against capital punishment. He appears to have been very careful to base his work upon facts and experience in other countries. He supported his views with collected evidence and statistics steering away from dramatic but insubstantial arguments. As with some of the other examples considered, in spite of his efforts Calvert's campaign was not to be a short intensive one. He died in 1933 without achieving substantive reform.[66] However the value of his work in focusing calls for abolition in terms of accurate information about the death penalty has been recognized as playing a crucial part in achieving the eventual law reform. Once again his work needs to be viewed as part of a continual process — it was begun by others, supported by others and carried on by others after his death.

IV. CONCLUSIONS

A range of examples of Christian service through law reform has been considered in this chapter. The achievements and frustrations seen in these examples may allow some general observations to be made about Christians and law reform. There is a clear call for justice and righteousness in the Bible. Christians cannot ignore this call and the churches cannot ignore their role in teaching about the application of that call. The efforts of organizations such as the Evangelical Alliance and the Churches Commission for Racial Justice together with publications such as *The Common Good* demonstrate an awareness of this duty in recent years.

Ultimately interpretation of the call to justice in individual lives is a personal matter. Christians are called to a variety of different types of service. Some have found and will find themselves called to seek justice through law reform. For some the call is strong and they are able to articulate it clearly. For others the call is indirect and they simply find

---

63 Potter, *Hanging in Judgment*, 205.

64 Tuttle, *The Crusade Against Capital Punishment*, 30,31.

65 E. Calvert, *Capital Punishment in the Twentieth Century*, 5th ed. (London, 1936).

66 Tuttle, *The Crusade Against Capital Punishment*, 32, 48, 143.

themselves in the right place at the right time to be involved. Whilst some of the Christians were originally unlikely candidates for their reforming work they ultimately found themselves with sufficient re- sources and support to carry out their share of the work. Those who have made the seeking of reform a priority have used a variety of means and normally these methods have involved being part of a wider movement or effort. Examples considered in this chapter included a parliamentary representative or figurehead role, a role issuing directly out of charitable work and an educating role providing research and information about required changes. Ultimately significant reform is the result of the collective work of a number of people. Christians need to be prepared to work with others including those who might be seeking similar ends but for completely different motives. That collaboration in itself is part of the spreading of the Gospel. Just as with other areas of Christian life, no easy route is guaranteed. In some of the examples considered those promoting reform had times of struggle on a personal level and perhaps even more significantly in the overall picture, found themselves at odds with other Christians who did not have the same conviction about their reforming work. Whilst those involved in law reform may often work with a personal awareness of the urgency of their work, the examples show that at times progress has been very slow indeed. It has been so slow that it has left those promoting the reform confused about their direction and feeling guilty about their lack of achievement. The exam- ples suggest that behind the ultimately successful campaigns there was much painstaking work. In the absence of some sort of 'moral panic' most law reform is slow. Christians cannot necessarily expect quick results.

The most striking aspect of some of the examples considered is the personal commitment of the reformers which drove them to take a particular path in trust. Perhaps it is this commitment and trust which should be the mark of the Christian law reformer. In his inaugural lecture in 1979, 'Promoting Change in the Legal System', Professor Michael Zander commented on the role of the would-be law reformer. In one part of his paper he suggested that law reformers can only promote those changes which appear to them to be necessary. Those proposing reform should not be concerned about judging whether the right time has yet arrived for the implementation of that reform. Others in authority can resist reform if they see fit. Professor Zander said that the law reformers' 'function is to propose; it is for others to dispose'.[67] Christian law reformers might add Proverbs 19:21: 'Many are the plans in the mind of man, but it is the purpose of the Lord that will be established.' Alterna- tively, in the words of the Living Bible, Proverbs 19:21 reads: 'Man proposes, but God disposes.'

[67] M. Zander, 'Promoting Change in the Legal System', (1979) 42 *Modern Law Review*, 491.

2

A Bill of Rights for the United Kingdom?

Julian Rivers[1]

I. INTRODUCTION

In broad outline, the justification for the existence of a bill of rights in a democratic constitution is as follows: human beings have moral rights simply by virtue of their being human, which it is the duty of all to respect. There are thus certain basic moral standards binding on all governments. Even a democracy, which takes as its practical standard of right the opinions of a majority of the governed, presupposes the existence of certain moral rights: a fundamental right to equality, the rights to vote and be elected, to participate in public debate, to form parties of like-minded people and so on. At least these rights need protecting from the potential excesses of democratic government. Thus on Ronald Dworkin's account,[2] for example, the root of Western constitutionalism is to be found in a fundamental right of all human beings to equal concern and respect. This expresses itself both in a majoritarian assessment of the common good and in an enhanced protection of those individual interests liable to be discriminated against in the majority's calculations.

The practical outworking of this theory is to establish a constitution built on the twin pillars of the rule of law and democratic government. The rule of law, on this account, ensures that the fundamental rights that impose moral limits to state action are stated in a bill of rights and are enforceable against the state. It is particularly appropriate that judges, who are insulated from the pressures of a democratic majority, are charged with protecting these rights. Democracy provides the legitimation for state action that occurs within the moral limits of the bill of rights. So in responding to democratic pressures, the legislative and executive branches of government are free to make and enforce law as they see fit, but under the oversight of a judiciary that enforces the moral boundaries of state action set out in the bill of rights.

[1] I am grateful to Paul Beaumont, David Clarke and Ian Leigh for commenting on an earlier draft of this paper.

[2] *Taking Rights Seriously*, (London 1977), 272–278; *A Matter of Principle*, (Cambridge, Mass, 1985), 196.

Practical arguments for change

The constitution of the UK does not reflect the theory just outlined, and it is often claimed that as a result the organs of government behave in a way that transgresses the acceptable moral limits of state action. Evidence for this can be found in the poor record of the UK before the European Court of Human Rights.[3] The solution that is normally suggested for this constitutional weakness is the enactment of the European Convention on Human Rights and Fundamental Freedoms as a UK Bill of Rights.[4] There is an important practical argument for the incorporation of the European Convention with its related protocols. This Convention is primarily an international treaty, creating pressure on the Government at an international level to ensure that the standards it contains are upheld. But its precise status within the legal systems of the UK is thoroughly unclear. If it were like any other international treaty one would expect it to have a limited effect in line with our dualist approach to international law.[5]

In England, the standard position is that the Convention is relevant in three situations: in the judicial development of the common law,[6] in the grant of discretionary legal remedies,[7] and in the interpretation of ambiguous statutes.[8] In Scotland, until recently, the narrower position obtained that the Convention would only be relevant as an aid to interpretation where the statute in question had specifically been enacted to implement a Convention obligation,[9] but the position now parallels that of England.[10]

---

[3]   S. Farran, *The UK before the European Court of Human Rights*, (London, 1996), 389–392.

[4]   The calls have been many and varied. See in particular M. Zander *A Bill of Rights?* (London, Sweet & Maxwell, 1997) 4th ed.; C. Campbell (ed.) *Do we need a Bill of Rights?* (London, Temple Smith, 1980); P. Wallington and J. McBride, *Civil Liberties and a Bill of Rights* (London, Cobden Trust, 1976); R. Brazier, *Constitutional Reform* (Oxford, 1991), ch. 7; D. Feldman, *Civil Liberties and Human Rights in England and Wales*, (Oxford, 1993) pp. 75–88. An excellent account of this matter can be found in the Constitution Unit's document, *Human Rights Legislation* (London, 1996).

[5]   *Rayner (Mincing Lane) Ltd v Department of Trade* [1990] 2 AC 418.

[6]   *Derbyshire County Council v Times Newspapers* [1992] QB 770 (CA), [1993] AC 534, [1993] 1 All ER 1011 (HL). See also *R v Secretary of State for the Home Dept. ex p McQuillan* [1995] 4 All ER 400.

[7]   *AG v Guardian Newspapers Ltd* [1987] 3 All ER 316 (HL).

[8]   *R v Secretary of State for the Home Department ex p Brind* [1991] 1 AC 696, at 747–8, 760–761.

[9]   *Kaur v Lord Advocate* 1981 SLT 322 per Lord Ross at 330.

[10] *The Petition of AMT for authority to adopt SR* Decision of the Inner House of the Court of Session (Lord President Hope) 26 July 1996, 1996 *Scottish Civil Law Reports* 897. I am indebted to Paul Beaumont for drawing my attention to this case.

There is in fact a range of judicial attitudes towards the European Convention. This is well exemplified by the *Derbyshire County Council* case[11] in which the courts had to decide whether a local authority could maintain an action against a newspaper for defamation in its own name, as a corporate body. The House of Lords concluded that it could not. While there was general agreement among the judges that it was appropriate to refer to the European Convention, in this case Article 10 on freedom of speech, where the common law was being developed, their use of the Convention ranged from the tightly constructed argument in reliance on Article 10 jurisprudence of Balcombe L.J.[12] to the fleeting reference of Lord Keith.[13]

Another uncertainty concerning the European Convention concerns its relationship to European Community law. Although the European Community cannot formally accede to the Convention, the European Court of Justice has repeatedly affirmed its commitment to ensuring the observance of general principles of law of which fundamental rights are an integral part. The European Convention is an especially significant expression of these rights.[14] European Community law is certainly binding within the domestic legal systems of the UK,[15] and so it has been argued that the European Convention is also binding within the English legal system in those areas of activity governed by European law.[16] But while a good argument can be made that Community law (which can have direct and superior effect in the UK) should be interpreted in line with the Convention where possible, it is not clear that the Convention is itself a source of rights in the UK just because the area in question is partly regulated by European Community law.

Even in those areas where certainty ought to exist, new doubts can arise. In *ex p Brind*[17] the House of Lords ruled that a minister did not have to take the European Convention into account in exercising his statutory discretion. Nonetheless, Lord Lester has recently suggested, entirely plausibly, that the publication of the new Civil Service Code,

---

[11] *Derbyshire County Council v Times Newspapers* [1992] 1 QB 770 (CA), [1993] AC 534, [1993] 1 All ER 1011 (HL)

[12] [1992] 1 QB 770 at 813–817.

[13] [1993] 1 All ER 1011 at 1021.

[14] Case 11/70 *Internationale Handelsgesellschaft* [1970] ECR 1125, [1972] CMLR 255; see most recently Opinion 2/94 [1996] ECR I-1759. See also Article F(2) Treaty of European Union 1992.

[15] *R v Secretary of State for Transport ex p. Factortame (no. 2)* [1991] 1 AC 603 at 658–9 (per Lord Bridge); *R v Employment Secretary ex p. Equal Opportunities Commission* [1995] 1 AC 1.

[16] N. Grief, 'The domestic impact of the European Convention on Human Rights as mediated through community law' [1991] *Public Law* 545.

[17] *R v Home Secretary ex p. Brind* [1991] 1 AC 696.

which expressly obligates government officials to comply with international and treaty law, has created a legitimate expectation that the Convention will be applied.[18] The precise impact of this is unclear, but, if correct, it would mean that a minister has at least enhanced duties to consult affected parties before exercising his discretion in a way that departs from the ECHR.[19]

The likelihood of reform

Since Sir Leslie Scarman's review of the British Constitution in 1974,[20] support for a Bill of Rights would appear to have grown steadily. This has developed out of a feeling of increasing confidence in the judicial regulation of executive and legislative action, nurtured by the growth of administrative and European Community law, and out of a perceived need to redress an imbalance in the British constitution, whereby the executive has become not only its motor, but most of the vehicle as well.

However, until recently there was no real likelihood of movement on this front since both Conservative and Labour parties were opposed, the one from a desire to maintain the current institutional balance, the other from a suspicion of judicial attitudes to socialist reform. The Liberal Democrats and their predecessors were the only substantial party to advocate a Bill of Rights for the UK.

The Conservative and Liberal Democrat views have not changed in recent years. The Conservative party remains committed to pragmatic and evolutionary constitutional change which does not include the enactment of a Bill of Rights,[21] while the Liberal Democrats would ultimately wish to see a new written consitution with a Bill of Rights enforced by a Supreme Court having the power to strike down any action in contravention of the Bill.[22]

For the Labour party, the step from democratic socialism to social democracy has been significant. In the late eighties and early nineties, the position of the Labour party was best described in their so-called white paper, *The Charter of Rights*. This clearly set out the intention of a future Labour government to enact 'individual and specific Acts of Parliament' to guarantee the rights set out in the Charter. In February 1993, the first issue of 'participation papers' entitled *Labour and the Constitution* invited the party to debate the arguments for and against

---

[18] Lord Lester of Herne Hill, 'Government compliance with international human rights law: a new year's legitimate expectation' [1996] *Public Law* 187.

[19] See Wade and Forsyth, *Administrative Law* (London, 1994) 418–420.

[20] *English Law: the new dimension*, (London, 1974).

[21] *Strengthening the United Kingdom, the Report of the CPC national policy group on the Constitution*, London 1996.

[22] *Policy Briefings* Nos. 6 and 8, 1995.

the enactment of a Bill of Rights.[23] By the 1995 party conference, the commitment of the Labour Party to prioritize the incorporation of the European Convention was established. This was reaffirmed in late 1996 in a consultation paper.[24]

In view of this commitment, and the Labour victory in the 1997 General Election, it is probable that the European Convention will be enacted as domestic law before the end of the millenium. Exactly what form that enactment will take is not clear. The 1996 consultation paper is obscure on whether judges will have the power to override statutes. The implication on page 6 is that judges would simply be required to interpret all legislation, so far as is possible, consistently with the Convention. But there is a suggestion on page 10 that Parliamentary sovereignty is exhausted in the ability to withdraw entirely from the Convention. If the courts treat the Convention as incorporated in the same way as they have treated the European Community Treaty as incoporated by the European Communities Act 1972, judges will be able to strike down statutes that they consider infringe the Convention. Indeed, one can still detect a certain unhappiness even among close supporters of the Labour leader. In a speech given by Lord Irvine of Lairg, now Lord Chancellor, to the Administrative Law Bar Association on 16 October 1995, the fundamental importance of the supremacy of Parliament and the need to exercise caution over the current development of judicial review was reasserted.[25] At first sight that would appear to sit uncomfortably with a commitment to enacting a Bill of Rights, a discomfort that Lord Irvine attempts to dispel by arguing that if the power of the judiciary is enhanced by enacting a Bill of Rights, it is all the more important to prevent the rise of judicial supremacism in the review of administrative action.[26] This argument is curious, to say the least.

In spite of these uncertainties, the enactment of some form of Bill of Rights is more likely now than it ever has been.

II. THE NATURE OF CONSTITUTIONAL RIGHTS

Political statements

The French Declaration of the rights of man and the citizen of 1789 proved to be a watershed in Western thought about the nature of justice. Article 2 of the Declaration provides:

---

[23] Issue No. 1 February 1993.

[24] Jack Straw MP and Paul Boateng MP, *Bringing rights home: Labour's plans to incorporate the European Convention on Human Rights into UK Law*, December 1996.

[25] Reproduced at [1996] *Public Law* 59.

[26] *Ibid.* at 77.

The final end of every political institution is the preservation of the natural and imprescriptable rights of man. Those rights are liberty, property, security and resistance to oppression.

Rights, on this account, are the building blocks of justice. Justice can be understood solely in terms of rights, and so the function of the state is to uphold and protect everyone's rights. Rights tell us how political institutions ought to behave.

At the end of the 18th century, such thought was deeply controversial. The reformist Bentham's comment about 'nonsense upon stilts'[27] is well known, as also is the conservative Burke's opposition.[28] Nonetheless, at an international and political level the view that justice can be stated in terms of rights is now widely accepted. The Universal Declaration of Human Rights (1948), echoing the French declaration, commences:

Whereas recognition of the inherent dignity and of the equal and inalienable rights of all members of the human family is the foundation of freedom, justice and peace in the world . . .

words which are repeated by the two International Covenants of 1966. And the three main regional conventions, the European Convention of Human Rights and Fundamental Freedoms 1950, the American Convention on Human Rights 1969 and the African Charter on Human and Peoples' Rights of 1981, all proceed on this basis, albeit with significant disagreement about what rights are actually to be included.[29]

There is thus a widespread perception that to be legitimate, moral and political debate needs to be cast in terms of rights, and that justice is a matter of rights. This applies as much to domestic as international affairs.

Philosophical foundations

The tenor of moral debate at a political and international level finds support in the large number of philosophers who now argue for the primacy of moral rights. Ever since John Rawls[30] and then Ronald Dworkin[31] attacked the hegemony of utilitarianism, an increasing

[27]   *Anarchical Fallacies*, Works Vol. 2, 501.

[28]   'As soon as this system [the rights of man] arrived among them, Pandora's box, replete with every mortal evil, seemed to fly open, hell itself to yawn, and every demon of mischief to overspread the face of the earth.' *Parl. Hist.* XXIX, 367, cited in C.C. O'Brien, *The Great Melody*, (London, 1992) 418–9.

[29]   A useful collection can be found in P.R. Ghandi, *International Human Rights Documents*, (London, 1995).

[30]   *A Theory of Justice*, (Oxford, 1972).

[31]   *Taking Rights Seriously*, (London, 1977).

number of philosophers have seen in human rights not just the outcome of a moral calculation, but the foundations of morality itself.

It is not difficult to see why this is so. Liberal political theory[32] usually takes the value of human autonomy as its foundation.[33] Even where liberalism has a more egalitarian cast, the 'right to equal concern and respect' is understood as a right to equal freedom.[34] The freely acting individual needs the space in which to live out his or her vision of the good life, and (more problematically) certain resources with which to be autonomous. Rights thus represent the necessary conditions for the development and exercise of autonomy, and become the public standard by which an individual's relationships with government and other individuals is to be evaluated. Moreover, autonomy is not simply the guiding value of politics, but can provide the foundation for a rationalist morality. Alan Gewirth's work is classic in this respect.[35] Gewirth attempts to build a complete moral theory on the fact of human agency, and ends up espousing a set of rationally necessary human rights.

However the conception of autonomy that underlies these justifications tends to include the freedom to choose what one will consider good. There is a 'right to moral independence',[36] and thus no objective good behind autonomy to which human freedom must be directed if it is to be moral. The set of rights derived from autonomy is thus anti-perfectionist. By this is meant that a vision of perfection (what is good) is eschewed in favour of a wide diversity of conceptions of the good life. Justice, not morality, is the supreme virtue of states and law, and justice means neutrality between competing conceptions of the good life. The state is not allowed to legislate simply on the grounds that some behaviour is seen as morally valueless or even morally reprehensible. Something more must be shown — the infringement of another's rights. So on principle it is wrong to legislate to prevent or discourage pornography,[37] or homosexuality,[38] or drug-taking,[39] and it is wrong to encourage

---

[32] 'Liberal' is understood broadly as expressive of the dominant political culture of the Western world.

[33] J. Raz, *The Morality of Freedom*, (Oxford, 1986) chs. 14 and 15; C.S. Nino, *The Ethics of Human Rights*, (Oxford, 1991) ch. 5; J. Feinberg, *Harm to Self*, (Oxford, 1986) ch. 18.

[34] R. Dworkin, 'Liberalism', in *A Matter of Principle*, (Cambridge, Mass, 1985) ch. 8.

[35] *Reason and Morality*, (Chicago, 1978). See also D. Beyleveld and R. Brownsword, *Law as a moral judgment*, (London, 1986), for an enthusiastic adoption of Gewirth's position.

[36] R. Dworkin, 'Do we have a right to pornography?' in *A Matter of Principle*, (Cambridge, Mass. 1985) at 353, 359–372.

[37] R. Dworkin, *A Matter of Principle*, ch. 17.

[38] Report of the Wolfenden Committee 1954; H.L.A. Hart, *Law, Liberty and Morality*, (Oxford, 1963).

[39] D.A.J. Richards, *Sex, Drugs, Death, and the Law* (Totowa, New Jersey 1982).

monogamous marriage, giving to religious and educational causes and so on, if the only reason for doing so is that some consider such lifestyles morally reprehensible or particularly valuable.

The instability of traditional constitutional rights

The constitutional enforcement of rights developed on the basis of a very limited conception of rights. Compare the language of the French Declaration with the American Bill of Rights, the first ten amendments to the US Constitution of 1791. For example, Article 1 provides:

> Congress shall make no law respecting an establishment of religion or prohibiting the free exercise thereof; or abridging the freedom of speech or the press or the right of the people peaceably to assemble, and to petition the Government for a redress of grievances.

The right contained in this article is an immunity, in that it insists that the state has no right to change the law in certain areas. Whatever Congress does, it shall not interfere with certain special interests, or alternatively, the state must go through certain procedures to interfere with those interests: 'nor shall any person . . . be deprived of life, liberty, or property, without due process of law'.[40] Rights on this account are a practical means of protecting the citizen from injustice, namely the injustice committed by an over-intrusive state. They tell you what the state should not do, not what it should do.

The judicial enforcement of constitutional rights developed during the nineteenth century in the United States on the basis of this second, limited, conception. Vested legal rights were not to be disturbed,[41] and in particular those rights deriving from the private agreements of individuals were protected via the 'contract clause'.[42] Early attempts to incorporate a set of basic natural rights into the Constitution via the 'privileges and immunities clause' of Article IV were laid to rest in the Slaughterhouse Cases of 1873.[43] The development of individual rights was thus in accord with the Supreme Court's power to uphold the division of jurisdiction between organs of government. In the same way as a court could strike down a statute for regulating an area in the exclusive jurisdiction of another legislature, so also it could strike out a statute for regulating an area in the exclusive competence of the individual. This may be contrasted with the French Declaration, which was a purely political document, urging the government to behave in a certain way. It only acquired significance as a legal standard within administrative law

---

40 Amendment V.
41 *Marbury v Madison* 5 US 137 (1803).
42 Sir M. Amos, *Lectures on the American Constitution*, (London, 1938), ch. 4; L. Tribe, *American Constitutional Law*, 2 ed, (New York, 1988), 547.
43 L. Tribe, *op. cit.* 528–532.

from the Second World War,[44] and in constitutional law from the mid–1970s.[45]

However, the course of the twentieth century has revealed a fundamental instability in the traditional limited conception of constitutional rights outlined above. Most significantly, it assumes an existing body of law that is already just: (e.g.) the legislature shall not interfere with the existing right peacably to assemble. Put the other way around, it assumes that the grossest injustices governments can commit consist of disturbances in the legal status quo to the detriment of the individual. It assumes that a basic minimum of justice is preserved in the state by the protection of immunities. This reveals quite clearly the debt traditional constitutional theory owes to John Locke. Locke argued that civil society is formed naturally by a communal act of enlightened self-interest, and that government is established to preserve the pre-existing natural rights of humans. The proper function of government is thus to protect the natural, spontaneous, legal order, and certainly not to interfere with it.[46] This is flawed. By way of example, one need only refer to the second case in which the US Supreme Court struck down a statute of Congress.[47] It had interfered with the right of property, disappropriating thousands of US citizens without any compensation. A clear case of injustice, it would seem, until one recalls that the property in question was another human being, a slave. The problems of this type of approach were most graphically revealed by the Court's dogmatic adherence to *laissez faire* economics in the New Deal era prior to 1937. Notoriously from this period, in *Lochner v New York*[48] (1905) the court had struck down a statute limiting the working hours of bakers to 10 hours a day and 60 hours a week.

Most people now accept that a basic minimum of justice cannot be ensured simply by upholding civil liberties. What we now have is a tension between the goal of a Bill of Rights, and the means it contains to reach that goal. The goal is to secure a basic minimum of just behaviour on the part of the state, by stopping it committing the worst injustices. But the means allowed is the inability to change the legal status quo. The problem is that sometimes the worst injustices are committed when the state does nothing. So the tendency to supplement the list of constitutional rights with other political rights is very strong; most modern Bills of Rights include rights other than liberties. Not only is one to be free from interference in matters of religion, speech and association, but one has rights of participation in procedures, rights to be protected from others and even rights to financial support. The state acts unjustly when it fails to give effect to such rights, and the categories of political and constitutional rights have become blurred.

[44] R. Brown and J. Bell, *French Administrative Law*, (Oxford, 1993) 205–223.
[45] J. Bell, *French Constitutional Law*, (Oxford, 1992), 29–33.
[46] Locke, *Two Treatises of Government* (1690) II. ix. 123–124.
[47] *Dred Scott v Sandford* 60 US 393 (1856).
[48] 198 US 45.

Judicial interpretation

A remarkable feature of Western constitutional jurisprudence over the last hundred years has been the willingness of judges charged with interpreting Bills of Rights to make the same move, in the face of a static text, from the traditional libertarian conception of rights to a fuller conception. At times this has been made possible by the 'chameleon-hued'[49] nature of rights, which enables the concept of a right to be the lynch-pin of some stunning *non sequiturs.* First in the US Supreme Court's second wave of activism from the 1950s,[50] then in Germany in the sixties and seventies,[51] then before the European Court of Human Rights in the seventies and eighties,[52] and now in Australia[53] and New Zealand,[54] judges have steadily expanded the scope of constitutional rights. This is hardly surprising. The traditional libertarian conception of constitutional rights is inadequate to ensure the minimum standards of justice, the language of bills of rights tends to be vague enough to support a variety of interpretations, and the political and philosophical environment is increasingly conducive to the use of rights in expressing moral positions. Examples of this are legion; three will have to suffice.

The first example comes from the European Court of Human Rights. Article 8 of the convention provides that 'everyone has the right to respect for his private and family life, his home and his correspondence', and that 'there shall be no interference by a public authority with the exercise of

[49]   W.N. Hohfeld, *Fundamental Legal Conceptions* (1919) ed. W. Cook, (New Haven, 1966), 35.

[50]   Significant landmarks in this process were *Brown v Board of Education of Topeka* 347 US 483 (1954) (racial segregation in public education a denial of 'equal protection') and *Griswold v Connecticut* 381 US 479 (1965) (married couples have a privacy right to use birth control devices). See generally M.J. Sandel, *Democracy's Discontent* (Cambridge, Massachusetts, 1996), chs. 2–4. It is only fair to note that American constitutional theorists appear to fall into two broad camps: those who insist that the Supreme Court has always found ways of enforcing what it takes to be the fundamental values of society, whether under a doctrine of natural law, substantive due process, or equal protection, and those who insist that there have been periods of relative faithfulness (and faithlessness) to the text. See L.F. Goldstein, *In Defense of the Text*, (Savage, Maryland, 1994), ch. 4.

[51]   F. Ossenbühl, 'Die Interpretation der Grundrechte in der Rechtsprechung des Bundesverfassungsgerichts,' NJW 1976, 2100.

[52]   D.J. Harris, M. O'Boyle, C. Warbrick, *Law of the European Court of Human Rights*, (London, 1995), esp. 7–9; See C. Gearty, 'The ECHR and the protection of civil liberties: an overview' (1993), 52 *Cambridge Law Journal* 89 for a good account of ECHR jurisprudence.

[53]   See below at 35.

[54]   See below at 35–36.

this right' except under certain conditions. This seems like a traditional liberty, but the court has consistently held that the state is under positive obligations to do certain things, for example to close a procedural gap in the law that prevented a man guilty of a sexual assault being prosecuted[55] and relieving marriage partners of their duty to live together in certain circumstances.[56]

The next example comes from the New Zealand Court of Appeal. A boy injured himself and suffered a life-threatening nosebleed. His parents, being Jehovah's Witnesses, refused their consent to a blood transfusion, and when the court overrode that refusal, sought to argue that this was in breach of their fundamental right to freedom of religion.[57] Gault J, giving the judgment of the court, accepted that the freedom of religious manifestation contained in Art. 15 of the New Zealand Bill of Rights Act 1990 included the right to take decisions concerning the health and medical treatment of a child. But this right was limited by the child's right to life in section 8. One had to engage in an act of 'definitional balancing' to ensure that one right was not so widely defined as to render another right empty.[58]

With respect, and, let it be said, agreement with the outcome, the argument is flawed. Section 3 of the NZBORA 1990 specifically provides that the rights and freedoms contained in the Act bind only the organs of government and those exercising public powers. The 'right to life' is in fact a right not to be deprived of life by the state without the due process of law and in accordance with the requirements of fundamental justice. If the parents had not taken their boy to hospital, and he had died, they might have rendered themselves criminally liable, but they would not have infringed the boy's 'right to life'. If the Act gives them the right against the state to determine appropriate treatment, the boy's right not to be deprived of life by the state is simply irrelevant, and the only reason for refusing to give effect to the parents' wishes is that in a free and democratic society, people's religious views cannot be allowed to destroy the life of their children.

Nor has the High Court of Australia remained immune from the same type of flawed reasoning. In 1992, the High Court discovered implicit in the Constitution certain limitations on the power of the legislature, arising out of the nature of democratic representation.[59]

---

[55] *X and Y v. Netherlands* (1985) ECHRR A91 para. 29.

[56] *Airey v Ireland* (1980) ECHRR A32 paras. 29–30.

[57] *Re J* [1996] 2 NZLR 134.

[58] *Ibid.* at 146.

[59] *Nationwide News Pty v Willis* (1992) 177 CLR 1; *Australian Capital Television v The Commonwealth* (1992) 177 CLR 106. And see H.P. Lee, 'The Australian High Court and implied fundamental guarantees' [1993] *Public Law* 606.

However, in the recent *Theophanous* case,[60] the majority move from the proposition that the power of the Australian Parliament is limited under the Constitution by the need to preserve representative government, in particular by a principle of freedom of political expression, to the proposition that there is a personal right to freedom of political expression that can remould the common law of defamation.[61] The constitutional right to freedom of speech is not just a freedom from governmental interference, but also a freedom from civil action by another individual. It is expressive of interpersonal relationships, as well as the relationship of individual to state.

To summarize so far, the Western world has developed a political culture in which it is believed that the requirements of justice can be exhaustively expressed in terms of rights. This receives philosophical support from those who believe that the foundations of political morality lie in the autonomous individual, which autonomy is the source of all legitimate demands on other human beings. Judges applying bills of rights tend to assume that their purpose is to uphold the minimum requirements of justice, and so adopt an expansive interpretation which embraces the political and philosophical positions outlined above. This interpretative strategy likewise finds support from liberal constitutional theorists.[62]

III. ASPECTS OF A CHRISTIAN POLITICAL MORALITY

Public morality: the central tradition

Pressure for a Bill of Rights is supported by a strong strand in modern political philosophy that justice as a political virtue[63] is separate from morality, requiring state neutrality between competing conceptions of the good life, by upholding a set of rights, derived generally from the value of individual autonomy. We can set this against what Robert George has called 'the central tradition' of Western thought, that it is indeed the function of the state to make people moral.[64]

The central tradition asserts that the purpose of all law, indeed of all power, is to encourage and assist people to live morally valuable lives. Like most Western ideas, this tradition has its roots in both Greek philosophy and Judaeo-Christian thought. So we find Plato saying:

---

61   per Mason C.J., Toohey and Gaudron J.J. at 130, Deane J. at 178.

62   e.g. D.A.J. Richards, *Toleration and the Constitution*, (Oxford, 1986); R. Dworkin, *Freedom's Law: The Moral Reading of the American Constitution*, (Oxford, 1996).

63   I am only concerned with justice as the characteristic of good political and legal institutions, and not, for example with justice as an attribute of God or a personal virtue. There are, of course, interesting connections to be made.

64   *Making Men Moral*, (Oxford, 1993).

When we examine the natural features of a country and its legal system, our ultimate object of scrutiny is of course the quality of its social and political arrangements. We do not hold the common view that a man's highest good is to survive and simply continue to exist. His highest good is to become as virtuous as possible and to continue in that state as long as life lasts.[65]

And Aristotle is more explicit:

It is clear then that a state is not a mere society, having a common place, established for the prevention of mutual crime and for the sake of exchange. These are conditions without which a state cannot exist; but all of them together do not constitute a state, which is a community of families and aggregations of families in well-being, for the sake of a perfect and self-sufficing life.[66]

The thought of Aristotle was largely adopted and Christianized by Aquinas in the 13th century, who saw the role of the state in training people for virtue and in creating the conditions favourable to living godly lives: 'Law is primarily a product of reason planning action to serve our ultimate goal of human happiness, and properly of happiness in common . . .'[67]

Happiness for Aquinas meant not pleasure but a state of virtuous flourishing culminating ultimately in the vision of God. The task of the king is to lead people to virtue by a gradual process: 'First of all to establish a virtuous life in the multitude subject to him; second, to preserve it once established; and third, having preserved it to promote its greater perfection.'[68]

The same idea, albeit somewhat muted, can also be found in the Protestant reformers, and coming more up to date, the tradition can be seen resurfacing in modern Natural Law writers such as John Finnis[69] at Oxford, Robert George[70] at Princeton and to a certain extent in some perfectionist liberal theorists such as Joseph Raz[71] and William Galston[72] although these latter have a conception of morality that is more in tune with current liberalism.

A Christian appraisal of the central tradition

The exponents of the central tradition have been almost exclusively Christian, but the tradition in one sense does not go far enough, and in

---

[65] *Laws*, iv. 707.
[66] *Politics*, iii. 5.1280b.
[67] *Summa Theologiae* IaIIae 90.2 (tr. T. McDermott, London, 1989, 280).
[68] *De Regno*, iv (i.15) [117], quoted in R. George *op. cit.* n.64 at 30.
[69] *Natural Law and Natural Rights*, (Oxford, 1980).
[70] *op. cit.* n.64
[71] *The Morality of Freedom*, (Oxford, 1986).
[72] *Liberal Purposes*, (Cambridge, 1991).

another sense can go too far. It does not go far enough in that it has tended to assume a two-stage morality. At one level there is a rational minimum of morality, that any human being ought to subscribe to, and can legitimately be required to live out (the 'natural law'). Beyond that is supererogatory morality that is only possible with the help of God's Spirit.[73] The morality that the state is supposed to enforce and encourage is the minimum standard.[74] This is particularly apparent in Finnis's recent and successful restatement: Religion is but one of seven 'goods', and seems to consist primarily of speculation about the divine.[75] It is not difficult to be sceptical about a division of morality into the rationally knowable and the divinely, and not generally revealed. Anthropologically it has proved difficult to establish any settled universal content to morality.[76] Perhaps the furthest we can go is to suggest that morality is organized into similar categories for people; there are few concrete situations which everyone would characterize as immoral.[77] At any rate, whatever universal agreement there might be is insufficient to guide legislation as a practical matter. Of course, this does not logically disprove the rationalist's case, but it does make it implausible. Furthermore, there is little in the New Testament to encourage such a division. Christ consistently set a standard of perfection,[78] which Paul was later to characterize in terms of a ninefold fruit,[79] nine virtues displayed by the person controlled by Christ's Spirit. For the Christian, to be moral is to be perfect in Christ, and one can never be satisfied with anything short of perfection. If it is the aim of the state to make people moral, it is the aim of the state to make people into mature followers of Christ, displaying his character, growing into perfection.

At first sight this conclusion would appear to go much further than those New Testament passages explicitly concerned with the role of the state. But a careful reading shows that government has both a negative and a positive role.[80] In addition the Roman state performed far fewer

---

[73]   Aquinas is ultimately responsible for this: F. Schaeffer, *Escape from Reason* (1968) in *Complete Works*, (Westchester, Illinois, 1982) Vol. I, 209–11.

[74]   To say that the standard is a 'minimum' is not to suggest that it does not contain virtues. One should recall Aquinas' fourfold list of natural virtues: prudence, justice, moderation and courage.

[75]   *Natural Law and Natural Rights,* 89–90.

[76]   M. Mead, 'Some Anthropological considerations concerning Natural Law' 6 Natural Law Forum 51.

[77]   '. . . recognition of natural rights to life, property and reproduction is found in all societies, although with profound variations in interpretation.' *Ibid.*, 64.

[78]   Matthew 5:48.

[79]   Galatians 5:22–23.

[80]   'He is God's servant to do you good' (Romans 13:4) and 'governors, who are sent by [the Lord] . . . to commend those who do right' (1 Peter 2:14).

functions than its modern day successor, which correspondingly needs a far richer morality to guide it. And finally, Christians today are enabled to participate in the state. We cannot suppose that Christians are to stop acknowledging Christ and loving their neighbour when they act in a 'public' capacity. Most importantly of all, we should not fall into the trap of supposing that the call to Christian perfection is only for those who acknowledge it. All are called to acknowledge Christ as Lord,[81] so 'Christian morality' must be universally binding, if not universally acknowledged. Love for one's neighbour is shown by a concern that he too grows up in Christ. So as a Christian voter, campaigner, legislator, governor, lawyer, judge, one's function is at root to see Christ glorified in each person's life. In this sense, the central tradition does not go far enough.

The limitations of state power

But the central tradition goes too far, if it fails to take seriously the limits on state power. I am most certainly not advocating a utopian theocracy. There are four groups of limitation on the ability of the state to lead people to Christ.

First, the state is limited by the nature of Christian morality itself. Chief among the characteristics of the Christian is selflessness. Christ himself did not insist on his 'rights' but rather 'emptied himself' and made himself nothing to secure our salvation.[82] From his followers he demands that they deny themselves, even giving up their rights, if necessary, to life ('take up your cross'[83]), physical integrity ('turn the other cheek'[84]), liberty ('carry the burden two miles'[85]) and property ('let him have your shirt as well'[86]). Key to Christian morality is the refusal to assert rights. But generosity and self-denial must be exercised spontaneously, they cannot be forced, and coercion is the principal mode of state action. The furthest the state can go is to recognize and reward such actions. Tax relief for charitable giving is an obvious example.

The second limitation on state power arises from the nature of faith. In propagating the gospel, Christians are to eschew the use of physical force,[87] using argument and example to persuade others of the truth.[88] Thus while it is not wrong to provide education in Christianity, it is wrong to insist that children attend.

[81] Philippians 2:10–11.
[82] Philippians 2:6–8.
[83] Matthew 16:24.
[84] Matthew 5:39.
[85] Matthew 5:41.
[86] Matthew 5:40.
[87] Luke 10:51–56.
[88] 2 Corinthians 10:4–5.

The third limitation arises from the need to establish structures that can be operated by sinful human beings. Democracy is not only expressive of a fundamental equality of humanity, it also provides a valuable check on the abuse of power. There is little enough in the New Testament concerning the substantive principles on which civil power is to be exercised. There is even less on the structure that the state must assume to be just. Nevertheless, there are both negative and positive reasons for arguing that power in the state must be dispersed among different organs. Negatively, power must be dispersed because of the temptations to abuse power to wrongful ends.[89] Positively, it must be dispersed because of the weight of responsibility involved in governing large numbers of people.[90] It is thus important to maintain a division of power both between state institutions and society and also between the organs of government. This is, of course, common ground with many non-Christians.

Finally, there are any number of pragmatic limitations on the enforcement of morality, depending on the resources available at the time, and the current moral standards of society. As Christians we know that the fundamental human problem is out of the reach of any human solution. The law can encourage and restrain, but it cannot change the human heart. So the morality that law presupposes cannot be too far out of line with social standards. Often, one will have to accept compromises that represent the best that can be done at the time; indeed, the pressure for moral consistency may have a detrimental effect if it forces the state to withdraw entirely from an area in which compromise is only ever possible.[91]

I would suggest that issues of the relationship between the law and Christianity can be considered by focusing on the interplay of the need to hold out Christianity as central to the state's morality and yet respect the limitations of state power.[92]

The nature of justice and rights

It follows from the account above that justice as a political virtue is not synonymous with morality. The state acts justly when it promotes true morality while recognizing the limitations of its power. It can act unjustly, either by acting immorally, or by ignoring the limitations of its role, in a sense by trying to be too moral. It is thus unjust to force people to

[89] Lord Acton's dictum is not quite correct, but absolute power gives greater scope for corruption to manifest itself.

[90] 'For lack of guidance a nation falls, but many advisers make victory sure.' Proverbs 11:14. See also Deuteronomy 1:9–18 and Exodus 18: 13–26.

[91] Aquinas, *Summa Theologiae* IaIIae 96, 1–3.

[92] See my *Cambridge Papers* on blasphemy (Vol. I No. 4) and religious establishment (Vol. III No. 4). These are available from *Cambridge Papers*, P.O. Box 27, Cambridge CB1 4GL.

worship idols (because that is immoral) and it is unjust to force people to worship Christ (because although worshipping Christ is good, attempting to force people to do it breaches the necessary limitations of state power).[93]

The fundamental issue raised by the adoption of a Bill of Rights is whether justice can adequately be expressed in terms of rights. The exact definition of a right is subject to some theoretical debate.[94] In the broadest sense, it is sometimes claimed that anyone who is the beneficiary of a duty has a corresponding right.[95] Closely related to this is the view that a right is an intrinsic interest or entitlement of a person.[96] More narrow is the view that to have a right is to have some degree of control over the enforcement of any corresponding duty.[97] If it is adopted, the interest theory must be qualified to a small extent in the direction of the will theory, in that it must be legitimate for the right–holder at least to draw attention to his or her interest, if they are capable of doing so. If there is some overriding reason why a person having a legitimate interest should not mention that interest (which is, after all, a form of enforcement), it is hard to see how that interest can be termed a right.

A Christian defence of rights could adopt the benefit-theory, arguing that rights are the necessary correlatives of duties.[98] Both spring into being simultaneously by virtue of humanity's relationship to God. But this fails to explain why duties we owe to God regarding, for example the environment do not give rise to animal and plant rights. Furthermore, once one accepts that there are some duties that do not give rise to corresponding rights, the notion of right becomes redundant, being merely a limited way of expressing a subset of duties.

A better defence of rights will focus on the intrinsic dignity of human beings made in the image of God.[99] On this basis one can distinguish

---

[93] Strictly speaking, we would probably want to characterize a law that was in principle good but unworkable because of a lack of social moral fibre (fourth limitation) as unwise rather than unjust, although the borderline with the need to persuade people of the rightness of laws (third limitation) is problematic. I am using 'justice' as a catch–all for 'morality-as-limited-by-the-nature-of-the-state'.

[94] See N.E. Simmonds, *Central Issues in Jurisprudence*, (London, 1986), ch. 8, for a good introduction. See also P. Jones, *Rights*, (London, 1994) ch. 2.

[95] W.N. Hohfeld, *Fundamental Legal Conceptions* (1966 ed.) p. 39.

[96] N. McCormick, *Legal Rights and Social Democracy*, (Oxford, 1982), ch. 8.

[97] H.L.A. Hart, *Essays on Bentham*, (Oxford, 1982), Essays 7 and 8.

[98] Thus C.J.H. Wright, *Human Rights: a Study in Biblical Themes*, Grove Booklets No. 31 (1979).

[99] Thus J.W. Montgomery, *Human Rights and Human Dignity*, (Edmonton, Alberta, 1986, 1995).

between animals (the beneficiaries of duties) and humans (the holders of rights). But even if one accepts such a foundation for rights, the following observations must be made:

a) *Humanity has no rights against God.* The just penalty for sin is death, understood primarily as separation from God.[100] The fact that Adam's sin did not lead to the immediate physical extinction of the human race is itself understood in Genesis as an act of God's unmerited grace.[101] There is no intrinsic right to life against God. The only sense in which rights–language is even conceivable in our relationship to God, is where God has graciously promised certain benefits. And we are indeed encouraged to hold God to his promises as an act of faith in his faithfulness.[102] Sometimes, modern translations of the Bible will use the language of rights (e.g. 'the right to be called the sons of God'[103]) but this is dangerous if it encourages anything other than an attitude of humility and gratitude for an interest that cannot legitimately be claimed as belonging intrinsically to us.

b) *All human relations are ultimately reflections of relationships with God: rights are therefore not primary.* Christians must understand morality as essentially tripartite.[104] What we do for others, we do out of obedience and love for God. Nowhere is this clearer than in David's reaction when he finally grasped the wrongfulness of his adultery with Bathsheba and murder of Uriah. The words could hardly be stronger: 'Against you only O Lord have I sinned.'[105] The harm and hurt we do to others pales into insignificance beside the affront to God. A breach of someone's 'rights' is primarily a breach of our duty to God. A secular morality has to understand all moral relationships in bipartite terms, which forecloses the possibility that two people might have duties towards each other, and no corresponding rights. The privity of contract problem, whereby a third party beneficiary under a contract stands to benefit from the fulfilment of the other parties' contractual duties (to each other), but cannot enforce those duties,[106] is a good picture of human relationships under God. This means that if we want to use the discourse of rights we must be aware that these are at root reflections of our duty to God, not the source of duties.

---

100   Genesis 2:17, Romans 6:23.
102   e.g. Malachi 3:10.
103   John 1:12.
104   C.J.H. Wright, *Human Rights: a Study in Biblical Themes*, Grove Booklets No. 31 (1979) 7–10.
105   Psalm 51:4.
106   *Tweddle v Atkinson* (1861) 1 B & S 393.

c) *Some aspects of morality cannot be cast in terms of rights.* This follows from the previous point. If one person wrongs another, that person has the duty to ask forgiveness, and the person wronged has the duty to forgive. But these are duties owed to God, and they cannot be recast in terms of human rights. We forgive because we ourselves have been forgiven the greater debt, not because we have rights to repentance or forgiveness.[107] More generally, the Christian virtues cannot be reformulated in terms of rights, because while there are undoubtedly many who will benefit from acts arising from someone's love, joy, peace, patience, etc. they cannot be said to be entitled to such acts. Furthermore, a belief that morality can be cast in terms of autonomy-based rights makes the immorality of self-regarding and consensual actions hard to grasp.[108] For example, the House of Lords recently upheld the convictions of adult men engaged in consensual sado-masochistic behaviour.[109] From a Christian perspective, to criminalize such actions may be imprudent, but it cannot be immoral. Yet what rights have they infringed? One evaluation is, on the contrary, that the state has infringed their rights by limiting their freedom of action.[110]

d) *Rights prejudice against communitarian benefits.* Just as an overemphasis on rights can make the encouragement of virtues difficult, so also it can make the use of common benefits as a reason for action suspect. Common benefits are often intangible, and while they affect the individual, they are not localized in the individual, and so are hard to capture as rights. Every workable bill of rights has to draw limits to individual rights, for example for reasons of national security or public health,[111] but the presumption is clearly in favour of the individual interest and against the public benefit. This contrasts markedly with the common judicial metaphor in the UK of 'balancing' rights and common interests.[112]

---

[107] Matthew 18:21–35.

[108] J. Feinberg, *Harm to Self,* (Oxford, 1986), especially ch. 17.

[109] *R v Brown* [1994] 1 AC 212, [1993] 2 WLR 556.

[110] D. Feldman, *Civil Liberties and Human Rights,* (Oxford, 1993), 517 (also drawing attention to the privacy interest overridden). However the European Court of Human Rights unanimously decided that the United Kingdom had not breached the European Convention on Human Rights, *Laskey, Jaggard and Brown v UK, The Times,* February 20, 1997.

[111] As in Articles 8–11 ECHR. See the discussion in O'Boyle, Harris and Warbrick, *Law of the European Convention on Human Rights,* (London, 1995), 285–301.

[112] A contrast that became apparent in the Thalidomide case: cf. *AG v Times Newspapers Ltd* [1974] AC 273, 301 and 319 with *Sunday Times v UK* (1978) 2 EHRR 245, 280–1.

e) *Legal rights are not necessarily the best means of enforcing morality.* Legal
    rights are very useful, in that they empower the person most interested
    in a certain outcome to enforce that outcome. Self-interest is har-
    nessed for the enforcement of morality. A bill of rights works on
    precisely the same principle of opening a procedure for individuals
    most affected by illegitimate state behaviour to prevent it. But one
    should not assume that this is always the best means of enforcing
    morality. In many cases the law uses communal enforcement agencies,
    most obviously in criminal law, or has to rely on unenforced
    obedience. A bill of rights tends to encourage an over-reliance on
    self-interest which is ultimately counter-productive, because it pro-
    duces a litigious and selfish spirit that is the very opposite of morality.

To summarize, the state is caught between a vision of perfection and a
sense of sin-ridden reality. Justice is the limited enforcement of morality.
But the claims of morality cannot be fully articulated in terms of rights,
nor can the subset of morality that is justice. The attempt to do so will
distort the proper role of the state.[113]

IV. CONSEQUENCES

Given that there are certain forms of behaviour which it is immoral for
a state to engage in, there can be little objection to attempts to prevent
such behaviour by the creation of a bill of rights. It is wrong for a state
to torture and kill, it is wrong for a state to punish a person without a
fair trial, and it is eminently sensible to create procedures by which
individuals who suffer under such regimes can appeal to independent
authorities to seek to prevent such behaviour. But if the enactment of a
bill of rights strengthens over-individualistic conceptions of justice, and
is itself treated as the foundation of justice, instead of only one aspect of
it, then it may contribute to a culture already hostile to aspects of the
proper role of law. Any bill of rights needs to be constructed to take
account of its potential dangers: this has consequences for its content,
interpretation, amendment and status.

Content

Older bills of rights tended to restrict themselves to the protection of
first-generation rights,[114] typically freedoms from an over-intrusive state.
Such rights are fairly straightforward to police, since typically they only
require us to establish what the state should not do. However, most people
agree that as a statement of basic justice, a bill of first-generation rights is

---

[113] See further J. Rivers, 'Beyond Rights: the morality of rights-language',
       Cambridge Papers Vol.6 no.3.

[114] i.e. civil and political liberties.

woefully inadequate. Hence many human rights documents include sec-ond[115] and third-generation[116] rights as well. It has already been suggested that justice cannot be completely formulated in terms of rights of any generation, but the inclusion of second- and third-generation rights in a bill of rights (as distinct from a human rights treaty) raises further practical problems. Third-generation rights between them cover the entirety of state activity. If a Supreme Court has to enforce such rights, it must potentially review the entirety of state activity. The danger is great that it becomes part of the legislature and the executive. In short, one undermines the separation of powers that is itself a bulwark against injustice, at worst creating an oligarchy of unelected judicial rulers.[117] This problem does not affect human rights treaties which as international documents do not specify how the state is to ensure that human rights are upheld. If we are to have a bill of rights, we must insist that it does not seek to do more than it reasonably can, which is to protect individuals from a certain, limited, type of injustice. This is not to claim that governments should not concern themselves with second- and third-generation 'rights'. They must do that and more. But a bill of rights is not an apt instrument to ensure the upright behaviour of governments in this field.

Interpretation

Even where bills of rights have been formulated in a limited way, we have already seen how judges applying bills of rights have tended to adopt expansive interpretations to ensure that the instruments interpreted fulfilled their avowed purpose of ensuring that justice is maintained. The breadth of potential interpretation makes the evaluation of specific proposals for inclusion in a Bill of Rights almost impossible. For example, South Africa's new Bill of Rights expressly includes a right of non-dis-crimination on grounds of sexual orientation.[118] The acceptability of this all depends on how it is interpreted: if it means that the employers cannot refuse to employ someone merely on the grounds of their orientation, that must be right, but if it means that homosexuals have a right to marry, we should be strongly opposed. The argument for homosexual marriage can already be made coherently on the basis of any right to equal

---

[115] i.e. economic and social rights.

[116] Third-generation rights are a broad and ill-defined category of 'solidarity rights' including the right to national self-determination, the right to a clean environment (discussed, below in D. Harte, 'A Christian Approach to Environmental Law?'), the right to peace and to disaster relief. In themselves they represent an unhappy attempt to squeeze important moral rquirements into the straitjacket of rights discourse.

[117] It is not uncomon to hear the complaint that Germany is governed from Karlsruhe, the seat of the Federal Constitutional Court

[118] Art. 9(3)

treatment or family life.[119] The relationship between text and decision is remarkably fluid. The danger of this fluidity is exactly the same as that besetting the desire explicitly to include second- and third-generation rights in a bill of rights, that it turns the supreme court into a universal appeal court, where everything anybody does can be subject to scrutiny. One way of resisting that is to insist that judges adopt methods of interpretation that bind them more closely to the text.

In the current hermeneutical climate, this is not going to be easy. Many are now arguing that the interpretation of texts is fundamentally unconstrained by the text itself, but is instead determined by the values that the particular interpretive community brings to the text.[120] Christian lawyers have to be clear on the consequences if this is true. Not only does it mean that judges cannot be constrained by the laws they are required to enforce, but it also has destructive consequences for any doctrine of divine revelation. There is no space here for a full consideration of these matters,[121] but three brief points should be made. Firstly, we cannot return to the idea that there is such a thing as a value-free, literal, interpretation of legal texts, especially of constitutional texts. The new hermeneutic is correct in asserting that our understanding of normative language is itself normatively determined. We do bring values to the text. However, secondly, a key interpretative value is fairness, in the sense of consistency with the history of interpretations of the constitutional text. It is open to a constitutional judge to unearth the moral position from which a bill of rights was written and adopt that position for the purposes of the case before him, even if it were he himself drafting the bill he would not have wanted the conclusion he now draws to be drawn. But, thirdly, it is in practice hard to resist an interpretation that is morally attractive, so long as it can plausibly be said to inform a particular text, even though it may not have informed a majority of those who drafted that text. There is, of course, a tension between the second and third considerations.[122]

If this account of adjudication is correct, we need both to insist on a 'conservative' reading of bills of rights, for the sake of the constitutional balance of power, and to develop Christian conceptions of political freedom and equality that can plausibly be said to stand behind the brief

119   The attempt has so far been unsuccessful under the European Convention: *S v UK*, (1986) 47 DR 274 (homosexual unions not 'family life' for the purposes of Art. 8.)

120   Most notoriously, Stanley Fish, *Is There a Text in this Class?* (Cambridge, Mass., 1980).

121   See D.A. Carson, *The Gagging of God*, (Leicester 1996) for an overview of the impact of hermeneutical pluralism.

122   This account of adjudication is Dworkinian. See in particular R. Dworkin, *Law's Empire* (London, 1986) chs. 9 and 10. See also T.R.S. Allan, 'Justice and Fairness in Law's Empire' (1993) 52 *Cambridge Law Journal* 64, ibid. *Law, Liberty and Justice* (Oxford, 1993), esp. chs. 2 and 4.

expressions of such rights, and that can guide the interpretation of such rights.

Amendment and derogation

One of the strongest pressures on a judiciary to shift the interpretation of existing law, is the failure of other formal means to amend it. The extreme difficulty with which the US constitution is amended[123] is a principal factor in the high degree of latitude Supreme Court judges have allowed themselves in interpreting their Bills of Rights. On the other hand, if a bill of rights is to fulfil its function of being 'fundamental law', it has to be preserved from amendment in the usual way. This is particularly important where the Executive has practical control of the legislature. The German solution of requiring a 2/3 rather than a simple majority in both houses of Parliament is a typical way of achieving the right level of flexibility.[124] And one could note in this context the suggestion that the Parliament Acts mechanism for passage of bills without the consent of the Lords could be revised to exclude a new bill of rights.[125]

Another way of ensuring flexibility consistent with the higher status of a bill of rights is to allow the legislature to derogate from the provisions of the bill, but only if done so expressly. This imposes a strong political pressure not to do so, but can allow for urgent exceptions without having to go through a formal process of amendment.[126] At the other extreme, it is also possible to establish levels of flexibility, marking out certain rights (or certain core elements of rights) as being totally immune from any change whatsoever.[127]

Status

One key issue that must be resolved if we are to have a bill of rights in the UK, is its status relative to primary legislation. Is it to be simply an Interpretation Act, or is it to grant the judiciary power to strike out offending legislation? If the latter is the case, the points that have already been made about interpretation become indispensible. A theory of limited interpretation is the only safeguard against judicial supremacy. But given current trends in interpretation, this is not a safeguard on which one wants to rely.

---

[123] Article V, US Constitution.
[124] Article 79 para. 2 German Basic Law.
[125] R. Brazier, *Constitutional Reform*, 141.
[126] This is the position in Canada: see Canadian Charter of Rights (Constitution Act 1982) s. 33. See also Constitution Unit, *Human Rights Legislation* (1996), 42.
[127] Art. 79 German Constitution.

The supremacy of Parliament was retained, as a matter of political compromise, in the New Zealand Bill of Rights Act 1990. Under s. 4 of the Act, the courts may not hold a statutory provision invalid or ineffective simply because it is contrary to the bill of rights. This section exists in an unhappy tension with the two following in which the rights protected are stated to be subject to such limitations as are necessary in a free and democratic society, and in which the courts are required to interpret statutes in accordance with the rights.

A majority of the Court of Appeal have taken the view that the legislative override only becomes relevant if the statutory provision concerned is not only inconsistent with one of the fundamental rights or freedoms, but is inconsistent with those rights and freedoms as limited by s. 5.[128] This view has the advantage of granting the judiciary power to allow the Bill of Rights some impact on a statutory regime, where the unlimited expression of the right would be inconsistent with that regime. But the view faces two difficulties. Firstly, it involves a forced reading of the text of the Bill of Rights Act. The natural reading of the text is that the standard of interpretation is the set of rights as unlimited. Secondly, and more importantly, the majority's view forces us to envisage a situation in which the court applies an Act of Parliament that is morally illegitimate: not only does it infringe a right, but does so in a way that cannot be justified in a free and democratic society. There is no moral space left within which the legislature can operate, and this creates pressure to remove the legislative override entirely. The minority's view makes sense as a matter of constitutional morality, because it gives the court a reason for adhering to the s. 4 legislative override. This reason is that the extent to which fundamental rights may legitimately be limited should be in the competence of the legislature, not the courts.

The lesson from New Zealand is that any bill of rights that preserves the ultimate supremacy of Parliament must contain within it a principled statement of the area within which Parliament can exercise final jurisdiction. I would suggest that it is the court's function to decide when a right has been limited, and whether the manner in which the right is limited is justified (i.e. procedural due process), but the question whether the limitation is in principle justifiable is one for Parliament and Parliament alone to decide. This role for Parliament should be ensured by explicitly stating that in limiting the exercise of a right, Parliament shall be presumed to be correctly assessing the needs of a democratic and just society. The issue of status turns on whether that presumption is irrebuttable (Parliamentary supremacy) or rebuttable on grounds the court finds convincing (judicial supremacy). A middle course might be to state that the presumption that

---

[128] *Ministry of Transport v Noort* [1992] 3 NZLR 260. See also *Ministry of Transport v Herewini* [1993] 2 NZLR 247.

Parliament has acted justly is only rebuttable on grounds of Wednesbury unreasonableness.[129]

V.   CONCLUSIONS: SOME TENSIONS OBSERVED

In concluding, three tensions that Christians thinking and working in this area face must be highlighted.

1.   There is the tension between the need to use existing language to communicate with others, while recognizing the limitations of that language. Rights language is predominant in current moral debate, and basic moral requirements can be cast in these terms. If the assertion of human rights prevents tyranny and injustice, so be it. And yet we need also to be wary of too close an embrace of a concept that is easily loaded with anti-Christian thought.

2.   There is the tension between the desire to legislate for the attainment of perfection, and the recognition of the sinfulness and limitations of human beings. We are caught, in Ronald Preston's apt words, between the politics of imperfection and the politics of hope.[130] This means that solutions are always provisional.

3.   There is the tension between the need to preserve institutional structures and the need to argue for correct substantive conceptions of justice. We want government to be restricted by the need to obtain the consent of the people, and we want government to adopt just laws. We want both to bind judges to the (flawed) texts of legal instruments in order to limit their power, and to persuade them to adopt interpretations of those texts that are substantively just.

There are no easy resolutions to these tensions. Our calling as Christian lawyers is to continue the struggle for a resolution for our time. I have argued in this paper that, in spite of its uses in restraining government injustice, the enactment of a bill of rights by its very nature skews the moral foundation of state action in a direction overly sympathetic to individual interests and overly hostile to duty, virtue, and the common good. Furthermore it too easily feeds off and promotes an autonomy-based moral and political philosophy that is frankly anti-Christian. There is much to be said for restricting the European Convention on Human Rights and Fundamental Freedoms to its current indirect role.

If a bill of rights is enacted, the only sure way of balancing power between the legislature and the judiciary is by restricting its function to

---

[129]   i.e. on the grounds that the limitation of a right is so unreasonable that no reasonable Parliament could have done so: *Associated Provincial Picture Houses Ltd v Wednesbury Corpn* [1948] 1 KB 223. But note that in practice this test is not as strict as it sounds.

[130]   *The Future of Christian Ethics*, (London, 1987), ch. 12.

that of an Interpretation Act. There should be no power to override statutes. Interpretation of any bill should also be 'conservative' in the sense of maintaining a high degree of consistency with earlier understandings of its meaning, although this does not relieve us from the need to develop Christian conceptions of political freedom and equality.

If we were to incorporate the Convention, in practice, most questions of content, interpretation and amendment would be foreclosed by the jurisprudence of the Strasbourg court, not always in the most appropriate way for this country. On balance, the focus of constitutional reform should be to strengthen the role and moral integrity of Parliament, and not to introduce a bill of rights.

3

A Christian Approach to Environmental Law?

David Harte[1]

I. WHERE DOES THE CHRISTIAN BEGIN?

For a Christian concerned with law reform there are two fundamental issues in identifying whether a Christian perspective on environmental law is appropriate. These are not peculiar to environmental law but are common to all areas of Law where it is sought to offer a Christian contribution. First, is there really a distinctive Christian perspective on the subject at all? Second, how can a Christian legal approach be articulated within the conceptual framework which is used by secular legislators and lawyers?

---

[1] In preparing this paper for publication, I have been particularly indebted to Professor Paul Beaumont, the editor of the volume, for reminding me that the relative nature of all secular legal systems is well demonstrated by the continuing differences between the law north and south of the Scottish border. At a number of points, it has been possible to amplify my own sketchy argument with valuable material which he has supplied, notably two articles referred to below; Donald A. Hay, 'Christians in the global greenhouse', (1990) 41 *Tyndale Bulletin* 107 and Francis Bridger, 'Ecology and eschatology: a neglected dimension', (1990) 41 *Tyndale Bulletin* 290. Also of considerable value has been an unpublished thesis presented by Colleen Lynn Theron, as part of the degree of LLM at the University of Aberdeen, 1996, 'What does the right to a decent environment mean? A jurisprudential overview.' The defects in the present paper, including any failure fully to take account of this material and the extensive literature which it cites, are however very much my own. Although written from an English perspective, the following discussion necessarily seeks to take account of the important European dimension to British Environmental Law. In a United Kingdom context the distinctive character of Scottish law makes any attempt to treat an area of law in a unified manner bound to be misleading. Much of the background to modern environmental regulation is found in those areas where the two jurisdictions differ significantly, notably land law.

An extreme Protestant view sees law as altogether distinct from the Gospel of Grace.[2] One may apply Christian insights to activities regulated by law, such as pollution, and use them as object lessons to illustrate the reality of sin. Thus, a study of law may underline the need for individual salvation, but it would be pointless to look for specifically Christian solutions in legal terms. A more moderate view may recognize a clear linkage between biblical teaching and the regulation of some areas of human activity but not others.

In the widest sense, there is a Christian perspective on everything. The one God is the Creator and the Lord of every aspect of life.[3] Sometimes, however, a Christian stance may simply mean choosing to have as little as possible to do with a particular activity, because it is inherently bad or of secondary importance.[4] On other occasions, or for some individuals, it may mean keeping away from areas of life for the sake of other Christians who may find those areas difficult to cope with.[5]

There are honourable traditions within Christianity of opting out from secular involvement. These include medieval and some modern monastic communities and miniature societies such as the Mennonites and the Amish. Such Christian communities have sought to insulate themselves as far as possible from secular institutions, including secular arbitration of any disputes between their members. Nevertheless, such communities may operate detailed and specific codes of conduct amongst themselves.[6]

[2] See the writing of Rudolph Sohm, referred to in Wilhelm Steinmüller, 'Divine law and its dynamism in Protestant theology of law' (1969) 8 *Concilium* (5) 13 and in H. Ridderbos, *Paul: An Outline of his Theology*, (1977, SPCK), 438–9. See too, Hans Dombois, 'The basic structure of Church law', (1969) 8 *Concilium* (5) 23.

[3] Ephesians 1:18–23 and Colossians 1:15–18.

[4] The priority will doubtless normally be concerned with concentrating on the positively good; Philippians 4:8.

[5] Romans 14:1–3. Note also, 1 Corinthians 8, on the proper attitude of the Christian to food offered to idols. As society becomes more secular, environmental and social concern is difficult to implement without incurring some element of moral ambiguity, for example where lottery money is needed for conservation projects, even ones involving church sites.

[6] The objection to secular law seems to be not so much to law but to Christians submitting themselves to non-Christian judges. See, 1 Corinthians 6:1–8. There is here an emphasis on not taking offence, in the spirit of Jesus' own teaching, notably in Matthew 5:38–48. There is also an emphasis on arbitration, mediation and negotiation rather than on formal judgment. However, the possibility of a Christian acting as judge between other Christians is clearly envisaged in the passage from 1 Corinthians and such arrangements are common today, whether under the full-blown legal model of the Roman Catholic Code of Canon Law or under the informal arrangements of a house church.

From an ecological point of view their farms, with abundant produce produced by traditional methods, can be models for modern organic agriculture.

If Christians do not opt out, to live in self-contained communities, they have to find a means of coexistence with the world, maintaining the difficult balance between being in the world but not of it.[7] In the West, there has been a tendency to assume that most sorts of work are 'safe' for Christians. It has been possible to carry out an interesting, or at any rate a remunerative occupation, without being forced to question whether what one is doing is right.

That has been so for lawyers generally and for those concerned with the environment, whether developers, architects, land managers or professional planners. Where societies have become more explicitly secular, and indeed anti-religious, the activities and underlying assumptions of such occupations are at risk. Short-term economic considerations and indeed corruption may be increasingly difficult to resist. Even without opting out from the secular world altogether, Christians may be driven to restrict themselves to a diminishing range of jobs and may feel compelled to concentrate as much time as possible in church fellowship.

Paradoxically, it may be in just such an era that Christians are called to be all the more fully involved in the world. Concern for the environment is a point of contact.[8] Secular people recognize the dangers faced by the planet. They experience environmental problems at first hand, pollution from neighbours' dogs on their doorstep[9] and noise through the next door wall.[10] Further, a proper legal regime for protecting the environment is necessary, if God's creation is to be treated with respect and if the world's resources are to be shared in the manner which the New Testament demands, as much as, and indeed even more than, the Old.

When Christians become actively involved in an area such as environmental protection, it is possible simply to treat the area as a forum for witness, by living a Christian life and testifying on a personal level. Even where secular values and categories are problematic, it is important for

[7] 1 John 17:9–26.

[8] See Hay, 'Christians in the Global Greenhouse', above, note 1, p. 112.

[9] See *Environmental Protection Act 1990*, Part IV and *Litter (Animal Droppings) Order 1991*, SI 1991 No. 961.

[10] The *Environmental Protection Act 1990*, s. 79(1)(g) generally regulates noise emitted from premises so as to be prejudicial to health or a nuisance. There is a host of other noise control provisions, e.g. the *Control of Pollution Act 1974*, s. 62 on loudspeakers, with a special exemption for ice cream vendors. The *Noise and Statutory Nuisance Act 1993* supplements existing controls and covers specific problems such as noisy burglar alarms. The *Criminal Justice and Public Order Act 1994*, ss. 63 ff. gives the police power to control noise from 'raves'.

Christian lawyers to engage with them, if they are to maintain contact with the world. Jesus gave the example for such dialogue with people as diverse as the woman at the well of Samaria[11] and the rich young ruler,[12] whom he met where they were and offered them the Gospel.

Seeking rules to express a Christian environmental ethic is a different matter, however, from sharing concern. With personal morality and perhaps with social affairs, there are well-recognized biblical principles which have been developed by the church in some detail. Despite all the differences, it is still possible to identify with the great range of human situations and experiences described in the Bible. Despite increasing differences, even between Christians, principles can be deduced from how the Bible handles those situations and the principles can feasibly be incorporated in modern legislation.

By contrast, regarding the environment detailed principles are more difficult to identify. However, there certainly are underlying Christian values and there are secular agendas which need to be tested against those values. A Christian perspective may add insights which others have failed to recognize. Also, it may help to provide the essential balance between apparently conflicting aims. This paper outlines the manner in which environmental law has emerged as an important category for lawyers. It seeks to identify underlying biblical values which appear to be relevant to environmental law. Questions are then raised as to what extent those values are consistent with the concepts employed in secular environmental law.

II.   THE EMERGENCE OF ENVIRONMENTAL LAW AS AN INCREASINGLY COHERENT BODY OF JURISPRUDENCE

This discussion is written from an English perspective but it would seem true to say, generally, that Environmental Law is a recently recognized category, both for comprehensive legislation and for systematic academic study. Historically, land use was long regulated, essentially as an aspect of private land law and through nuisance actions.[13] However, public interest in matters like land pollution was also recognized from early days. Thus, in the fourteenth century, there were Acts of Parliament prohibiting the

---

[11]   John 4:4–42. Although this is a passage of more direct relevance to family law reform it offers a challenging starting point for a meditation on the significance of water, a substance which is of lasting symbolic power as a fundamental environmental medium.

[12]   Luke 18:18–23.

[13]   In the 1970s, the importance of the interrelationship of private land law and modern environmental regulation was emphasized by Patrick McAuslan in his influential *Land, Law and Planning*, (1975, Weidenfeld and Nicolson).

deposit of filthy rubbish on the edge of cities and, in the sixteenth century, the burning of coal was similarly restricted to control atmospheric pollution.[14] Modern environmental regulation really originated at the time of the Industrial Revolution. Thus, the provision of sewers and the control of housing density were steps taken to deal with cholera and other health hazards which preoccupied the 1840s and 1850s. This legislation was dominated by reformers such as Edwin Chadwick.[15] It was seen as eminently necessary for practical reasons, but, unlike the abolition of the slave trade, factory legislation, prison improvement and other areas of later eighteenth century and Victorian legal reform, emerging environmental law does not appear to have been influenced explicitly by Christian beliefs.

A key aspect of traditional environmental law, both the protection of private property interests and anti-pollution and other public health legislation, was that it was *ad hoc* and reactive. There was no grand theoretical objective of protecting the environment for its own sake or out of a sense of any responsibility to honour God's creation. The protection of property was justified in terms of safeguarding order and prosperity and that appears to have been supported by the churches as part of a general policy of upholding the civil powers, in accordance with such texts as Romans 13. Doubtless a high level of sanitation was also seen as self-evidently good. It was of course said that 'cleanliness was next to godliness'. In very general terms, private property law and public health law served to maintain a basic level of environmental protection which was at least consistent with the biblical principle 'Thou shalt love thy neighbour as thyself'.[16] However, the judges were equally ready to justify exploiting natural resources in the interests of expanding national wealth, at the expense of degrading the environment.[17]

---

[14] See *An Act for the Punishment of them which cause corruption near a city or great town to corrupt air*, 1388, cited by McAuslan, *Land, Law and Planning*, 34. Rather different examples of early environmental legislation prefigure modern conservation law related to the control of agricultural pests; see the Scottish illustrations by Colin Reid, *Nature Conservation Law*, (1994, W. Green), 2.

[15] R.A. Lewis, *Edwin Chadwick and the Public Health Movement 1832–1854*, (1952, Longmans).

[16] The link was not made explicit, as it was for common law liability in negligence, by Lord Atkin in the exceptional case of *Donoghue v Stevenson* [1932] A.C. 562. That case was significant not least because of its origins in Scotland and its unifying effect on the law of the two jurisdictions. Lord Atkin himself was Welsh and in ecclesiastical circles is recalled as a leading opponent of the disestablishment of the Welsh church.

[17] A classic illustration was *Salvin v North Brancepeth Coke Co.* (1874) 9 Ch. App. Cas. 705.

During the second half of the twentieth century a much more coherent framework for environmental protection has been developed. The first, and still probably the most significant aspect of this, is the system of development control under Town and Country Planning legislation. This was imposed in England and Wales by the *Town and Country Planning Act 1947*[18] and, since then, planning permission has been required for any significant new development, whether building a new house or an extension to a factory, opening a quarry or turning an office block into a church! There is an elaborate system of central government policies and of plans made by local authorities for their respective areas which must be taken into account when planning applications are considered.[19]

Over the second half of the twentieth century, a number of other special regimes were developed. Water abstraction was subjected to licensing by the *Water Resources Act 1963* and was linked to the control of water pollution. Water pollution had originally been left to private nuisance actions, but was recognized as a form of public nuisance and was specifically regulated by a series of statutes, particularly the *Clean Rivers Acts*.[20] Serious poisoning of the atmosphere had been given some attention, notably by the *Alkali Act* of 1863 and 1874,[21] and more recently by the *Clean Air Act* of 1956 and 1968.[22]

The demands of nature conservation led to legislation in the nineteenth century, with the *Sea Birds Preservation Act 1869*, at a time when the demand for feathers on ladies' hats was threatening whole populations of birds. The public importance of wild and beautiful areas of the countryside was recognized in the *National Parks and Access to the Countryside Act 1949*. Further protection for plants, birds and animals, and particularly for wildlife habitats, has been provided by what is now the *Wildlife and Countryside Act 1981*,

---

[18] See the separate *Town and Country Planning, Scotland, Act 1947* and now the *Town and Country Planning (Scotland) Act 1972*.

[19] The principal primary legislation for England and Wales is now the *Town and Country Planning Act 1990*. For those unfamiliar with the subject, a clear and well illustrated introduction is Victor Moore, *A Practical Approach to Planning Law*, edition 5, (1995, Blackstone).

[20] An early attempt to ban pollution in rivers by the *Rivers Pollution Prevention Act 1876* was a failure. A system for licensing industrial and sewage discharges was introduced by the *Rivers (Prevention of Pollution) Act 1951*. This system was extended by a number of later Acts, particularly the *Control of Pollution Act 1974*.

[21] See the consolidating *Alkali Act* of 1906.

[22] The emergence of modern environmental law, particularly with regard to pollution control and the present law is thoroughly explained in David Hughes *Environmental Law*, third edition, (1996, Butterworths).

Part I.[23] Parts of the built environment were also recognized as needing conservation. A statutory system for listing buildings of historical or architectural merit, dating from earlier in the century, was toughened up as an aspect of modern planning controls, following the Second World War.[24]

[23] Another excellent and very readable introduction to Environmental Law is, Simon Ball and Stuart Bell, *Environmental Law*, third edition, (1995, Blackstone). This includes several chapters on nature conservation. A good introduction, specifically to that area of environmental law is Colin Reid, *Nature Conservation Law*, see above, note 14. Nature conservation has been furthered by significant European Community Directives; Directive on the Conservation of Wild Birds, 79/409/EEC (OJ 1979 L 103) and Directive on the Conservation of Natural Habitats and of Wild Fauna and Flora, 92/43/EEC (OJ 1992 L 206/7) These provisions seek to implement wider international agreements, notably the Ramsar Convention on Wetlands of International Importance, 1971 and the Bern Convention on the Conservation of European Wildlife and Natural Habitats, 1979. For the application under national law, see the provisions for sites of special scientific interest under the *Wildlife and Countryside Act 1981*, ss. 28 and 29 and also the *Natural Habitat Regulations 1994*, SI 1994 No.2716.

[24] Listed buildings law is of particular interest from a church point of view. In England at any rate, half the grade I listed buildings and many grade II buildings are churches but they are dealt with outside the ordinary planning system by the churches' own systems, under what is known as 'the ecclesi-astical exemption' from listed building control; see the *Planning (Listed Buildings and Conservation Areas) Act 1990*, part VI. A full account of Listed Building Law which gives clear coverage of the church system and its relationship to the secular system is Charles Mynors *Listed Buildings and Conservation Areas*, 2nd edition, FT Law and Tax, 1995. For the corresponding provision in Scotland, see the *Town and Country Planning (Scotland) Act 1972*, s. 54. Although the church systems are often criticized by church people as expensive bureaucracy they are considerably cheaper than the secular system would be and allow far greater freedom for reordering historic church interiors to meet the needs of modern worship and outreach. The exemption was originally negotiated by the Church of England as custodian of the main collection of ancient church buildings in Britain and because the Church of England already had a well established system in the Faculty Jurisdiction (see G. and H.L. Newsom *The Faculty Jurisdiction of the Church of England*, third edition, (1993, Sweet and Maxwell)). To maintain ecumenical parity, the exemption was granted to all religious denominations in England and Wales and not just to the Church of England. With increased interest in building conservation, the Secretary of State for Culture, Media and Sport now has the power to withdraw the exemption where a denomination fails to operate an adequate system itself; *Planning (Listed Buildings and Conservation Areas) Act 1990*, s. 60(5), SI 1994 No. 1771 and Department of the Environment Policy and Planning Guidance 15, para. 8.4. All major denominations now have their own approved schemes in place.

Alterations to listed buildings and their surroundings are subject to stricter control than under ordinary planning law. In 1974, listing of individual buildings was supplemented by the concept of conservation areas of architectural or historic interest, where strict controls are imposed over any demolition of buildings and where trees are specially protected.[25]

A major feature of Environmental Law in the UK during the last two decades has been its progressive rationalization. A series of statutes have introduced what amount to comprehensive codes for water resources,[26] protection of the atmosphere from pollution,[27] and control of land fill.[28] The *Environmental Protection Act 1990*, Part I, imposed a new system of integrated pollution control for supervising all forms of pollution from large scale industries. Regulation has been increasingly centralized, with licensing and prosecutions for environmental offences now being concentrated largely in the hands of a unified Environment Agency for England and Wales which was set up under the *Environment Act 1995*.[29] Regulatory functions have been clearly separated from the management of resources and the provision of services which are left to commercial undertakers. This is particularly true with water and waste disposal.[30] Further developments have been made as a result of International Conventions. European Community Law has set progressively more rigorous standards for environmental protection and conservation both of species and of natural resources. These standards are increasingly integrated into UK Law.[31]

[25] See now, *Planning (Listed Buildings and Conservation Areas) Act 1990*, Part II. For protection of trees generally, cf. tree preservation orders under the *Town and Country Planning Act 1990*, s. 198 and generally ss. 197–214, with commercial regulation of felling under the Forestry Act 1967.

[26] See now the *Water Resources Act 1991*. See too the *Water Industry Act 1991*. These Acts consolidated recent changes in the statutory framework for the management and regulation of water resources, including privatization of supply and distribution. Less extreme, but hotly contested, changes were introduced in Scotland by the *Local Government etc (Scotland) Act 1994*, overhauling the *Water (Scotland) Act 1980*.

[27] Industrial pollution is largely dealt with as an aspect of integrated pollution control, under Part I of the *Environmental Protection Act 1990*. However, local authorities also have extensive policing powers over low scale atmospheric pollution, notably under the *Clean Air Act 1993*. For local authority control over noise nuisances, see the *Control of Pollution Act 1974*, Part III, and the *Environmental Protection Act 1990*.

[28] The rules for the disposal of solid waste are now provided in the *Environmental Protection Act 1990*, Part II.

[29] S. 1 ff. A separate Scottish Environment Protection Agency is set up under s. 20ff.

[30] See notes 26, 27 and 28, above.

[31] Stanley P. Johnson and Guy Corcelle, *The Environmental Policy of the European Communities*, (1995, Kluwer International); Gerd Winter *European Environmental Law*, (1996, Tempus). See also note 23, above.

The policy underlying modern UK environmental legislation was most fully reasoned in the Conservative government White Paper of 1990, *This Common Inheritance*.[32] Subsequently, there were annual updates to that report. The main policy statement by the Labour Party is *In Trust for Tomorrow*.[33] Significantly, in both main policy documents, Christians would recognize an awareness of the idea of stewardship. There is shared recognition of the priorities of pollution control, conservation of limited natural resources and planning for public sharing of land use.

There are, also, a number of areas which tend to be singled out by all parties as particularly worrying, doubtless where politicians have sensed public concern and want to demonstrate that they are 'doing something'. Many of these concerns, although huge, are remote.[34]

Dealing with them is so complex that there is a danger of politicians merely saying the right thing. Such problems are often international, and indeed of global concern. Tighter controls by one country may put it at an economic disadvantage.[35] Thus, depletion of tropical forests and destruction of the polar areas are both recognized as of great importance in *This Common Inheritance*,[36] but they can only be tackled with effective international co-operation and it may be relatively difficult to raise concern amongst people living thousands of miles away.[37] By contrast, pollution, in its various forms, is more obviously damaging at a national level and can be dealt with there. Its global dimension, such as damage to the ozone layer and global warming, may, therefore, be more readily recognized by the public.

Concerns, at a national level, over problems which pose global risks to humanity as a whole are particularly appropriate for a concerted European approach. The international fears for the global environment where agreement and action seem most likely to be converted into effective policies are those where the country causing harm can be shown as likely to suffer early direct consequences itself. However, even here there are tensions between long-term rhetoric and immediate political pressures, particularly

---

[32]   Cm. 1200.

[33]   The Labour Party B/034/94.

[34]   On the nature of environmental problems, see Malcolm Newson (editor), *Managing the Human Impact on the Natural Environment, Patterns and Processes*, (1992, Belhaven).

[35]   See generally on international environmental law, P.W. Birnie and A.E. Boyle, *International Law and the Environment*, (1992, OUP) and P.H. Sand, *The Effectiveness of International Environmental Agreements*, (1992, Grotius).

[36]   Above, note 32.

[37]   It may be that conservation of endangered species of large animals, whether whales or elephants, has more direct popular appeal, at least in some Western countries, which may add support for an international ban on whaling and on trading in ivory.

economic restraints. Inevitably, in government documents, there may seem more of a tendency to compromise, because economic pressures are more immediate than the environmental danger.[38]

III. THE BASIS FOR A CHRISTIAN LEGAL CONTRIBUTION

Historically, Christians appear to have had disconcertingly little concern for the environment. Nature was largely regarded as wild and dangerous, requiring taming.[39] Buildings, gardens and agriculture mattered, but mineral abstraction, and latterly industrial pollution, do not generally seem to have been challenged prophetically, as morally dubious, despite the long-term damage which they cause. This may not be surprising when one considers the failure of the church to expose other ills near at hand, and sometimes a tendency even to justify them. Without going any further back in time, there were major examples in the nineteenth and twentieth centuries which had both a social and an environmental dimension. These included the annihilation of North American Indians and other native populations[40] and the Highland Clearances, where the established Church of Scotland does not seem to have raised any real questions over the large scale evictions involved.[41]

These are, of course, sweeping generalizations. There have always been some prophetic voices raised and prophecy is demonstrated in the Bible to be a lonely activity. For the most part, Christians have doubtless suffered from short sightedness which has prevented them from recognizing wrongs close at hand, not because Christians are peculiarly bad, but because they have always been part of the society they live in. They are preoccupied with trying to do

---

[38]   For the faltering impetus to control emissions which are harmful to the atmosphere, see Hughes, *Environmental Law* (above, note 22) 122 f. Hughes shows how the United Nations Conference on Environment and Development, in 1992, produced a firm commitment to control, which appears not to have been followed through in the Intergovernmental Panel on Climate Change in 1994 and the 'Berlin Mandate' of 1995. On the other hand, carbofluorocarbons from refrigerators and aerosols threatening the atmosphere have been the subject of more concerted control following international agreements.

[39]   There are examples to the contrary. Thus, Martin Luther showed a profound awareness of nature as an expression of God's continuing activity in the world; see, e.g., Jaroslav Pelican, *Luther's Works, the Companion Volume*, (1959, Concordia) 165 and Luther's Commmentary on the Sermon on the Mount, (1530–32) W, XXXII, *Luther's Works* 21, 126.

[40]   Dee A. Brown, *Bury my Heart at Wounded Knee*, (1971, Holt, Rinehart and Winston). Note too the acquiescence in Apartheid in South Africa, especially by the Dutch Reformed Church.

[41]   John Prebble, *The Highland Clearances*, (1963, Secker and Warburg).

their own immediate work and living their own lives as well as possible. What can be said is that nature became popular as a source of inspiration for art and literature for the Romantic Movement in the eighteenth and nineteenth centuries. However, this movement may be regarded as largely secular or deist and, at any rate, not in any way distinctively Christian.

The injunction in Genesis, even before the fall, was 'Be fruitful and multiply, and replenish the earth, and subdue it and have dominion over the fish of the sea, and over the fowl of the air and over every living thing that moveth upon the earth.'[42] This idea of dominion and subjugation has been characterized by critics as essentially exploitative and therefore destructive of nature.[43] Apologists admit that the Hebrew word for 'subduing' in this context may have a tough emphasis. However, it has been pointed out that this contentious word is applied to the raw earth. What is grown in the earth is referred to more benignly: 'cultivation is the means to fruitfulness'. The picture is one of human 'co-operation in and serving the natural order'.[44]

The famous passage in the first chapter of Genesis may have inspired industry and technological innovation, especially since the eighteenth century, but neither industry nor technology are necessarily destructive. Nature itself is amazingly prodigal in what it seems to waste. Biblical references to pruning vines are a reminder of this.[45] The allegation that Christianity has supported the abuse of nature ignores the biblical emphasis on responsible stewardship and also the biblical account of sin, which explains why abuse is only to be expected and is a distortion of God's original intention. What is significant here is that, following the fall, the stewardship of the earth became a burden.[46] The concept of

[42] Genesis 1:28.

[43] E.g. Ian L. Harg, *Design with Nature*, (1969, Doubleday), quoted in, John Stott, *Issues Facing Christians Today*, (1984, Marshalls), ch. 6, 'Our Human Environment'. For other critics see Lynn White Jnr., 'The historical roots of an ecological crisis', *Science* 155, (10 March 1967) 1204.

[44] Donald A. Hay, 'Christians in the global greenhouse', (1990) 41 *Tyndale Bulletin*, 107, at 117. Hay provides valuable references to both sides in the debate. Among the defenders of the Christian position see: I. Barbour (ed.) *Western Man and Environmental Ethics*, (1973, Addison-Wesley, Mass); J. and J. Barr, 'Man and nature – the ecological controversy and the Old Testament', *BJRL* 55 (1972) 9–32. For a positive assertion of the concept of stewardship see: H.P. Santmire, *The Travail of Nature*, (1985, Fortress Press, Philadelphia); R. Atfield, *The Ethics of Environmental Concern*, (1983, Blackwell, Oxford) and W. Granberg-Michelson, *A Worldly Spirituality: The Call to Take Care of the Earth*, (1984, Harper and Row, San Francisco).

[45] E.g. Leviticus 25:3.

[46] 'Cursed is the ground for thy sake; in sorrow shalt thou eat bread; in sorrow shalt thou eat of it all the days of thy life; thorns also and thistles shall it bring forth to thee; and thou shalt eat the herb of the field; in the sweat of thy face shalt thou eat bread, till thou return unto the ground; for out of it wast thou taken; for dust thou art, and unto dust shalt thou return' Genesis 3:17–19.

human dominion of nature was distorted from stewardship to exploitation. A fully biblical perspective recognizes this as part of the reality of sin, not a justification for sinning.

An awareness of the reality of sin may itself have contributed to the Christian failure to take a lead in environmental protection. Jumping from the beginning to the end of the Bible, the book of Revelation looks forward to the destruction of nature, when the heavens shall depart 'as a scroll when it is rolled together'.[47] The evangelical emphasis, until quite late in the present century, has concentrated on salvation of the individual, to the extent that both social issues and wider material concerns have tended to be ignored. This is inadequate, from a biblical perspective. The second letter to the Thessalonians provides the antidote, by warning the Christian reader not to be preoccupied by the prospect of the end of the world, but to get on with living the Christian life in the present.[48]

The attitude of some Christians to the prospect of global environmental disaster may seem reminiscent of the response of King Hezekiah when Isaiah prophesied that the kingdom of Judah would be overthrown by the Babylonians. Isaiah's prophecy was prompted by learning that Hezekiah had just given an unrestricted guided tour of Jerusalem to a party of Babylonian ambassadors. Hezekiah's seemingly complacent reaction to the prophecy was: 'Is it not good if peace and truth be in my days?'[49]

Although the churches in the nineteenth century may not have made a concerted effort to protect the environment, it is significant that they did actively challenge the social evils of slavery and the abuse in factories of women and children as discussed by Teresa Sutton above. It is also significant that this coincided with great times of revival. More recently many of the negative stereotypes of Christianity in modern British society have been partially offset by a renewed evangelical sensitivity to social issues which was established at the Keele Conference in 1967. Certainly, since the late 1960s, there have been plenty of Christian voices expressing environmental concern.[50] The second Evangelical Congress, at Nottingham

---

47 Revelation 6:14; cf. Isaiah 34:4. However one is to understand the rich imagery of the book of Revelation, there can be no doubt that it vividly and remarkably anticipates the whole gamut of environmental problems which face the world at the dawn of the Third Millennium. See especially chapters 8, 9 and 16. These passages had an immediate impact for a lecture on problems facing environmental law delivered by the present writer during the Gulf War, when the oil reserves in Kuwait were opened up to pollute the sea, and oil wells were set on fire, hiding the sun for hundreds of square miles.

48 2 Thessalonians 2, especially verse 1 and 2. Significantly, this teaching is set in the context of a very stark warning of the reality of the end of things, see chapter 1, especially verses 7 and 8.

49 2 Kings 21:19

50 See e.g. John Stott, *Issues Facing Christians Today*, above, note 43.

in 1977, included Global Stewardship as one of its themes.[51] The emphasis there was very much on human need in a shrinking world. Other British evangelical Christian writing has showed a clearer concern for the earth itself.[52]

A fundamental attack on Christian environmental ethics is made by those who reject the idea of a sovereign God as the Creator of nature. This approach is linked with 'New Age' philosophies.[53] Such critics, when they are religious, tend to pantheistic and, in an extreme form, may personify nature itself as a sort of mother goddess. This is fundamentally alien to the Christian understanding of the God who created nature, but became part of it, simply as an individual man, in the person of Jesus.[54] To such thinkers the passage in Revelation which speaks of the destruction of nature may seem negative and indeed irresponsible.[55] However, as always, if the Bible is read as a whole there is in fact a balance. The book of Revelation goes on to prophesy that, after the first heaven and the first earth have passed away, there will be a new heaven and a new earth.[56]

---

[51]   John Stott, *Obeying Christ in a Changing world*; Philip King 'Global Steward-ship', ch. 6, in Vol. 3, Bruce Kaye (ed.), *The Changing World*, (1977, Collins).

[52]   E.g. E.F. Schumacher, *Small is Beautiful*, (1974, Abacus).

[53]   A valuable source book here is Joseph R. Des Jardins, *Environmental Ethics*, (1993, Wadsworth), see particularly, at 103, the reference to Lynn White Jnr. 'The Historical Roots of our Ecological Crisis', *Science*, 155 (March 1967): 1203–1207. See also references in Hay 'Christians in the Global Greenhouse', above, at note 2, particularly J. Lovelock, *Gai*, (1970, O.U.P.), and J. Lovelock and S. Epton, 'The quest for Gaia' in J. Gribben (ed.), *The Breathing Planet*, (1986, Basil Blackwell and the New Scientist, Oxford).

[54]   Pantheism may be identified in the concept of 'Deep Ecology', explored by Des Jardins in his *Environmental Ethics* (see above) ch. 10. See here, particu-larly, Arne Ness 'The Shallow and the Deep, Long-Range Ecology Move-ment', *Inquiry*, 16 (1973): 95–100; *Ecology Community and Life Style*, translated by Rothenberg, (1989, Cambridge University Press). For the more Christian antecedents in this approach see Des Jardins *Environmental Ethics*, ch. 7. A biocentric approach originated with Albert Schweitzer, *Civilisation and Ethics*, (1946, A. & C. Black). A more recent exponent of a biocentric approach to environmental ethics, rooted in traditional Western thought, is typified by Paul Taylor, *Respect for Nature*, (1986, Princeton). I am indebted for further references to the unpublished thesis presented by Colleen Lynn Theron, referred to above at note 1, particularly C. Stone, *Earth and Other Ethics*, (1988, New York, Harper Row), George Sessions (ed.), *Deep Ecology for the 21st Century*, (1995, Boston, Shambhala).

[55]   Revelation 6:14.

[56]   Revelation 21:1ff.

A fundamental question here is to what extent this new heaven and new earth envisage a disjunction from the old or may rather consist in a transformation to which human stewardship should be actively directed. As Francis Bridger has written, 'the other side of the eschatological coin is less concerned with doom but more concerned with continuity'.[57] If the Bible is accepted as the authoritative word of God, then clearly human beings can not bring about a transformation of the world by themselves. However, it may not necessarily follow that the dramatic biblical language of destruction means that God will simply abandon his original creation. Again, Bridger suggests that, from a Pauline perspective, God may not so much overthrow the natural order as vindicate it.[58]

The non-Christian ecological movement which criticizes Christianity for promoting destruction of the earth reproves its opponents for being anthropocentric.[59] But, biblical environmental ethics are Christocentric. 'They testify to the vindicating acts of God in creation and redemption.'[60] The Christian ecological perspective is fundamentally superior to the earth-bound approach of the New Age. However, whether one views the world as very much a temporary phenomenon, where stewardship must still be exercised until the final account is taken at the last judgement, or whether one envisages a more progressive transformation of nature, one thing which does seem to be lacking is any explicit attempt to analyse, from a Christian perspective, the present state of Environmental Law and the directions in which it may be going.

IV.   ESTABLISHING A CONCEPTUAL FRAMEWORK

The first basic issue for Christians concerned with law reform in a particular area is to establish a general biblical approach. The second basic issue is the problem of using appropriate categories and terminology in

[57]   See especially Romans 8:18–30 and Colossians 1:15–20. For discussion of these passages and their implications see, Francis Bridger, 'Ecology and eschatology: a neglected dimension', (1990) 41 *Tyndale Bulletin*, 290. Bridger offers an approach which looks forward beyond that presented by Hay in 'Christians in the global greenhouse'. He includes references to a further wide range of literature, notably Jurgen Moltman, *God in Creation*, (1985, SCM, London).

[58]   The parallels are abundant. After the Resurrection, it was striking that Christ's physical body maintained a continuity with his earthly body; see e.g. Matthew 28:9; Luke 24:30 and 42–43, and John 20:27 and 21:13. Taking a different point, Jesus made clear that he had not come to destroy the Law of the Old Covenant but rather to fulfil it; Matthew 5:17 and see Luke 16:17.

[59]   See the references given by Hay in 'Christians in the global greenhouse', above, note 1.

[60]   Francis Bridger, above, 301.

communicating with the secular world. It may be possible to analyse a given environmental problem in Christian terms. In some cases there may seem a definite Christian responsibility to aim for particular policies. However, the problem remains of relating a Christian analysis to a practical programme for law reform. To do this it is first necessary to ensure that an appropriate conceptual framework is available. Only then will it be possible to offer an effective, reasoned critique of secular proposals for law reform and, more proactively, take the initiative in calling for specific reform.

There can be no doubt that the categories in which people think affect the way they think. That, of course, is far from saying that words are more important than the ideas they express. But the Bible is living proof of the power of 'the word'. Christians recognize the Bible itself as the living word of God. Jesus himself is explicitly referred to as 'the Word'.[61] The form which God chose for the Incarnation is immeasurably important. Also, where the Bible treats of matters such as legal rules and the environment, it would seem important to consider the manner in which it does so.

One aspect of this is that the Bible is selective. That may itself be important, if we are looking at law where there does not seem to be much clear biblical input. As we shall consider below, the absence of an explicit treatment of a particular topic may itself suggest that there are no absolute rules in that area. Nevertheless, there may be some spiritual lead-in there is rarely, if ever, a blueprint. The very fact that rules in the Old Testament are spelled out in what may seem a jumble warns against any temptation to go back to them in a legalistic sense, as if they were texts to be applied by a system of strict legal interpretation. On the other hand, the often seemingly scattered nature of biblical texts allows them to be taken as fragments, each of which may prompt meditation. This, in turn, may lead to the recognition of principles which are applicable today.

The ancient dietary laws may seem to be irrelevant in the light of the New Covenant, but they were originally given for a purpose. The fact that God chose those rather than other rules to distinguish the people of Israel from their neighbours may well have much to teach us today.[62]

---

[61] Λογος; John 1:1 and 1 John 1:1.

[62] The distinction between clean and unclean animals in Leviticus 11 has long been discarded by the Christian Church (see Acts 15:28–29). However, these rules may well have had an important practical purpose for good health. By contrast, other discreet rules have been maintained as of continuing effect (e.g. in Leviticus 18 and 20, dealing largely with human sexual behaviour). There is a liberal tendency to argue that with modern developments, such as contraception, the sexual rules which may be found in the Bible are now outdated, as well as the old dietary ones. By contrast, a biblical approach may suggest that both sets of rules reflect underlying principles which are as valid today as ever, although both need to be constantly reassessed, so that the principles can be applied effectively in modern conditions.

Concepts such as the jubilee have implications for modern land management and property regimes.[63] Less obvious passages in the New Testament may have environmental implications which lawyers, as much as
other Christians, will do well to ponder; for example, the mysterious,
acted-out parable of the fruitless fig tree,[64] or the miracles of the loaves
and fishes[65] and the stilling of the storm.[66]

The detailed rules for beautifying the Tent of Meeting,[67] and, later,
the account of the construction of the Temple,[68] may teach a good deal
about the importance of maintaining aesthetic standards. Concepts which
are difficult to measure risk being left out of consideration in environmental law. Thus, promoting good design and amenity is at a disadvantage
when set against matters which can be more readily measured in monetary
terms and where increasingly specific regulations have been introduced,
such as those aimed at the elimination of pollution. Aesthetics are not
only difficult to measure but difficult to find agreement on. Thus, there
is public concern to preserve old and beautiful buildings, but there is also
a desire to make them accessible to the public and there is a concern that
'pickling' obsolete architecture should not hamper development of new
jobs and products for the market.[69]

It is a striking aspect of environmental law in various jurisdictions that
it seems to have little to say about aesthetics. This is also an ambivalent
subject for Christians. There is a puritan element which regards beauty
as a matter of indifference or a snare of the devil. On the other hand,
there is at least as powerful a tradition which sees beauty as a spiritual
medium bringing human beings closer to God the Creator. This is
underlined by Jesus' own upbringing in the carpenter's workshop.

In English law, provision to preserve buildings and the countryside for
their aesthetic appeal is incorporated into the planning system. Yet,
planners and judges have tended to shy away from recognizing any
objective, aesthetic principles. Even when a proposed new building is
considered likely to add aesthetically to a village, permission to build it
is likely to be refused if it will breach the formal cordon limiting
development within the existing village envelope. Approval for building

---

63 Leviticus 25. This also relates environmental concerns with proper concern
    for the poor.
64 Matthew. 21:19–21 and Mark 11:13–14 and 20–24.
65 Matthew 14:17; Mark 6:38; Luke 9:13 and John 6:9; Matthew 15:34 and
    Mark 8:7.
66 Mark 4:39.
67 Exodus 36:8–39: 43.
68 1 Kings 6:1–7:51 and 2 Chronicles 3:1–4:22.
69 See *Journal of Planning Law*, Occasional Papers, *A Future for Old Buildings?*
    (1977) and *Making the Most of Our Heritage?* (1989) 32–69.
70 See *Lord Luke of Pavenham v. Minister of Housing and Local Government* [1968]
    1 Q.B. 172.

within the village may be correspondingly easier, even though it may be aesthetically much less worthy.[70]

Aesthetic judgement has been seen as essentially a subjective matter on which there really are no objective principles.[71] Doubtless, it is true that canons of aesthetics are as elusive as biblical rules for protecting the environment, but the pursuit of a beautiful, as well as a healthy, environment, accessible to all, may be seen as an eminently Christian task.[72] Architects may have competing aims but it is possible to bring these out into the open so that they can be properly set against each other. Thus, in what may be considered the milestone case of, *Save Britain's Heritage v No. 1 Poultry Ltd*, the House of Lords accepted that it was permissible to replace a grade II listed building on a prominent site in London with a new building by an outstanding modern architect.[73] However, this was on the basis that the competing aesthetic and conservation considerations had been scrupulously weighed.

In the countryside, there is a similar tension between different concepts of conservation, and between conservation generally and public access. On the one hand, there is public interest in conserving wildlife species and in protecting beautiful areas of countryside. There is also increasing pressure for greater public access rights and simply for greater freedom to develop land. Indeed, to some, wildlife conservation seems an expensive luxury. A good illustration of such conflict occurred in *Beebee's* case.[74]

Poole Borough Council proposed to revive a planning consent for house-building at a site on the edge of Canford Heath, a remaining fragment of the Egdon Heath of Thomas Hardy's Wessex novels. The proposal was resisted by the British Herpetological Society, which protects creatures such as lizards. The opposition was backed by the World Wildlife Fund. These bodies challenged the council on the basis that it had failed to take proper account of the fact that the land had recently been included as part of a Site of Special Scientific Interest under section 28 of the *Wildlife and Countryside Act 1981*. Schiemann J. dismissed the conservation bodies' application for judicial review. Although there had been breaches of the conservation procedures, the council had adequately considered the conservation value of the site and had been entitled to put houses first.[75]

---

71   *Winchester City Council v. Secretary of State for the Environment* 29 P. & C.R. 1 and 31 P. & C.R. 576.

72   In the specialist context of whether a new altar by Henry Moore should be installed in a major church by Sir Christopher Wren, see *Re St Stephen Walbrook* [1987] Fam. 146.

73   [1991] 1 WLR 153, [1991] 2 All E.R. 10.

74   *R. v. Poole Borough Council ex parte Beebee and others* (1991) 3 *Journal of Environmental Law* 293.

75   A postscript to the case was that Michael Heseltine, the then recently reappointed Secretary of State for the Environment in John Major's first cabinet, called in the Borough Council's scheme and quashed the consent. Significantly perhaps, his passion is trees and he has planted a fine arboretum around his own home.

An important aspect, here, is establishing a principled physical infrastructure. There are key public services, such as power lines, water and roads, which have been largely controlled by government agencies for most of the second half of the twentieth century. These have, conspicuously, been the subject of privatization by recent Conservative governments.[76] Even under central or local government control, doubtless because of Treasury pressure, there has been a tendency to concentrate on cost considerations in building and managing this infrastructure. On the large scale, road bypasses and new power lines for the National Grid have tended to be constructed with the main emphasis on cheapness, giving rise to a series of increasingly militant protests. On the small scale, it is difficult to find road furniture or any other clutter from these services which display any aesthetic sensitivity.

To some Christians these may seem trivial matters. However, others may see them as a significant illustration of a lack of sensitivity for the creation and for the Creator himself. With privatization, regulatory functions are now generally exercised by independent public agencies, but their concerns seem largely limited to ensuring safety and preventing commercial exploitation of natural monopolies by overcharging. There may be scope for a Christian contribution in injecting a more definite concern for amenity and an explicit aim to seek beauty and good design through environmental law.

There are frequent statutory references to the need to take account of conservation and amenity, but such formulae tend to be couched in such general terms that there is little prospect of them being enforced through court proceedings.[77] A model for a more tangible requirement to upgrade the environment, or at least to make sure that it is not made worse, may be found in the *Planning (Listed Buildings and Conservation Areas) Act 1990*. Thus in exercising their powers with respect to buildings or land in a conservation area, a planning authority is required to pay special attention 'to the desirability of preserving or enhancing the character or appearance of that area'.[78] It would, in theory, be possible to emphasize amenity in planning law by requiring that, on any planning application, consideration should be given to the desirability of ensuring that the proposed scheme should at least not detract from the character of the area.

---

[76] See, notably, the water privatization legislation for England and Wales now consolidated in the *Water Resources Act 1991* and the *Water Industry Act 1991*. Operation of the national grids for electricity and gas has also been privatized and the government has provided for new roads, at any rate, to be constructed as private toll routes.

[77] E.g. *Water Resources Act 1991*, s. 16, as amended by the *Environment Act 1995*.

[78] S. 72. See, however, the restricted interpretation which has been put on this requirement; *South Lakeland District Council v. Secretary of State for the Environment* [1992] 2 A.C. 141. See here also *Planning (Listed Buildings and Conservation Areas) Act 1990*, s. 66.

Another aspect of the legal framework for environmental management is the scope for bodies, such as charities, which can hold land in perpetuity and are helped by tax concessions. Churches and other religious foundations are examples of these bodies, as are secular organizations, such as the National Trust or the National Trust for Scotland. In a money-obsessed world, where resources can easily be siphoned out of a country and governments encourage conspicuous personal expenditure, these organizations provide opportunities for alternative accumulations of wealth, with altruistic purposes. Christians are prepared to invest in organizations for evangelism and for the relief of poverty. In the long-term, preserving and improving the physical amenities of city and countryside may be an equally important witness. Devising the most effective system of trusts is an important challenge for Christian property lawyers.

Programmes for reform in the British system to introduce legal change depend on rational presentation of arguments and on the development of a measure of consensus. A Christian perspective may at least help to refine the arguments on both sides of a debate and to ensure that the conclusion is reasonable and is accepted with a good grace. The extent to which there is any specifically Christian agenda for environmental law reform is debatable. In many cases there may be no one right, or 'Christian', answer. However, it should be possible to determine whether secular solutions are at least compatible with Christian imperatives. Where a balance is to be struck, the conflicting principles need to be analysed and their respective compatibility with Christian principles evaluated.

For example, where it is proposed to construct an impressive new building in place of a modest old listed one, all other factors being equal, there may seem to be no objective solution to the choice between preserving the present structure and encouraging architectural originality. Or, there may seem to be no clear answer where there is a choice between conserving a piece of open country which is a habitat for wildlife and building houses which may be more expensive to build elsewhere. However, asking fundamental questions may enable an individual Christian to see more clearly which scheme would be right; in the first case, whether an old or a new building would better glorify God, or, in the second, whether retaining a place of peace and beauty and protecting the species there or building new homes will best meet human need in the long-term.

Biblical texts cannot be used today in a rigid, legalistic manner. Secular legislators and those who apply the secular law will not recognize that the Bible has any innate authority. On the other hand, a text may be used to express a rule which is contained in the secular law in such a way as to keep the biblical framework in the public mind. The reminder that 'the Bible says it too' may provide a feeling of solidarity which the modernist can welcome and this can predispose the same person to consider the truths expressed in other biblical texts more sympathetically.[79] Significantly,

[79] The classic example is Lord Atkin's reference to 'the neighbour' in *Donoghue v Stevenson*, see above, note 16.

environmental law is very much an area where it can be claimed that 'the Bible says it too'.

Often, and especially in areas of sexual morality, Christian principles are raised to oppose legal change. By contrast, where the Christian sees secular proposals for legal reform as good or acceptable, there may be a tendency to leave the well-meaning secularists to get on with it. This can be dangerous. Where the emphasis is not quite right, there may be a greater readiness on the part of the secularist to accept correction on matters of detail, than there would be to back down over a proposal which Christians oppose as fundamentally wrong. Also, if Christian discourse is accepted as relevant and valuable in one area of law reform, that can benefit the general climate and make society more receptive to Christian voices elsewhere. Not to engage in the debate across the field marginalizes the church and makes it generally less effective in its mission.

Although the Bible does not offer rules in anything resembling a coherent code, the nearest it gets to one is the Ten Commandments. Their unique character says something very important about the priority to be given to the principles which they enshrine, over any other laws. But even here application may vary from time to time and, place to place. No modern code can be composed using even the Ten Commandments as if they were chapters or volume titles. Christian lawyers are bound to use legal categories, rather than biblical ones. Normally, this means categories which have been devised by text-book writers or in legislation, increasingly produced by non-Christian authors. It is difficult to change those categories. Nevertheless, where new ones are being laid down, it may be particularly important to seek to influence them as well as the detailed rules which they contain.

In practice, secular categories may be innocuous. Indeed, it may be possible to relate them, explicitly, to a Christian perspective, and this seems so with environmental law. There, some categories reflect objective facts which would seem consistent with the medieval Christian understanding of nature. Study of environmental law is generally organized according to the media of air, water and solid waste disposal into the earth. Thus, the *Environmental Protection Act 1990* defines 'the environment' in terms of three media: land, water and air. The Act deals with these in turn, although less fully with water and air, because these are covered by other legislation.[80] This is reminiscent of the ancient concepts of the four elements. Even fire, the fourth element, can be identified with energy, as a major subject for environmental law. The ancient idea of the four elements was doubtless

[80]   Each medium calls for a different protective regime, but the *Environmental Protection Act 1990* is a milestone, as it recognizes that no one medium can be treated exclusively, in isolation. The Act sets up the system of integrated pollution control, providing a comprehensive system for large industrial undertakings which are likely to pose major environmental problems. This allows 'the best environmental option' to be worked out in disposing of industrial waste products from such undertakings. See now the 1996 EC Directive on integrated pollution control, 96/61/EC OJ 1996 L257/26.

taken by the Medieval Church from classical rather than from biblical sources. However, they are an aspect of the divine order embodied in nature, as recognized in theological thought.[81]

Some new environmental law concepts, particularly some originating from the EC, may readily commend themselves to a Christian lawyer. One, which overrides some deeply entrenched attitudes in the UK, is the 'precautionary principle'. This envisages that steps should be taken to guard against pollution or other environmental harm if there is a possibility of such harm, and not only where it is a virtual certainty.[82] This gives primacy to conservation. It implies that there should be a burden placed on developers to show that any schemes which they propose will not cause harm, rather than waiting to see whether the opponents' fears are justified, by which time it is too late to do anything.[83]

The precautionary principle has an affinity with some Old Testament provisions. The rule against cooking a kid in its mother's milk, which is repeated three times in Exodus and Deuteronomy, has obvious parallels with feeding cows meal made from parts of other cows rejected for human consumption.[84] When this practice was associated with the bovine disease BSE and then with the related human CJD, European Community law was used, in a manner reminiscent of the general biblical ban, to impose blanket restrictions requiring the destruction of all cows which could possibly be affected rather than leave any risk to human health.[85]

---

[81] See A.C. Crombie, *Augustine to Galileo: The History of Science A.D. 400–1650*, (1952, Falcon, London) and J.D. Bernal, *Science in History, Vol. I: The Emergence of Science*, (1969, Penguin) esp. 174 ff. Although scientific understanding has long abandoned the ancient concept of four elements they have resurfaced as a model for understanding the material world, for example in Architecture; see, Gottfied Semper, *The Four Elements of Architecture and Other Writings*, translated by H.F. Mallgrave and W. Herrman, with an introduction by H.F. Mallgrave, (1989, Cambridge).

[82] See further, Cm 1200 at 11 and *R. v. Secretary of State for Trade and Industry, ex parte Duddridge* (1995) 7 *Journal of Environmental Law* 224.

[83] The principle is accepted as UK government policy in *This Common Inheritance*, Cm. 1200, see 11. However it is not borne out in case law; for example, *R. v. Secretary of State for Trade and Industry, ex parte Duddridge* (1995) 7 *Journal of Environmental Law* 224, concerned with whether precautionary steps should be taken to guard against the risk of leukaemia which might be occasioned by exposure to electromagnetic fields under electric power lines; and *North Uist Fisheries Ltd v. Secretary of State for Scotland* (1992) 4 *Journal of Environmental Law* 241, concerned with the degree of risk necessary before designation of a Site of Special Scientific Interest.

[84] Exodus 23:19 and 34:26 and Deuteronomy 14:21.

[85] See Case C-180/96R *UK v Commission* [1996] 2 CMLR 1. Another example here could be the question of whether the rule in the Ten Commandments in Exodus 20:4 and Deuteronomy 5:8 against making 'likenesses' may have more relevance today to genetic engineering than to works of art.

V.   A CHRISTIAN PERSPECTIVE ON THE CONCEPT OF ENVIRONMENTAL RIGHTS

Sometimes, being forced to use secular categories may pose problems for the Christian lawyer. Such problems may arise where well-established concepts are adapted in new ways. An example is where environmentalists seek to expand the fundamental categories of rights.[86] Thus, writers outside and sometimes antipathetic to the Christian tradition seek to claim rights on behalf of animals,[87] or even trees,[88] or some larger concept of nature. Such an idea of rights tends to imply that human beings are merely part of a continuum of natural beings.[89] It can amount to denying that human life has particular significance, in that it expresses the image of God.[90] UK law has resisted attempts to introduce such ideas. Significantly, there has been reluctance by judges dealing with applications for judicial review on environmental matters to recognize standing on the part of any applicant who lacks some clear human relationship with the site concerned.[91]

Christians would applaud the extensive law designed to safeguard nature and to protect animals from abuse including, especially, cruelty. A topical example of this is the *Wild Mammals (Protection) Act 1996*. However, concepts of specific rights for non–human creatures can all too easily slip into the vacuum left by secular refusal to acknowledge the sovereignty of God. Animals, in particular, can be treated as if they were another category which should be afforded rights in the same way as slaves, children and the mentally disabled.[92] This approach can lead to the undermining of the sanctity of human life, as where human beings who lack their complete faculties may be considered less deserving of protection than healthy animals.[93]

---

[86] I am indebted in the following section of this paper for insights and an extensive review of the relevant literature by Colleen Lynn Theron in an unpublished thesis presented as part of the degree of LLM at the University of Aberdeen, 1996, 'What does the right to a decent environment mean? A jurisprudential overview'.

[87] See, notably, P. Singer, *In Defence of Animals*, (1985, Blackwell, Oxford).

[88] See the US case concerned with the Mineral King Valley in the Sequioa National Park, US Supreme Court Reports (1971) 31 L Ed. 2d 638; also C. Stone, 'Should trees have standing? Towards legal rights for natural objects' (1972) 45 *Southern Californian Law Review* 450–501.

[89] See Des Jardins, *Environmental Ethics* (above, note 53) chapters 5 and 6.

[90] See here D.R. Schamann and l.T. Polacheck, 'The case against rights for animals', (1995) 22 *Boston College Environmental Affairs Law Review* (4) 747.

[91] *R. v. Secretary of State for the Environment, ex parte Rose Theatre Trust Co* [1990] 1 Q.B. 504. Cf *R. v. Poole Borough Council ex parte Beebee and others* (1991) 3 *Journal of Environmental Law* 293.

[92] See here J. Feinberg, 'The rights of animals and unborn generations' in W. Blackstone (ed.), *Philosophy and Environment Crisis*, 1974, Georgis University Press 43–68; C. Stone, *Earth and Other Ethics*, (1988, New York, Harper and Row).

[93] See Singer, above, note 87.

The concept of rights has been used very differently by a number of recent writers as a tool for maintaining environmental protection on a large scale. Here, Christians would clearly seem to have a responsibility to be associated with the protection of future generations of human beings.[94] But, there is a major problem of how to justify legal steps to protect the interests of those who do not yet exist. Christians may believe that future generations do exist already in the mind of God, but this will hardly cut much ice in the secular world, given the reluctance of society even to recognize rights in unborn children.

With regard to future generations, failure to recognize God as the determinant of morality, and ultimately the authority for law, is particularly worrying. The secularist may strain the concept of rights so as to justify measures designed to protect the future. Appropriate rights to protect the environment and as yet unidentified people can be conceptualized as group rights.[95] This approach appears to represent a certain political understanding of human solidarity for ends which are selected by those who appoint themselves to speak for the group. The concept may be used to link environmentalists with civil liberties pressure groups.[96]

For Christian lawyers it may be appropriate to emphasize the legal rights in those who are in a position of stewards or trustees. Nevertheless, the idea of rights in beings other than human persons is questionable. From a Christian perspective it may amount to substituting for the authority of God, that of ecological or civil liberties activists. These claim, on their own initiative, to identify the rights to be protected and the manner in which they are to be enforced against simply human claims. The 'deep ecology' approach to environmental ethics treats the earth as a system to be respected for its own sake and human beings as no more than one species amongst all the others. Exponents of this approach exclude the idea of God as Creator and the earth as part of that creation committed to human stewardship. However, they can recognize that the use of rights as an end to further the protection of the environment is

---

[94] Des Jardins, *Environmental Ethics* (above, note 53) chapter 4.

[95] See J.T. McClymonds, 'The human right to a healthy environment; an international legal perspective', (1992) 37 *New York School Law Review* 583–633; J. Symonides, 'The human right to a clean, balanced and protected environment' (1992) 20 *International Journal of Legal Information* 24; J. Downs, 'A healthy and ecologically balanced environment: an argument for a third generation right' (1993) 3 *Duke Journal of Comparative and International Law* 351–385; P.W. Gormley, 'The right to a safe and decent environment', (1988) *Indiana Journal of International Law* 327.

[96] J. Nickel, 'The human right to a safe environment: philosophical perspectives on its scope and justification' (1993) 18 *Journal of South African Law*, 177–184.

flawed because it is essentially anthropocentric, depending upon self-appointed stewards.[97]

A relevant concept, here, which is of particular interest from a Christian perspective, and which appears to be in tune with the idea of stewardship, is that of *Sustainable Development*. It is applauded by the UK government in *This Common Inheritance*.[98] It envisages that there will be continuing development, but that the destruction of irreplaceable assets will be restrained. Instead it emphasizes the creation of new resources which will extend the benefits of development to all humanity, rather than fuelling the consumption of the few.[99]

In the classic analysis of legal relationships, rights are balanced by duties.[100] However, literature which focuses on human rights can obscure the other half of the equation, including the duties which those with rights themselves owe. From a Christian perspective, the rights of other individuals are eminently worthy of respect and protection but they must be treated with caution where they are made a vehicle for imposing the ideologies of one group on others. By contrast, an emphasis on duties stresses that the first priority is to carry out God's will. Christians may misinterpret his will, but they believe that there is, ultimately, a secure foundation for rules to protect the environment which aim to carry out his purposes. In the last resort, the rights to environmental protection are the rights of God himself, but, from the point of view of his human agents, what matters is identifying the duties which define the human role in carrying God's will into effect.

The need to emphasize environmental duties rather than rights is the conclusion reached by Theron: 'By replacing the phraseology of a right with a duty we are not derogating from the importance of protecting the environment. Instead we are introducing a perspective that is more in line with our moral conceptions, without challenging the basic framework of our legal institutions. By moving away from rights we may also be challenging a rights' culture that associates rights claims with mere self-interest.'[101]

An emphasis on rights is particularly evident in civil law. By contrast, the enforcement of duties without reference to correlative rights is a normal characteristic of criminal law. The English system of criminal justice is unusual in allowing scope for the individual citizen to bring prosecutions, in most types of cases, against those who have broken their

[97] C. Giagnocavan and H. Goldstein, 'Law reform or world reform: the problem of environmental rights' (1989/90) *McGill Law Journal* 345.

[98] Cm. 1200.

[99] See further, the Report of the World Commission on Environment and Development (The Bruntland Report), *Our Common Future*, 1987.

[100] W.N. Hohfeld, 'Some fundamental legal conceptions as applied in judicial reasoning', (1913) 23 *Yale Law Journal*, 16.

[101] Note 1, above, p. 36. See the discussion by Julian Rivers, above, p.41

duty to the public at large by committing a criminal offence. On the other hand, modern systems of environmental regulation depend on the exercise of administrative discretion in which the individual member of the public has little opportunity to take part.[102]

Typically, only a local planning authority can serve an enforcement notice ordering a developer to remove an unsightly new building for which he did not obtain planning permission.[103] Public administrative law gives some scope for the ordinary member of the public to play a role in formulating policies, such as those in development plans,[104] and to take part in decision-making by such means as public inquiries on planning proposals.[105] However, judges have tended to limit the role of the public by the courts' reluctance to recognize their *locus standi* to challenge decisions in proceedings for judicial review.[106] The assumption seems to be that the public may only play a part in environmental regulation where they are given a definite right to do so. This contrasts with the traditional view of the criminal law that it is the duty of every citizen to assist in the enforcement of the law.

Developing a Christian perspective on environmental law reform could see a shift to a culture emphasizing responsibility for maintaining and improving the quality of the environment. At one end of the scale this could mean citizens ensuring that litter and graffiti were removed from the streets. At the other end it could involve a sense of obligation to take part in development plan consultations and in inquiries on specific planning proposals.

Part of the Christian emphasis in the choice of categories for Environmental Law is therefore likely to be on duties to protect and respect the environment, laying the emphasis on responsibility, rather than rights. Here, European Community Law offers further encouragement with its emphasis on the principle of 'making the polluter pay'. This implies that those responsible for creating waste and industrial damage should be obliged to clear it up, rather than making a quick profit and leaving a dangerous and devastated landscape.[107] The principle may have been

[102] See here Patrick McAuslan, *The Ideologies of Planning Law*, (1980, Pergamon), especially the Introduction, where he distinguishes between the traditional legal concern to protect private property, the public interest expressed through government officials and elected representatives and the populist interest of concerned members of the public.

[103] *Town and Country Planning Act 1990*, s. 172.

[104] *Town and Country Planning Act 1990*, Part II.

[105] *Ibid.*, e.g. ss. 16, 20, 42 and 79.

[106] See *R. v. Secretary of State for the Environment, ex parte Rose Theatre Trust Co.* [1990] 1 Q.B. 504.

[107] For an example of this principle see the tax on land fill introduced by the *Finance Act 1996*, ss. 64 ff. See also proposals for 'carbon taxes' on fossil fuels aimed at reducing the 'greenhouse effect', OECD, *Environmental Taxes in OECD Countries*, (1995, OECD). See too, Cm 2426 at para. 3.16.

established late in the day but it does at last redress the approach of the Common Law during the heyday of unfettered enterprise in the Industrial Revolution.[108]

VI. BIBLICAL PRIORITIES, SECULAR ABSOLUTES AND CHRISTIAN RELATIVISM

Any biblical text requires to be read against what can be understood of the historical setting when it was written. When a matter is mentioned in the Bible, it is raised in a particular place and at a particular time. The significance of time and place is the stuff of hermeneutics which gives added significance and applicability to a text rather than reducing its value. Where the Bible refers to an area of life such as the environment in a fragmentary way, this does not mean that it is a matter of little concern to God. Rather, it suggests that the principles relevant to such an area may properly vary considerably from time to time and place to place. An awareness of this may enable Christian lawyers to be forward looking and innovative.

The idea of desirable variation in the law is expressed in the concept of subsidiarity. This is one of the features of European Community Law, and means that, so far as possible, decisions, including legislation, should be made locally, as close to the grass roots as possible. This helps to accommodate diversity and to allow for maximum freedom of choice by local communities. The concept, in fact, appears to have originated in Christian Canon Law, recognizing the diversity of rules appropriate to local churches.[109]

A proper Christian relativism may apply to major legal institutions which are taken for granted as permanent in particular societies. Notably, there is a deep-seated debate between Christian traditions over the right attitude to private property.[110] The Commandments against stealing and

---

[108] See note 17, above.

[109] See for example *Encyclical of Pius XI*, 1931 'Let the public authority leave to the lower groupings the care of lesser matters where it would expend an inordinate effort'. See, today, the Ten Principles under which the Roman Catholic Code of Canon Law 1983, was produced: James A. Coriden, Thomas J. Green and Donald E. Heintschel, *The Code of Canon Law: a text and Commentary*, (1985, Paulist Press), 6 and 312.

[110] The very extensive literature on the philosophical nature of property and its justification includes a range of Christian attitudes, from active disapproval of the concept of private property to its acceptance as an essential requirement for human advancement, effectively as an instrument of what theologians may term Common Grace. For a variety of different approaches to property, see, for example: Samuel L. Blumfield, *Property in a Humane Economy*, (1974, Illinois); Lawrence C. Becker, *Property Rights; Philosophic*

against covetousness are both central here.[111] They imply that property rights should be a permanent feature of any legal order. However, that does not mean that there is a single most suitable regime, say for land management. Thus, very restrictive concepts of private property may have been historically justified, notably at the time of enclosures in English villages, when it was essential to protect limited natural resources at crucial stages of development. During the eighteenth century, especially, virtually all agricultural and grazing land which had previously been shared by the occupants of a village was allocated permanently to individuals under a series of private Acts of Parliament.[112]

The biblical view is the realistic one that sin is a part of the human condition, so there will be a tendency to abuse rights over land, however those rights are distributed. Enclosures may have been necessary to provide more food for a growing population, but they indisputably caused much hardship to those who were given little or no share in the enclosed land. On the other hand, giving freedom to all to use the land can certainly result in it being irreparably damaged. This is the well-known 'problem of the Commons'.[113] The extent to which it may be ecologically damaging to override private rights in land is likely to be brought very much into focus if the new government seeks to introduce extensive public rights to roam over open private land.

Other major legal institutions which have important environmental implications suggest that relativism is central to any system of justice in balancing conflicting interests. Notable here is the concept of protecting 'reasonable enjoyment' of property rights in land through the law of nuisance. It is still arguable that the law of private nuisance can be a more effective regime for furthering the balanced use of land and for ensuring its conservation than transferring control to any 'public' body.[114]

The idea that the legal protection afforded to a neighbourhood may change with the character of the area is a particular example of relativism

[110] cont.
Foundations, (1977, Routledge Kegan Paul); D.R. Denman, *The Place of Property*, (1978, Geographical Publications); C.B. Macpherson, *Property: Mainstream and Critical Positions*, (1979, Oxford); James O. Grunenbaum, *Private Ownership*, (1987, Routledge Kegan Paul); Kevin Gray, *Elements of Land Law* (1st edition), (1987, Butterworths); John Brewer and Susan Staves (eds.), *Early Modern Conceptions of Property*, (1995, Routledge).

[111] Exodus 20:15 and 17 and Deuteronomy 5:19 and 21.

[112] See W.G. Hoskins, *The Making of the English Landscape*, (1977, Hodder and Stoughton), ch. 7; also R.A. Dodgson and R.A. Butlin (eds.), *The Historical Geography of England and Wales*, 2nd ed., (1978, Academic Press, London).

[113] William F. Baxter, *People or Penguins: The Case for Optimal Pollution*, (1974, Columbia).

[114] See Elizabeth Brubaker, *Property Rights in the Defence of Nature*, (1995, Earthscan).

in modern nuisance law. The prospect of such change has been made potentially less arbitrary through integration of nuisance law into the planning system, but, even so, change can produce apparent unfairness. This is shown in the contrasting cases of *R v Exeter County Council ex parte Thomas*[115] and *Gillingham BC v Medway (Chatham Dock) Co.*[116] In the *Exeter* case, it was decided that a local planning authority could properly give planning permission for a new housing development, even though the likely consequence was that this would make existing industrial users liable to nuisance claims for smell or noise. In the *Gillingham* case, it was shown that, conversely, a grant of planning consent for a noisy transporter terminal could change the character of the area so as to make reasonable noise, which would previously have been a nuisance to neighbouring householders.[117]

A further inherently relative concept has recently been made explicit by European Community Law. That is the 'principle of proportionality'. It is evident in UK legislation which is based on EC Directives. Thus, the *Environmental Protection Act 1990* requires large industrial plant to apply BATNEEC (best available techniques not entailing excessive cost).[118] Under section 7 of the Act, licences for major industrial processes are to include conditions spelling out such techniques which are required in respect of the relevant works. The reference to cost makes clear that the requirements are essentially relative.

The principle of proportionality is also apparent in case law applying European nature conservation legislation.[119] In '*The German Dykes Case*', the Commission of the European Communities brought an action in the Court of Justice of the European Communities, in Luxembourg, claiming that major dredging works in a National Park in Germany were in breach

[115]   *R v Exeter County Council ex parte Thomas* [1991] 1 Q.B. 471, [1990] 1 All ER 413.

[116]   *Gillingham B.C. v Medway (Chatham Dock) Co.* [1993] Q.B. 343, C.A.

[117]   The limits of the *Gillingham* case were indicated in *Wheeler v Saunders Ltd* [1996] Ch. 19, [1995] 2 All E.R. 697, C.A., where a small planning consent for enlarging a piggery was held not to amount to a change in the character of the neighbourhood, so it did not legitimize what would otherwise be a nuisance.

[118]   BATNEEC had an early precursor in UK legislation, in the concept of 'Best Practicable Means', which were required to prevent pollution, for example *Alkali, etc, Works Regulation Act 1906*.

[119]   Another good environmental example is '*The Danish Bottles Case*'; Case 302/86 *Commission of the EC, supported by UK v Kingdom of Denmark*, [1988] ECR 4607. For explanation see (1990) 2 *Journal of Environmental Law* 89. There it was held that a severe quota on imported drinks from elsewhere in the EC which did not use standard, reusable, Danish bottles, was not justified to protect the environment. The importers should be allowed to set up their own reclamation arrangements.

of a Special Protection Area for birds, because they would cause deterioration to the habitats of rare birds such as avocets.[120] The Court held that a Special Protection Area could be altered in size, 'only in exceptional circumstances', but such circumstances did apply in the case because of the danger of floods and the need to protect the coast line. Also, the works would actually have ecological benefits in creating new salt flats for birds. On the other hand, economic concern for the fishing port of Greetsiel would not have been enough, by itself, to justify damaging the bird habitats.[121]

Proportionality can be seen as a dilution of absolute standards. However, although it is important to beware of relativism where there are clear biblical rules, where there are not, a balance seems entirely consistent with a Christian approach. Christians are bound to differ over where the balance should be struck, as are individuals of all persuasions. However, from a Christian perspective, nature itself is not absolute, even though it should certainly be respected.

As a general observation, case law may leave a freer hand for a wide ranging systematic development of principle than does a code determined by principles worked out abstractly in advance. Where *ad hoc* legislation evolves into a principled system, the principles may be more effectively worked out than if the law was laid down initially in a comprehensive code. Inevitably, in a newly developing field, such as environmental legislation, UK law is increasingly dominated by ready-made codes with their origins in Europe. Of course, even in code-based systems of law, revisions of codes are to some extent influenced by experience of decided cases. Also, case law from the Court of Justice of the European Community appears to have the authority of Common Law precedent. The generally applicable principles, such as proportionality, are therefore being laced through the whole system.

From a Christian perspective, concepts, such as reasonableness in nuisance and proportionality in enforcing strict environmental controls, are examples of legal flexibility where that seems perfectly acceptable. However, legal protection of the environment for its own sake does seem to be more deeply embedded in European Community Law than in English Law. Recent examples of cases from the Court of Justice of the European Community show that the protection of the environment has attained the status of a master principle in secular law. This is very

120 Case C-57/89 *Commission of the EC v. Federal Republic of Germany, supported by the UK* [1991] ECR I–883; For comment see (1992) 4 *Journal of Environmental Law* 139. The case turned on the interpretation of Article 4.4 of the EC Birds Directive 1979, 79/409/EEC OJ 1979 L 103/1.

121 SPAs have now been subsumed in the wider category of SACs (Special Areas of Conservation) under the Habitats Directive 92/43/EEC OJ 1992 L206/7. The criteria for modifying SACs has been widened, specifically to include economic considerations to some extent; see Article 6(4).

welcome if it is kept consistent with Christian teaching to respect creation and to exercise proper stewardship over it. However, proportionality may prevent even such a master principle from getting out of hand.

The master principle of environmental conservation and the manner in which it may be qualified was illustrated in the *German Dykes* case, where the court at Luxembourg held that incursions could only be made into a Special Protection Area for birds in exceptional circumstances.[122] In the subsequent *Lappel Bank* case, the Luxembourg court underlined the point. There, the British Secretary of State recognized the Medway Marshes as wetlands deserving classification as an SPA under the 1979 Birds Directive. He recognized that an area known as Lappel Bank was part of the site which was important for birds, but he excluded it from the designation because he considered it more important to allow the Bank to be developed as an extension to the port of Sheerness. The RSPB challenged this exclusion on the grounds that once an area was acknowledged as meriting designation it must be designated, even though in exceptional circumstances designation could then be removed.

The Divisional Court refused an application for judicial review and this was upheld by Hirst and Steyn LL.J. in the Court of Appeal, on the basis that it was self-evident that the EC must have assumed that the governments of Member States could decide not to designate areas, provided they had reasons for doing so, and such reasons could clearly include economic factors.[123] By contrast, Hoffmann L.J. did not consider the matter self-evident, although he accepted that if the economic considerations were exceptional they could justify overruling the demands of nature conservation. On that basis the RSPB appealed to the House of Lords, and the House referred the case to Luxembourg. The Luxembourg court has now followed the recommendation of its Advocate General and ruled that refusal to confirm the designation can not be justified by economic factors.[124] However, as the House of Lords refused to restrain the work on the new port extension going ahead pending the appeal, the Luxembourg ruling might seem a rather hollow victory.

The *Lappel Bank* case showed that the English courts generally did not regard the EC legislation on wildlife conservation as giving priority to the importance of wildlife in designating sites as SPAs. However, Luxembourg has now established that the Birds Directive did create that priority. It may be suggested that the Luxembourg approach seems more in accordance with the biblical attitude to creation than was the approach

---

[122] Note 120, above.

[123] *R. v. Secretary of State for the Environment, ex parte RSPB*, (1995) 7 *Journal of Environmental Law* 245.

[124] C-44/95 *R v Secretary of State for the Environment, ex parte RSPB* [1996] ERC I-3805, [1996] 3 CMLR 411; for comment see (1997) 9 *Journal of Environmental Law* 168.

of the English Court of Appeal.[125] On the other hand, it would be dangerous to give excessive weight to the conservation of species or sites which happen to have been selected as worthy of conservation by European or national officials, just as it is dangerous to assume that freedom to make the maximum profit is necessarily in the best public interest.[126]

VII. CONCLUSION: ENGAGING WITH THE PROBLEM AND IDENTIFYING PRIORITIES FOR REFORM

Although there may not be a 'Christian Environmental Law', it does seem possible to claim a distinctive Christian perspective on environmental law. The Bible does not prescribe a legislative programme but it does establish definite values for environmental stewardship. Also, a Christian perspective provides realism as to the prevalence and the depth of sin. This emphasizes the necessity for law to confront both local and global environmental problems. It also warns against reliance on particular human programmes for reform. Each change must continually be monitored against basic biblical principles, to test whether it will tend to glorify God and to better the lot of humanity. Familiarity with the full range of Scripture may prompt insights into particular problems, such as the threat to environmental health from a disease like BSE. It may also emphasize the fundamental importance of considerations such as amenity and beauty, which financially hard-pressed governments may consider mere luxury.

If Christian lawyers are to contribute effectively to environmental law reform, they are obliged to use the categories and the terminology of secular law. However, they must do so critically. Some concepts which

[125] The Habitats Directive, 92/43 EEC, does allow for de-designation in certain circumstances. As far as new Special Conservation Areas are concerned, there is still flexibility for Member States in proposing sites for selection. However, if a Member State indicates that a site is worthy of designation under the Birds Directive, it would seem that the effect of the *Lappel Bank* case is that the site ought to be given protection under the Habitats Directive. The position now is that, for any development in a protected area, planning procedures must be followed before it can be judged that economic or other considerations justify withdrawing protection again. In particularly sensitive areas which have been designated as European areas, the proposal can only be justified on economic grounds where the European Commission accepts those are exceptional.

[126] The potential injustice of selecting a site for conservation and causing unexpected economic loss to the owner is well illustrated in *Amalgamated Investment Property Co v John Walker* [1976] 3 All E.R. 509; but see how the injustice in that case has been guarded against in future, *Planning (Listed Building and Conservation Areas) Act 1990*, s. 6.

are taken for granted, such as the very idea of rights, may need to be treated with caution if they are used in new ways as a basis for protecting the environment. A Christian emphasis on duty and responsibility may be theologically sounder and may have more practical effect.

Often a secular approach to law reform and the concepts used in the secular law will be fully compatible with a Christian vision for the environment, although care must be taken not to treat any principle as absolute without clear biblical warrant. Here, the influence of European Community Law has been heartening, for example with the establishment of the 'precautionary principle' to guard against possible harm, rather than controlling it only after it has been demonstrated that it is harmful. Another key example is 'the polluter pays' principle which requires that the polluter should bear the cost of coping with pollution, if possible, by ensuring that he pays to avoid it in the first place and, otherwise, to clear the pollution up afterwards.

Christian concern is naturally global, rather than merely national, let alone parochial. The worldwide Christian community, therefore, has a particular responsibility to understand and implement a vision of sustainable development, which will increasingly enable all the world's people to enjoy its riches fully, but without destroying them. Christians worldwide are also in a position to press for vital measures which are required at an international level. These would doubtless include curbs on the pollution which continues to fuel the greenhouse effect and protection for threatened forest areas, through such measures as restriction on the trade in hardwoods. International measures can only be expressed effectively through the national law of individual states where the local Christian lawyers may play a part in formulating and calling for appropriate measures.

For the Christian lawyer with a concern for the environment there is much scope for developing a strategy for effective reform, in accordance with biblical insights. Ultimately, however, it may be important for Christians, in general, to consider whether stewardship of the environment amounts merely to the guardianship of a wasting asset or whether stewardship, including environmental law, will itself lead, under God's direction, to a transformed universe. In the early days of the church, expectancy of the imminent ending of the world spurred evangelists to spread the Gospel. Now, at the beginning of the Third Millennium, the Gospel has been preached throughout the world. It could be that the time is ripe for the church to draw a new vision from Scripture, not simply of saved individuals but of the world itself redeemed, to glorify its Creator[127].

---

[127]   Whilst this chapter was in press a number of relevant publications have become available. These include Tony Sargent, *Animal Rights and Wrongs: A Biblical Perspective*, (1997, Hodder and Stoughton); Michael S. Northcott, *The Environment and Christian Ethics*, (1997, CUP); Ghillean Prance, *The Earth under Threat: A Christian Perspective*, (1997, Wild Goose); Hugh Montefiore, *Time to Change: Challenge for an Endangered Planet*, (1997, Bible Reading Fellowship).

4

Whose Life Anyway? A Re-Examination of Suicide and Assisted Suicide

John Warwick Montgomery[1]

I. INTRODUCTION

English common law is a conservative tradition. Judges are loath to play the role of legislators and Parliament is hesitant to enact legislation on controversial social issues. Thus law reform is not currently pending in the United Kingdom in regard to suicide or assisted suicide — in spite of the debates which such proposals and actual legislation have elicited in civil law and other common law jurisdictions. This chapter endeavours to determine whether, in principle, legal liberalization ought in fact to be introduced for the benefit of those wishing to terminate their lives.

A generation has passed since the first appearance of Brian Clark's television play, *Whose Life Is It Anyway?* (1972), followed in 1978 by the moving stage production starring Tom Conti at London's Mermaid Theatre. The play turned out to be prophetic. Under the caption, 'US Courts Uphold Right to Assisted Suicide,' the London *Times* reported on 9 April 1996:

> The right of terminally ill Americans to commit suicide with the help of a doctor has been upheld by two federal appeal courts. The landmark rulings on the East and West Coasts have brought a controversy that has long been simmering to the forefront. A national debate is emerging on the medical, legal and theological implications. The issue is almost certain to go to the Supreme Court where the justices will be asked to decide if the dying have a constitutional right to ask a doctor for assistance in ending their lives. . . . The federal appeal court in San Francisco voted 8–3 to annul a law barring assisted suicide that dated back 140 years in Washington state. The court said that competent adults have a constitutional right to seek help in choosing 'a dignified and humane death rather than being reduced to a child-like state of helplessness'. The ruling was followed by a similar finding in New York.[2] The

---

[1] An earlier version of the present chapter was published in *Nexus: A Journal of Opinion* (Chapman University School of Law, Anaheim, California), Vol. I, No. 2 (Fall, 1996).

[2] *Quill v Vacco*, 80 F. 3d 716 (2d Cir. 1996) (footnote inserted for this book).

judges said it made no sense that doctors could pull the plug on life-support systems at a patient's request, but were not allowed to prescribe lethal doses of drugs for those who wanted them.'

Clearly the issues at stake are of the most fundamental importance for human rights. Equally plain is the impossibility of treating the suicide/assisted-suicide question in a hermetically sealed legal compartment: root values are at stake, so there is no choice but to combine jurisprudential with serious ethical and theological analysis. The need for such treatment is particularly evident from the 9th Circuit (Washington) opinion, so we shall start there.

II.   THE 'COMPASSION IN DYING' JUDGMENT

The most striking aspect of the *en banc* opinion in *Compassion In Dying v State of Washington*[3] is not the substantive conclusions reached but the style of reasoning displayed. The Court by no means restricts itself to an analysis of precedents or to the fundamental Constitutional issues (due process, the state interest, the liberty interest, etc.): a painfully superficial overview of historical attitudes towards suicide provides the background for a discussion of 'current societal attitudes.' Here the Court gives considerable weight to polls and statistical surveys. We are informed, *inter*

[3]   79 F. 3d 790 (9th Cir. 1996); 1996 WL 94848 (9th Cir. [Wash.]). The US Supreme Court in early January heard oral arguments in an appeal against this decision and that in *Quill*, note 2 above. A United Press International release of 8 January 1997 reported:

> The Supreme Court indicates it might be a long way from approving physician-assisted suicide, as key justices suggest they have problems with the issue. The Supreme Court heard argument Wednesday on two lower court rulings that struck down bans on doctor-assisted suicide in New York and Washington states. Justice David Souter, considered a leader of the court's liberal wing, from the bench asked lawyers why the court shouldn't wait for society to resolve the issue politically. Souter told one lawyer advocating the right to doctor-assisted suicide, 'Why not wait? We are not in the position to make the judgment now that you want. It would just be guesswork' without more information. Chief Justice William Rehnquist told lawyers that a ruling on physician-assisted suicide would bring on the same emotions as abortion, adding, 'You're going to have those (pro and anti-abortion rights) factions fighting it out in every session of the legislature.' And Justice Anthony Kennedy, usually a swing vote, said doctor-assisted suicide would cause 'fear' among those who might be pressured to take their own lives. Citing a New York task force study on the issue that has been widely used in briefing the court, Kennedy told assisted-suicide advocates, 'The autonomy (for the individual) that you seek is illusory . . . In fact you will be introducing fear into medical facilities. That's what I get from that New York report.'

On 26 June 1997, the US Supreme Court did in fact reverse both decisions. Chief Justice Relinquist delivered the Court's judgment, which was unanimous albeit with separate concurring opinions: 117 Sup. Ct. 2258.

alia, that 'polls have repeatedly shown that a large majority of Americans — sometimes nearing 90% — fully endorse recent legal changes granting terminally ill patients, and sometimes their families, the prerogative to accelerate their death by refusing or terminating treatment,' that 'polls indicate that a majority of Americans favor doctor-assisted suicide for the terminally ill,' and that 'according to a survey by the American Society of Internal Medicine, one doctor in five said he had assisted in a patient's suicide.' Not surprisingly, the Court's venture into sociology concludes with a value-laden reference to the 'growing movement to restore humanity and dignity to the process by which Americans die.'

The Court is at pains throughout to emphasize its dependence on *Roe v Wade,* e.g.: 'In examining whether a liberty interest exists in determining the time and manner of one's death, we begin with the compelling similarities between right-to-die cases and abortion cases.'[4] One of the most 'compelling similarities' between *Compassion In Dying* and *Roe v Wade* lies in the common sociological focus of the decision-making in the two cases. In *Roe,* shallow historicizing (abortion has been opposed only by the Hippocratic school and by Christians, so it cannot be rejected out-of-hand in a pluralistic society today) is made the basis of sociological judgment: 'This holding is consistent with the relative weights of the respective interests involved . . . and with the demands of the profound problems of the present day.'[5] No attempt is made to deal with the essential ontological question: 'We need not resolve the difficult question of when life begins.'[6] Just as *Roe* sacrifices the personhood of the foetus to the vagaries of contemporary sociological pressure,[7] so *Compassion In Dying* allows opinion polls to substitute for a principled determination of the worth of a dying patient's life.

Two observations need to be made concerning this common reasoning style. First: legal judgments are, by definition, 'ought' statements; they do not describe a state of affairs but declare a binding standard. Thus whenever judges base their opinions on sociological or statistical considerations they commit the venerable naturalistic fallacy (sometimes termed, appropriately, the sociologist's fallacy): they suppose that one can derive the 'ought' from

---

[4] Need it be pointed out that just as there is no unqualified US Constitutional right to privacy justifying the taking of foetal life, so there is no unqualified 'liberty interest' justifying the taking of one's own life or assisting others to do so? My right to privacy or to liberty is always limited by the effects of my actions on other individuals and on the body politic in general.

[5] *Roe v. Wade,* 410 U.S. 113, 165 (1973).

[6] *Id.* at 159.

[7] J.W. Montgomery, 'Abortion and the Law: Three Clarifications', in *New Perspectives on Human Abortion,* Hilgers, Horan, and Mall eds. (1981) 281–92; *Slaughter of the Innocents* (1981); 'The Rights of Unborn Children', 5 *Simon Greenleaf Law Review* (1985–1986) 23–72.

the 'is' — that the normative is derivable from the descriptive. But fifty million Frenchmen (or two-hundred million Americans) can be *wrong* — and often *are*. To allow abortion on demand because a majority of people favour it is the functional equivalent of decriminalizing tax evasion because most people hate income tax. And to reason that because many people now think suicide or assisted suicide is permissible and that a certain number of physicians do in fact help the terminally ill on their way, such practices are legally justifiable, is utterly fallacious. *Vox populi* has never been, and has not suddenly become, *vox Dei*.

Secondly, the jurisprudence of *Roe v Wade* and *Compassion In Dying* is not classic common-law jurisprudence at all, but a relatively recent deviant, which, however, has virtually captured the field in America. The greatest exponent of so-called American Legal Realism, Karl Llewellyn, argued that since (in his view) law is but a means to social ends and courts are in reality engaged in a process of rationalizing precedent and principle to achieve contemporary social goals,[8] judges should substitute for the nineteenth century 'formal style' (where the real grounds for decision are concealed behind an appeal to formal reason and supposedly objective values) the 'grand style' (where one straightforwardly identifies the roots of the law in social needs). Llewellyn was convinced that by the 1960's the grand style had come to prevail, at least in American appellate courts.[9] Recently, Atiyah of Oxford and Summers of Cornell, in a major comparison of the English and American common law traditions, have distinguished two visions: the classic English 'formal vision' in which courts rely on precedent, commit themselves to principled decision-making, and leave law-making to the legislature (Parliament); and the modern American 'substantivistic model' in which judges confidently make law based on policy-orientated considerations.[10] Ronald Dworkin has pointed out the extreme dangers of policy-orientated, judicial lawmaking, where judges become deputy legislators and policy rather than principle comes to prevail on the bench.[11] *Compassion In Dying* would appear to represent the latest example — and a particularly egregious one — of this sad trend in the higher courts of America.

But if principle rather than social policy is to be our proper guide, then we must look in depth at the jurisprudential background of the suicide and assisted-suicide question.

---

8   K. Llewellyn, *Jurisprudence: Realism in Theory and Practice* (1962) 55–57.
9   K. Llewellyn, *The Common Law Tradition: Deciding Appeals* (1960) 35 ff.
10 P.S. Atiyah and R.S. Summers, *Form and Substance in Anglo-American Law: A Comparative Study of Legal Reasoning, Legal Theory, and Legal Institutions* (1991).
11 R. Dworkin, *Taking Rights Seriously* (1978) 82–92; *Law's Empire* (1986) 221–24, 244. On Dworkin's approach to the abortion issue, as set forth in his book, *Life's Dominion*, see J.W. Montgomery, 'New Light on the Abortion Controversy?', (1993) 60/7 *New Oxford Review* 24–26.

III. THE LAW OF SUICIDE AND ASSISTED SUICIDE

The common law traditionally punished suicide as a criminal act, and aiding and abetting suicide is still criminalized in most common law jurisdictions. The grounding for the legal doctrine was to be found in both civic and theological principle. Sir Matthew Hale wrote in his authoritative *History of the Pleas of the Crown* (late seventeenth century):

> *Felo de se* or suicide is, where a man of the age of discretion, and *compos mentis*, voluntarily kills himself by stabbing, poison, or any other way. No man hath the absolute interest of himself, but 1. God almighty hath an interest and propriety in him, and therefore self-murder is a sin against God. 2. The king hath an interest in him, and therefore the inquisition in case of self-murder is *felonicè & voluntariè seipsum interfecit & murderavit contra pacem domini regis.*[12]

Sir William Blackstone, in the first general textbook of the English common law, the *Commentaries* (eighteenth century), made the same points with greater eloquence:

> The law of England wisely and religiously considers, that no man hath a power to destroy life, but by commission from God, the author of it: . . .the suicide is guilty of a double offence: one spiritual, in evading the prerogative of the Almighty, and rushing into his immediate presence uncalled for: the other temporal, against the king, who hath an interest in the preservation of all his subjects.[13]

And, at the beginning of the nineteenth century, East declared in his *Treatise of the Pleas of the Crown:*

> The last kind of felonious homicide is that against a man's own life, which denominates the party slaying himself *felo de se.* This is where any one wilfully or by any malicious act causes his own death. The law regards this as an heinous offence, though the party himself may at first view appear to have been the only sufferer: for as the public have a right to every man's assistance, he who voluntarily kills himself is with respect to the public as criminal as one who kills another. It is equally an offence against the fundamental law of society, which is protection. The law has therefore ordained as severe a punishment for it as the nature of the case will admit of, namely, an ignominious burial in the highway with a stake driven through the body; and a forfeiture of all the offender's goods and chattels to the king.[14]

As for assisted suicide, Sir James Fitzjames Stephen states the historic common law position:

---

[12] Hale, *P.C.* I, 411–12 (chap. xxxi). *Cf.* W. Hawkins, *P.C.* I, 67–69 (chap. xxvii) (1716).

[13] *Bl. Com.* IV, xiv, 3. For theological selections from Blackstone and Hale, see J.W. Montgomery, *Jurisprudence: A Book of Readings* (4th ed. 1992) 277–81, 331–38.

[14] East, *P.C.* I, 219 (chap. v, sec. 5).

Suicide is held to be murder so fully, that every one who aids or abets suicide is guilty of murder. If, for instance, two lovers try to drown themselves together, and one is drowned and the other escapes, the survivor is guilty of murder.[15]

In that connection Stephen makes comparative reference to the nineteenth century German *Strafgesetzbuch*, Art. 216, 'which, in providing for the punishment of various cases of homicide, says: — "If a person is induced to kill another by the express and serious request of the person killed, he must be imprisoned for not less than three years" (and by Article 16 not more than five).'[16]

The deterrent of forfeiture of lands or goods belonging to the one who kills himself was removed in 1870 as a result of the abolishing of forfeitures for felony in general (33 & 34 Vic. c. 23). The custom of interring the suicide at a public crossroads also disappeared in the 19th century, again as a result of legislation (4 Geo. 4, c. 52; 45 & 46 Vic. c. 19).

The twentieth century has seen suicide reduced from a felony to a misdemeanour and ultimately decriminalized entirely in most common law jurisdictions; in England the latter occurred as late as 1961 by way of the Suicide Act of that year. *Attempted* suicide has also been decriminalized; Glanville Williams makes the pregnant comment:

> Although it is now universally conceded to be useless and harmful to punish those who attempt suicide for any reason, because the punishment of one who attempts suicide can only increase his depression and render a renewed attempt more likely, prevailing opinion still holds that it is right and efficacious to punish those who assist suicide (or who kill with consent), even though they act from the strongest humanitarian motives. This seems to show that the more relaxed attitude toward the person who attempts his own suicide is based on limited pragmatic considerations and does not signify any abandonment of the traditional condemnation.[17]

Where suicide itself does not exact any legal opprobrium, there is a certain superficial logic (we shall later see how superficial it indeed is!) to the view that assisting suicide should also be free of legal penalties. Thus the distinguished nineteenth-century French criminalist Faustin Hélie wrote:

> La loi n'a point incriminé le suicide. Le fait de complicité est-il punissable? La négative est évidente, puisqu'il n'y a pas de participation criminelle à un fait qui ne constitue en lui-même ni crime ni délit.[18]

---

15 J.F. Stephen, 3 *A History of the Criminal Law of England* (1883) 104.

16 *Id.* at 106.

17 G. Williams, 'Suicide', 8 *Encyclopedia of Philosophy* 44 (P. Edwards ed. 1967).

18 F. Hélie, *Pratique criminelle des cours et tribunau, résumé de la jurisprudence sur les codes d'instruction criminelle et pénal*, pt. 2 ('Code pénal'), (1877) 299.

Glanville Williams sees clearly the resolution of this apparent paradox that 'if one person can lawfully commit suicide, why should it be an offence for another to help him?' — it is 'because we still think suicide immoral'.[19]

Indisputably, however, secular, pluralistic Western societies at the very end of the twentieth century are less and less inclined to regard suicide as immoral — and so they are more and more inclined to decriminalize aiding and abetting the suicide of others. The Netherlands offers a well-known case in point. Though Article 293 of the Dutch Penal Code classes voluntary euthanasia as one of the 'serious offences against human life' in Title XIX of the Code, assisted suicide is known to have become an established part of medical practice in the Netherlands since the early 1970s. Two court decisions in 1986 (one from the Hague Court of Appeal, the other from the Dutch Supreme Court) have created a defence of 'necessity', absolving physicians from prosecution as long as the voluntary euthanasia conforms to certain guidelines.[20] And now we have the two US federal appeals court decisions which would, but for their reversal by the US Supreme Court, have provided parallel death-on-demand possibilities in America — to operate in tandem with abortion-on-demand as established throughout the United States in 1973.

[19] G. Williams, *Textbook of Criminal Law* (1978) 531. *Cf.* his *The Sanctity of Life and the Criminal Law* (1957).

[20] *See* J. Keown, 'The Law and Practice of Euthanasia in the Netherlands', (1992) 108 *Law Quarterly Review* 51–78. The London *Times* reported (13 April 1996) that by the time Australia's Northern Territory's euthanasia act entered into force on 1 July 1996, a physician in Darwin should have developed a software program making it possible for a terminally ill patient to take his own life by pressing the return key on his laptop computer (the subject will be connected to a syringe driver, linked in turn to the laptop; when the appropriate command is activated, a lethal dose of barbiturate will be injected into the subject's bloodstream). 'The Church and prolife lobbyists fear that the law will make Darwin the death capital of Australia, if not the world, attracting hundreds of terminally ill people to the Northern Territory.' Church Net UK News Service announced on 16 August 1996 that the 'NSW [New South Wales] Council of Churches has called on the Prime Minister to examine ways to establish a uniform, national anti-euthanasia policy, far beyond the perimeters proposed in *The Territories (Protection of Human Life) Act 1996* [A Federal Private Member's Bill to overturn the Northern Territory legislation]. Council President, Rev. Ross Clifford said today, 'The Council of Churches fully supports the draft content of the proposed private members Bill but for any anti-euthanasia legislation to really work effectively, a national perspective must be adopted through the co-operation of all states and territories exercising their own legislative power.' . . . He added, 'Without a unified policy, any move to reverse the Northern Territory legislation would be thwarted if any other State passing

Clearly there are value questions of gigantic proportion to be faced in determining whether such a trend ought to be supported or opposed. Let us now turn to such an evaluation.

IV. A THEOLOGICAL PERSPECTIVE

It is not by chance that the decriminalization of suicide and (much more recently) of assisted suicide coincides with the modern post-Reformation era of Enlightenment secularism. Voltaire regarded the suicides of Brutus, Cassius, and Marc Antony as victories over nature.[21] Montesquieu *(Considérations sur les causes de la grandeur et de la décadence des Romains* [1734]) admired the Roman practice of suicide which allegedly 'gave every one the liberty of finishing his part on the stage of the world in what scene he pleased'.[22]

[20] *cont.*
pro-euthanasia legislation allowed people from other States to freely access the Act.'

Mr. Clifford, who is also a NSW and Northern Territory Solicitor and Barrister, provides the following updated information on the Australian situation (fax of 28 November 1996 to this author): 'With respect to the Northern Territory of Australia Rights of the Terminally Ill Act the Supreme Court of the Northern Territory dismissed the appeal. As a consequence a member of our Federal Parliament (Mr Andrews) has presented to our Federal Parliament the Euthanasia Laws Bill 1996 to overturn the Territory Euthanasia provisions. The House of Representatives, our Lower House and where the power resides, is still debating the Bill (maybe they will vote in December). Our Senate which is made up of senators from our states has referred the matter to a committee, one reason being is the question of state rights — the power of the Federal Parliament to overrule a state/territory. The committee will not report before February 24, 1997 and no vote in the Senate will take place before then. Commentators feel the Lower House will support the Andrews Bill but the Upper House is doubtful. Our Federal High Court has determined not to hear the issue until the parliamentary process is complete. As a matter of interest our New South Wales parliament had a debate on the issue (no Bill just a debate) and voted overwhelmingly against euthanasia. Our Premier, Mr Carr, has written to me as President of the NSW Council of Churches, to indicate "after the debate I cannot see euthanasia legislation being enacted in our State." He expressed a strong public voice against euthanasia.' For Mr. Andrews's first reading speech on the Federal Bill, see the Appendix to this chapter. The House of Representatives passed the Bill, see *The Times*, 10 December 1996, as did the Senate, see the *Financial Times*, 25 March 1997, overturning the Northern Territory euthanasia legislation.

[21] Voltaire, 'Of Suicide', 17 *Works* 165 ff. (4th ed. T. Smollett transl. 1772).

[22] Montesquieu, 3 *Complete Works* (1777) 86–87.

David Hume — better known for his attempt to undercut all arguments from miracles, such as Christ's resurrection from the dead, as proofs of religious truth — elaborated Montesquieu's arguments. In his *Essay on Suicide* (1783) he concluded that 'the life of a man is of no greater importance to the universe than that of an oyster'[23] — a position directly contradictory to that of Jesus, not so incidentally, who declared that 'you are of more value than many sparrows' (Matthew 10:31).

Schopenhauer, in his treatise *On Suicide*, claimed that taking one's own life should be regarded neither as a crime nor as a sin since 'it is quite obvious that there is nothing in the world to which every man has a more unassailable title than to his own life and person.'[24] (Note how this argument parallels that of the Pro-Choice advocate who claims that a woman has an absolute right to do as she wishes with her own body.)

In our time, atheist Antony Flew defends suicide and assisted suicide on the twin grounds that to keep sufferers from a quick death is ethically cruel and that no human being can disregard the aspirations, wishes, and interests of another human being without denying that person's true worth, even when the consequence is the cessation of the other's life.[25] Humanist philosopher Sidney Hook argues:

> We may define the good differently, but no matter what our conception of the *good* life is, it presupposes a physical basis — a certain indispensable minimum of physical and social well-being — necessary for even a limited realization of that good life. Where that minimum is failing together with all rational probability of attaining it, to avoid a life that at its best can be only vegetative and at its worst run the entire gamut of degradation and obloquy, what high-minded person would refuse the call of the poet mourir entre les bras du sommeil? We must recognise no categorical imperative 'to live,' but 'to live well.'[26]

The problem with such views is that, stimulating as they may be, they do not necessarily represent more than the opinions of the thinker who sets them forth. Wittgenstein was surely correct in principle when

23 D. Hume, 2 *Philosophical Works*, T.H. Green and T.H. Grose eds. (1874–1875) 406 ff. For a critique of Hume's argument against miracles, see J.W. Montgomery, *The Shape of the Past* (1975) 288–98 and *Faith Founded on Fact* (1978) 43–73.

24 A. Schopenhauer, *Studies in Pessimism* (2d ed. T.B. Saunders transl. 1891) 43–73.

25 A. Flew, 'The Principle of Euthanasia', 4 *The Plain View* (1957) 189–90. My critique of Flew's antimiraculous argumentation may be found in J.W. Montgomery, *Faith Founded on Fact* (1978) 52 ff.

26 S. Hook, 'The Ethics of Suicide', 37 *International Journal of Ethics* (1927) 173 ff. Such sentiments are commonly expressed in the popular pro–euthanasia literature, e.g. D. Humphry, *Final Exit: The Practicalities of Self-Deliverance and Assisted Suicide for the Dying* (1991).

he observed that 'ethics is transcendental,'[27] that is, any genuine ethic would have to rise above the level of human opinion and have an absolute justification for the values it proclaimed. Inevitably, therefore, we must go beyond philosophical opinion to the consideration of religious — theological — answers to the question of whether life ought to be terminated by the individual himself, with or without the aid of others.

But what religion or theology can assist us here? Religious claims are hardly identical and indeed are often mutually incompatible.[28] Moreover, not a few religious positions have historically been indifferent to the value of individual human life[29] and little concerned with what modernly we call human rights.[30] Greco-Roman polytheism, for example, had no difficulty with suicide — or, for that matter, infanticide by the exposing of unwanted children.[31]

We turn to Christian theology both on the ground that it offers a defensible case for transcendent revelation[32] and because it has provided the basic value system for the entire Western culture and, at least from the time of Justinian in the 6th century, the ethical foundations of both the common and the civil law traditions.[33] To ignore the Christian perspective on suicide and assisted suicide, therefore, would be folly, for it would entail cutting ourselves off not only from our heritage but also from the most fruitful potential source for resolving these very difficult value questions.

---

[27]　L. Wittgenstein, *Tractatus Logico-Philosophicus* para. 6.41–6.421 (1971). For the implications of this truth in jurisprudence and legal ethics see J.W. Montgomery, 'The Case for "Higher Law", (1979) 6/2 *Pepperdine Law Review* 359–80 and *Law and Morality: Friends or Foes? An Inaugural Lecture* (1994).

[28]　See J.W. Montgomery, *The Suicide of Christian Theology* (1970) and *Christianity for the Toughminded* (1973).

[29]　J.W. Montgomery, *Giant in Chains: China Today and Tomorrow* (1994) 101–36.

[30]　J.W. Montgomery, *Human Rights and Human Dignity* (1986) 105 ff.

[31]　This was also the position of Epicureanism and (with the exception of Cicero, whose natural law views and ethic had close affinities to biblical religion) Stoicism. Seneca argued, for example, that 'just as I shall select my ship when I am about to go on a voyage, or my house when I propose to take a residence, so shall I choose my death when I am about to depart from life' (*Epistolae morales* LXX, 11).

[32]　J.W. Montgomery, *Where is History Going?* (1969), *Human Rights and Human Dignity* (1986) 131–60.

[33]　See H.J. Berman, *Law and Revolution: The Formation of the Western Legal Tradition* (1983), especially chapter 4 ('Theological Sources of the Western Legal Tradition').

Biblical revelation is directly opposed to suicide, on the twin and related grounds that human life is infinitely precious and that it comes about as a gift of the divine Creator and Redeemer of mankind, who therefore alone has the right to terminate it.[34] 'All they that go down into the dust shall kneel before Him: and no man hath quickened his own soul' (Psalm 22:29–30, Book of Common Prayer). 'Naked came I out of my mother's womb, and naked shall I return thither: the Lord gave, and the Lord hath taken away; blessed be the name of the Lord' (Job 1:21, AV). Every instance of suicide in Scripture is related to spiritual collapse, from Saul to Judas (I Samuel 31:4; II Samuel 17:23; I Kings 16:18–20; Matthew 27:5; Acts 1:18).

The contrast with contemporary secular thought could hardly be greater. As in the case of abortion, the modern secularist here insists on the autonomy of the individual. One's personal choice is the absolute, before which all other considerations may be sacrificed. Such a viewpoint is well illustrated by the closing exchange in *Whose Life Is It Anyway?* between the judge and the tetraplegic seeking to have his life-support machine shut down:

> *Judge*: But wouldn't you agree that many people with appalling physical handicaps have overcome them and lived essentially creative, dignified lives?
>
> *Ken*: Yes, I would, but the dignity starts with their choice. If I choose to live, it would be appalling if society killed me. If I choose to die, it is equally appalling if society keeps me alive.
>
> *Judge*: I cannot accept that it is undignified for society to devote resources to keeping someone alive. Surely it enhances that society.
>
> *Ken*: It is not undignified if the man wants to stay alive, but I must restate that the dignity starts with his choice. Without it, it is degrading because technology has taken over from human will.[35]

The classical theologians of orthodox Christianity, such as Augustine, have set themselves firmly against such autonomous reasoning: man does not exist for himself alone, but for his God and for others, as in our Lord's well-known summary of Old Testament teaching (Matthew 22:37–40, and parallels):

> Thou shalt love the Lord thy God with all thy heart, and with all thy soul, and with all thy mind. This is the first and great commandment. And the second is like unto it, Thou shalt love thy neighbour as thyself. On these two commandments hang all the law and the prophets.

---

[34] J.W. Montgomery, 'Do We Have the Right to Die?', *Christianity Today* 469–79 (January 21, 1977), and 'Human Dignity in Birth and Death: A Question of Values', 7 *International Journal of Value-Based Management* (1994) 147–58.

[35] B. Clark, *Whose Life Is It Anyway?* (1978) 78.

Thus, as might be expected, any limited support in today's church for voluntary euthanasia has come from situationists who do not recognize the existence of absolute biblical principles (e.g. Joseph Fletcher, *Morals and Medicine*).[36] St. John-Stevas so well summarizes the Christian theological position that he deserves to be quoted *in extenso*:

> Christians put forward three arguments for condemning euthanasia. The basis of the Christian position is not, as is sometimes stated, that life has an absolute value, but that the disposal of life is in God's hands. Man has no absolute control over life, but holds it in trust. He has the use of it, and therefore may prolong it, but he may not destroy it at will. A second point made by Christians is that no man has the right to take an innocent life. 'The innocent and just man thou shalt not put to death', says Exodus 23:7 . . . The only occasion when a Christian may take the life of a human being, is when he is an unjust aggressor against an individual or the common good.
>
> Suffering for the Christian is not an absolute evil, but has redeeming features. It may be an occasion for spiritual growth and an opportunity to make amends for sin. Lord Horder in the House of Lords debate in 1950 drew attention to this aspect of pain. 'To call the function of a doctor who helps a patient to achieve that degree of elevation of spirit an intolerable burden — as the euthanasia advocate is apt to call it — seems to me to be disparaging one of the very important duties that a doctor has to perform.' At the same time the Christian recognizes suffering as an evil in the natural order, and is under a duty to relieve it where possible, although not at any price. . . .
>
> A third cause of Christian opposition to euthanasia is the 'wedge' argument. In its strict form, this states that an act which if raised to a general line of conduct would injure humanity, is wrong even in an individual case. In its more popular sense, it means that once a concession about the disposability of innocent life is made in one sphere, it will inevitably spread to others.[37]

To be sure, Christian theology has been well aware of the moral ambiguities that plague the suicide issue — as they do all ethical issues in a sinful and fallen world. What about martyrdom — or the giving of one's life to save the lives of others? Scholastic theologians have employed the so-called 'doctrine of double effect', noting that the good result in such instances can be seen to derive not from the suicide itself but from the motivation or objective act that led to it. This rather convoluted reasoning should not, however, be allowed to obscure the basic theological point: suicide is always an evil, never a good. In certain limited circumstances, it may be a lesser of evils, but a lesser evil is never somehow magically transmuted into a positive good.

The Christian position on suicide and assisted suicide is grounded in an acidly realistic view of fallen human nature. Because of the self-centredness characteristic of all human beings since the Fall of our first

---

36   See J. Fletcher and J.W. Montgomery, *Situation Ethics: True or False* (1972).
37   N. St. John-Stevas, *Life, Death and the Law* (1961) 271–73.

parents, to normalize or legalize the aiding and abetting of suicide is an act of utter naïvety and folly. Owing to original sin, we are all subject to fallibility, laziness, and perversity. Where voluntary euthanasia is allowed, a gilt-edged invitation is provided for the manifestation of these characteristics. The patient and/or the physician may err in diagnosis of the true medical condition and the chances of survival. The patient and/or his loved ones may simply tire of life and of the care needed to sustain it. Those who will survive the patient may even be motivated by greed or by the potential benefits accruing to them from the patient's early demise.

All of these considerations are particularly magnified in our modern secular society, with the intense psychological and social pressures it puts on its members: the supposed absolute right to health, success, and happiness. No one should have to endure a moment of unnecessary suffering! High suicide rates in the Scandinavian welfare states illustrate the neurotic side of the problem today, and the increasing number of teen suicides in America should make us attentive to the need societally to restrain rather than approve the facile termination of life. In this area as in all others, the secularist suffers from a high dose of naïve rationalism: he assumes that suicide and the aiding and abetting of suicide will occur for the best of reasons. In point of fact, precisely the opposite is far more likely, given the self-centredness characteristic of us all. Perhaps the last thing we need is unlimited autonomy where matters of life and death are concerned.[38]

Are we saying that the Christian position is unqualifiedly condemnatory of assisted suicide — that no concessions are warranted even when extraordinary means are being employed to keep a patient alive? As already noted, Christian ethics is perfectly willing to recognize that in a sinful and fallen world suicide, unassisted or assisted, may rarely constitute a lesser of evils (e.g. in war, where the suicide of a captured prisoner might be preferable to a period of torture during which he would surely reveal strategic information leading to massive loss of other lives; or, medically, where only one life-support machine is available and the only way for it to benefit a young person in need is for it to be disconnected from a willing, terminally-ill elderly patient). But these limiting cases do not ever yield a principled justification of suicide or assisted suicide *per se* — nor sufficient ground for legislative approval of such acts. Hard cases still make bad law.

[38] A particularly sad recent example of misplaced autonomy was the death of the seven-year-old child pilot Jessica Dubroff in April, 1996. The London *Times* reported (13 April) that in spite of criticisms that allowing her to pilot a plane in severe weather conditions to break a record displayed 'bad adult judgment' and raised the spectre of 'the motives of highly ambitious parents', her mother justified the little girl's choices in these words: 'She should have been up there. She had a freedom which you can't get by holding her back. . . . She went with her joy and her passion, and her life was in her hands. . . . I beg people to let children fly if they want to.'

As for 'pulling the plug' — removing extraordinary means of keeping a patient alive — one faces the tremendous difficulty of defining what is in fact 'extraordinary'. Surely the use of a feeding tube, so as to keep a dying patient alive, is not abnormal medical treatment, any more than is the bringing of a tray of food to a patient whose legs have been amputated. In the English case involving the removal of life support from comatose Tony Bland,[39] the Court's opinion has been rightly criticized on this very ground:

> Lord Goff's reasoning is, with respect, vulnerable to at least three major criticisms. First, why is pouring food down a tube 'medical treatment'? What is being treated? Further, the analogy between tube-feeding and mechanical ventilation is unpersuasive. A ventilator assists a patient to breathe but a tube does not assist a patient to digest, and it replaces, rather than assists, swallowing. Moreover, the withdrawal of a ventilator does not prevent the patient from breathing spontaneously but the withdrawal of tube-feeding results in certain death. And if the delivery of food by tube is medical treatment, is the removal of waste products by catheter and enema also medical treatment? Secondly, even if tube-feeding is medical treatment, why is it futile? Is it not achieving its purpose of nourishing the patient? To hold that the treatment is futile because the patient will not recover consciousness is surely to confuse the worthwhileness of the treatment with the worthwhileness of the patient's life.[40]

Arthur Hugh Clough, a fairly muddy-minded English poet of the nineteenth century, wrote the oft-quoted couplet:

> Thou shalt not kill; but need'st not strive
> Officiously to keep alive.

But what is 'officious'? The usual response is that anything beyond self-support is artificial, mechanical, and therefore legitimately disposable. Thus, in *Whose Life Is It Anyway?*:

> *Judge*: Certainly, you're alive legally.
>
> *Ken*: I think I could challenge even that.
>
> *Judge*: How?
>
> *Ken*: Any reasonable definition of life must include the idea of its being self-supporting. I seem to remember something in the papers — when all the heart transplant controversy was on — about it being alright to take someone's heart if they require constant attention from respirators and so on to keep them alive.[41]

In principle, however, the 'artificiality' of life-sustaining procedures does not alter the suicide or assisted-suicide scenario in the slightest. Would it

39   *Airedale NHS Trust v Bland* [1993] AC 789.

40   J. Keown, 'Doctors and Patients: Hard Case, Bad Law, "New" Ethics', (1993) 52 *Cambridge Law Journal* 210.

41   B. Clark, *Whose Life Is It Anyway?* (1978) 76.

be any less murder if, instead of shooting a person, we deprived him of his iron lung or of his insulin on the ground that these are 'artificial' means of keeping him alive? If doing such things to another would be homicide, then doing them to oneself would just as certainly be suicide. A little reflection on the question of 'dependence' will reveal that no one — at any stage of his or her existence — is really independent of others or of the environment, 'natural' or 'artificial' (if the distinction really has any meaning). We depend upon others, including manufactured devices, for our very survival. (If you doubt this, try not using your boiler this winter.) Far more unites the terminally ill patient, the foetus, and the healthy, adult reader of this chapter than separates them. All three are dependent, and their dependency, instead of offering a potential ground for destruction or self-destruction, is a common bond. 'Never send to know for whom the bell tolls;' John Donne reminded humanity: 'it tolls for thee.'[42]

V.   THREE OBJECTIONS AND A CONCLUSION

Several major objections can be raised to the position espoused here but they are all readily answerable.

Private morality or public concern for the right to life

H.L.A. Hart maintains that the suicide and assisted-suicide issue should remain a matter of private morality — that such sensitive ethical decisions should not be legislated.[43] This is precisely the approach Ronald Dworkin takes to abortion: as a religious question, it should not be subjected to the interference of the state or its laws.[44] But, as I have argued over against Dworkin,[45] where life is in the balance, the state and its law must intervene in order to prevent egregious violations of human rights.

---

[42] It may be that the judicial confusion on the legitimacy of doing nothing so as to allow a patient to die versus the culpability involved in stopping a proper medical treatment derives from the unfortunate Common Law doctrine of nonfeasance: the notion (rejected in the Continental Civil Law) that one can with impunity refuse to assist a person in peril — that culpability attaches only when one commences to assist and then negligently does not continue to do so. This distinction is as conceptually bad and ethically immoral as the effort to distinguish between 'active' and 'passive' euthanasia. See A. D'Amato, 'The Conflict Between Legal and Moral Obligation: the "Bad Samaritan" paradigm', in his *Jurisprudence: A Descriptive and Normative Analysis of Law* (1984) 287–303, and J.W. Montgomery, *Human Rights and Human Dignity* (1986) 186–87.

[43] H.L.A. Hart, *Law, Liberty and Morality* (1962).

[44] R. Dworkin, *Life's Dominion* (2d ed. 1994).

[45] See note 11, above.

Slavery was a highly disputed religious question, but should the state therefore have stood neutrally apart, permitting those who saw nothing the matter with slavery to keep their slaves?[46] The right to life is enshrined in international covenants and conventions as the most fundamental of human rights; we must not let it be eroded by jurisprudential indifferentism. Argues Keown:

> The notion of a worthless life is as alien to the Hippocratic tradition as it is to English criminal law, both of which subscribe to the principle of the sanctity of human life which holds that because all lives are intrinsically valuable, it is always wrong intentionally to kill an innocent human being. This principle is, by contrast, rejected by the so-called 'new' (consequentialist) morality which openly espouses the notion of the 'life not worth living'.[47]

Victimless act or harming others

It is said that suicide and assisted suicide are 'harmless acts' — acts that impact only the terminally ill patient — and therefore should be subject to his absolute and untrammelled control. Stephen notes the common view (though he feels uncomfortable with it) that 'suicide is the only offence which under no circumstances can produce alarm'.[48] This is essentially the position of Joel Feinberg, who in Chapter 27 of his influential *Harm to Self* (Volume III of *The Moral Limits of the Criminal Law*)

> . . . examines from a special perspective the problem of voluntary euthanasia. In particular it [the chapter] considers the effects on voluntariness of 'understandable depression,' and concludes that depression need not vitiate the voluntariness even of a choice of death, provided certain other conditions are met, and that only a kind of defective reasoning — the 'catch 22 arguments' — can seem to show the contrary. On the larger question of the moral permissibility of active euthanasia generally, after considering the role of living wills and durable power of attorney, the chapter concludes that the only possible reason for maintaining the present absolute prohibition is that it is necessary to prevent mistakes and abuse. If there is no such necessity then there is no morally respectable reason to interfere with the liberty of an autonomous person to dispose of his own lot in life, even if his choice is for death.[49]

Though Glanville Williams regards suicide as 'a practice freely consented to that does not harm others,'[50] he concedes that assisted suicide could

---

46   See T. Sutton, 'Christians as Law Reformers in the Nineteenth and Twentieth Centuries', Chapter 1 above at pp 13–15.

47   J. Keown, (1993) 52 *Cambridge Law Journal* 211.

48   J.F. Stephen, 3 *A History of the Criminal Law of England* (1883) 107.

49   J. Feinberg, *Harmless Wrongdoing*, xix (1988).

50   G. Williams, 8 *Encyclopedia of Philosophy* (P. Edwards ed. 1967) 44.

well have a dark side to it: 'There is a case for punishing those who assist suicide by young people (who may go through a temporarily difficult phase, and whose suicide is a cruel blow to parents), or who *persuade* others to commit suicide, or use fraud, or assist the act for selfish reasons.'[51]

The mention here of parents suffering from the suicide of their children should remind us that suicide never occurs in a social vacuum. Indeed, because of the interlocking character of human life — the fact that man is inherently a social animal — there are strictly no immoral acts that hurt only the perpetrator. 'Harmless wrongdoing'[52] is a contradiction in terms, as even lighthearted playwright Noël Coward fully recognized.[53] One of the most touching testimonies to this truth where suicide is concerned is found in the first of Lord Chancellor Hailsham's autobiographies, and it warrants much reflection:

> I am moved at this stage to add a footnote about suicide. I had thought of remaining reticent on the subject, but I am impelled to write about it in the hope that at some time someone will read, and heed, my words. My dear brother Edward committed suicide, and there is a sense in which I have never recovered from the blow. He was in every way a delightful person, brave and talented beyond the lot of man. He rowed for Leander, was President of the Oxford Union, earned and received a Double First, was MP for Eastbourne, the author of at least one best-selling book, and a rising member of the Bar. He could not have failed, had he lived, to play an important, perhaps even a decisive, part in the history of the country. He killed himself one spring day in our home in Sussex with my 20-bore shotgun which, when I had been a little younger, had been my most prized possession. I will not waste time discussing what led him to do it, except to say that the last phase was insomnia, or to say why I have never failed to blame myself without mercy for my failure to prevent him doing it. I only write this in order to express my profound and passionate conviction that suicide is always wrong if only for the misery it inflicts on others. Bereavement is one thing. The pain at bereavement is the price we pay for love, and high as that price is, it is not one which one grudges paying when bereavement is suffered. But bereavement by suicide is some-thing altogether different and leaves an incurable wound. If only Edward had known the pain he was inflicting on us all who were left behind, and the ceaseless and incurable self-condemnation we all felt so that even now forty years later I cannot bear the burden of it, he would never have done what he

---

[51] G. Williams, *Textbook of Criminal Law* (1978) 531.

[52] Joel Feinberg's title to Volume IV of his *The Moral Limits of the Criminal Law* (see note 49 above).

[53] This is one of the central themes of Coward's frequently revived play, *Present Laughter* (acting ed. 1949), e.g. 25–26:

> *Garry*: I don't do any harm to anybody.
> *Liz*: You do harm to yourself and to the few, the very few who really mind about you.'

did and, if by reading this some other unhappy family may be saved from woe so intolerable, this book will not have been in vain. As it is, Edward is in the hands of God, and no doubt he is wholly forgiven, since if our poor natures can wholly forgive him as we do, how much more will the infinite compassion of the Saviour take him to his arms. But suicide is wrong, wrong, wrong, and Christians were amongst the first to recognize the fact. Their spiritual insight is to be recognized as among the proofs, as well as the consolations, of Christianity.[54]

Pluralism and the risks and consequences of assisted suicide

Finally, we are told that, even granting the moral power of Christian objections to suicide and assisted suicide, one has no right to impose such views on a pluralistic society. One might reply, in the words of the Psalmist (16:4, *Book of Common Prayer*): 'They that run after another god shall have great trouble.' If the Christian world-view is correct in its understanding of human nature — both as to man's inherent dignity and as to his existing corrupted state of selfishness — then to disregard these facts societally, even in a pluralistic society, is to court disaster. Professor Kamisar, a non-Christian, has shown on purely secular, pragmatic grounds that the biblical prohibitions against suicide and assisted suicide are fully warranted. He points up the difficulty of establishing genuine consent when the patient is suffering from severe pain; the risk of incorrect diagnosis — with, in this case, irreparable consequences; and the real possibility of carrying out euthanasia on a patient who could subsequently have been cured by new medical developments. Kamisar further elaborates the classic 'wedge' argument: to condone euthanasia is inevitably to reduce respect for the sanctity of human life in general.[55]

The practical soundness of these arguments — and the confirmation they offer of the validity of the Christian stance on suicide and assisted suicide — comes from the most detailed study to date of the legally sanctioned practice of euthanasia in the Netherlands. Here there is ample empirical evidence of the slippery slope, practically, logically, legally, and ethically. The study concludes that in the Netherlands, with 'standards' (note well!) roughly the equivalent of those advocated by the Compassion In Dying organization and other American euthanasia groups,

54   Hailsham, *The Door Wherein I Went* (1975) 60–61. *Cf.* his more recent *A Sparrow's Flight: The Memoirs of Lord Hailsham of St Marylebone* (1990), and the chapter devoted to him in R. Clifford, *Leading Lawyers' Case for the Resurrection* (1996) 70–81.

55   Y. Kamisar, 'Some Non-Religious Views Against Proposed "Mercy-Killing" Legislation', (1958) 42, *Minnesota Law Review* 969–1042. Glanville Williams characteristically attempted to refute Kamisar's arguments in 'Mercy-Killing Legislation — A Rejoinder', (1958) 43 *Minnesota Law Review* 1–12.

. . . euthanasia is being practised on a scale vastly exceeding the 'known' (truthfully reported and recorded) cases. There is little sense in which it can be said, in any of its forms, to be under control. As Leenen has observed, there is an 'almost total lack of control on the administration of euthanasia' and 'the present legal situation makes any adequate control of the practice of euthanasia virtually impossible'.[56]

The same considerations have been shown to apply to the so-called 'living wills'. Jerome Wernow of the University of Leuven, Belgium, has irrefutably demonstrated that:

> The current content and legal acceptance of these documents is largely a product of what once was known as the Euthanasia Education Council, now called Concern for Dying. A scrutiny of their rationale for the use of the living will exhibits a presuppositional strain of thought similar to that espoused by the proponents of suicide throughout history. Tenets like self-determination and primacy of health as life's essential values are similar to the bases for advocacy of suicide found in Seneca, the Stoics, the Humanist Movement and Social Darwinism.[57]

Conclusion

And where do such philosophical conceptions take us? A concluding story — true, but no less parabolic for that — may provide an answer.

Some years ago when I served as Director of Studies at the International Institute of Human Rights, founded by René Cassin, in Strasbourg, France, one of the guest lecturers was a New York lawyer who delivered a series of lectures on 'The Right to Die'. She expected a very positive response from the avant-garde student audience. She was shocked to find just the opposite reaction, particularly among international students from the Third World. Their point was that in their countries the struggle for the right to life had hardly been won — after ages of paganism in which the individual counted for next to nothing. Anything that would facilitate death at the expense of life was therefore anathema.

The 9th Circuit opinion in *Compassion In Dying* is well aware that life issues are interconnected: voluntary euthanasia is linked with abortion throughout the opinion. What the Court appears blissfully ignorant of is that, because of the seamless garment of human dignity, facilitating death

---

[56] J. Keown, 'The Law and Practice of Euthanasia in the Netherlands', (1992) 108 *Law Quarterly Review* 51–78. See our text at note 20 above. For an updated treatment of Keown's material in book form, together with valuable essays on the subject by other specialists, see L. Gormally (ed.), *Euthanasia Clinical Practice and the Law* (1994). Keown's latest treatment of the subject is his article, 'Euthanasia in the Netherlands: Sliding Down the Slippery Slope?', (1995) 9 *Notre Dame Journal of Law, Ethics & Public Policy* 407 ff.

[57] J.R. Wernow, 'The Living Will', (1994) 10 *Ethics & Medicine* 27–35.

in any way facilitates it in every way. Owing to human selfishness, there is a built-in tendency toward social entropy: we find it easier and more convenient by far to kill than to keep alive. The law is supposed to protect us from ourselves in this respect, not make it easier for us to destroy each other or ourselves. If we err, let us err on the side of preserving life.

Law reform is not *per se* a positive good. Its value depends squarely on the value of the changes proposed. The absence of current UK legislation or serious legislative proposals to facilitate dying may not be most helpfully explained by the conservative temper or alleged lack of philosophical reflection on the part of legislators and the English legal community. Rather, it is best seen as signifying a deeper appreciation than one encounters today in many other legal contexts that the life one saves (societally and individually) may be one's own.

VI. APPENDIX TO CHAPTER 4:

Current House Hansard (Australia), 9 September 1996. Page: 3670 (PROOF)

EUTHANASIA LAWS BILL 1996

First reading

Bill presented by Mr Andrews.

Mr ANDREWS (Menzies) (12.54 p.m.) — Mr Acting Speaker, I presented the Euthanasia Laws Bill 1996. Last year, the Northern Territory became the only place in the world to legalise what proponents describe as voluntary euthanasia — in reality, intentional killing and assisted suicide. Whether intended or not the act, passed by a legislature representing less than one per cent of the national population, has a direct impact on other Australians.

Far from its operation being limited to Northern Territory residents, people have travelled from elsewhere seeking to use the act. This then is a national issue. Let there be no doubt about what the Northern Territory has done.

The Northern Territory act is not about the discontinuance of futile or heroic treatment. It is not about the refusal of burdensome or unwanted medical attention. It is not about the appointment of an agent to make decisions about treatment for an incompetent person. And it is not about the provision of modern, pain-relieving palliative care. The Northern Territory act is about one thing — the use of a lethal injection to bring about the immediate death of another. This, Mr Acting Speaker, is a Commonwealth bill to stop lethal injections.

Four reservations expressed about the draft bill have been met. The new bill does not single out the Northern Territory; it enacts a law to the extent of the Commonwealth's power. The bill does not invalidate the Territory's Natural Death Act. This bill is solely about euthanasia and no other matter. And this new bill has no retrospective effect.

The bill restates two clear principles about the treatment of the dying and the disabled in our society. First, the bill states that the legislative assemblies have no power to make laws which permit or have the effect of permitting the form of intentional killing of another called euthanasia — which includes mercy killing — or the assisting of a person to terminate his or her life. Secondly, the bill confirms that the legislative assemblies do have power to make laws with respect to the withdrawal or withholding of medical or surgical measures for prolonging the life of a patient, and of medical treatment in the provision of palliative care to a dying patient — but not so as to permit intentional killing.

These principles reflect the state of the law throughout Australia, with the notable exception of the Northern Territory. Every other state and territory has laws which proscribe intentional killing and assisted suicide. Where these issues have been addressed in recent years — in Victoria, South Australia and the ACT — euthanasia has been rejected. Plans to legalize it in New South Wales were dropped in the face of overwhelming parliamentary opposition. The national approach to rejecting the intentional killing of the terminally ill and assisted suicide is therefore reflected in this Commonwealth bill.

By enacting its legislation, not only has the Northern Territory re-jected this national approach; it has ignored the findings of every major committee of inquiry in the world, it has cast aside the ethical principles of the world medical profession, it has rejected the tenets of every major religious group, it has ignored the concerns of its own Aboriginal people, and it has turned a blind eye to the evidence of widespread abuse of euthanasia in the Netherlands. The Northern Territory has also failed to do two things which could reasonably be expected of a legislature concerned about caring for the dying.

First, there has been no attempt to introduce modern refusal of treatment legislation as in Victoria and South Australia. Instead, the Northern Territory clings to its Natural Death Act, antiquated legislation which originated in America two decades ago. Hence there are no provisions for the appointment of agents to make medical decisions on behalf of a person who becomes incapable of doing so. Secondly, the standard of palliative care in the Northern Territory is totally inadequate.

Instead, the Northern Territory chose to bypass a caring response for all dying people and to legalize assisted suicide for a few. The Commonwealth parliament clearly has the constitutional power — and, I believe, the duty — to enact this bill. I commend it to all honourable members. I present the explanatory memorandum.

Bill read a first time.

Mr ACTING SPEAKER — In accordance with standing order 104A, the second reading will be made an order of the day for the next sitting.

5

A Christian Vision for Corporate Governance

Stephen Copp

I. INTRODUCTION

This chapter[1] concerns the way in which companies should be run. It was first offered under the title 'Corporate Governance — A Christian Response to the Moral Vacuum'. On reflection this was considered to be too negative and condescending. Companies have provided the Western world at least (and also countries such as Japan) with a very high standard of living. They have played an important role in enabling it to withstand totalitarianism, whether in the form of fascism or communism. Companies are irrevocably bound up with the lives of countless Christians, whether as owners (and remember those who have pension plans can be counted as this), consumers or employees. The title was, therefore, changed to 'A Christian Vision for Corporate Governance'. Nonetheless, there seems to be a widespread belief that all is not well in the corporate world. Corporate governance has stolen the imagination of company lawyers and academics and professionals from many other disciplines as one of the key subjects to study as we progress towards a new Millenium although it appears that some scepticism may be developing in respect of the 'corporate governance industry'.[2] It is hard to open academic journals on business-related matters without finding one or more articles on the subject. This is more than a reaction to a negative perspective that all is

---

[1] The writer wishes to thank Professor Kevin McGuinness, Steele Raymond Professor of Business Law at Bournemouth University, for his helpful comments on the draft of this paper, as well as other colleagues, and finally, the editor and anonymous referee. The usual disclaimer applies. The position is stated as at 1 September 1996, although it has been possible to include some later material. Unfortunately it has not been possible to take into account some significant developments, including the Labour Party election victory, the Preliminary Report of the Hempel Committee, and the speech of the Archbishop of Canterbury to the Trades Union Congress in September 1997. All biblical references are to the New International Version (Hodder & Stoughton, 1986).

[2] See 'Corporate governance "must not stifle UK plc" ' *Accountancy*, December 1996, 21.

not well in the corporate world and is perhaps fired by the fundamental and thought-provoking questions raised.[3]

This paper deals with three main questions:

What shortcomings are revealed by the debate on corporate governance?
Is there a response based on Christian teaching to these?
If so, what response should be given?

The approach taken has been to review a wide range of topical materials reflecting the breadth of the contemporary debate on corporate governance from across a range of disciplines. The response of Christian teaching to these shortcomings has been based on a review of some major trends in Christian thinking and the Biblical narratives. As a consequence inevitably it has not been possible to do more than give an overview on a subject where there is a vast literature crossing disciplinary boundaries. What it is hoped that this chapter will achieve is to introduce the general reader to the nature of these important issues and provoke thought and debate.

II. WHAT IS MEANT BY CORPORATE GOVERNANCE?

It is difficult to define a term such as corporate governance as opposed to describing its use. There are three common approaches. Parkinson[4] uses it to refer to 'the **processes** of supervision and control . . . intended to ensure that the company's management acts in accordance with the interests of the shareholders'. The Cadbury Committee,[5] which was only concerned with the financial aspects of corporate governance, defined it as '. . . the **system** by which companies are directed and controlled'.[6] In contrast, Monks and Minow[7] define it as 'the **relationship** among

3   See, for example, C. Handy, 'What is a company for?' *Royal Society of Arts Journal*, March 1991: 'What is a company really for today? Do our rules and institutions reflect that purpose, or do they, perhaps, get in the way? Things do outlive their purpose, and what was once sensible may now seem crazy. We do not have to be slaves to our history,' cited R. Sparkes, *The Ethical Investor* (HarperCollins, 1995) 227.

4   J.E. Parkinson, *Corporate Power and Responsibility, Issues in the Theory of Company Law* (Clarendon Press, 1993) 159. Emphasis added.

5   The Cadbury Committee was established in May 1991 by the Financial Reporting Council, the London Stock Exchange and the accountancy profession and issued the report, *The Financial Aspects of Corporate Governance* ('the Cadbury Report') (Gee 1992) in December 1992. This contained a Code of Best Practice, directed primarily to the boards of directors of all UK listed companies.

6   *The Cadbury Report*, para. 2.5. Emphasis added.

7   R.A.G. Monks and N. Minow, *Corporate Governance* (Blackwell, 1995) p. 1. Emphasis added.

various participants in determining the direction and performance of corporations. The primary participants are (1) the shareholders, (2) the management (led by the chief executive officer), and (3) the board of directors . . . Other participants include the employees, customers, suppliers, creditors and the community.' The third of these approaches has been adopted in this chapter for the following reasons. Firstly, it is submitted that the role of relationships is central to an understanding of corporate governance. Secondly, it well reflects the international and multidisciplinary debate taking place on the role of the company and what some regard as the stakeholders (a term considered later in this paper) in a company.[8]

Even though this definition is useful for working purposes it is important to appreciate its limitations. Firstly, the debate on corporate governance tends to extend not to all companies but only to listed companies.[9] The reason for this is that in such companies ownership and management will be substantially separated[10] and there may, therefore, be a perception that management lacks effective controls. Such companies tend also to be of greater public interest because of their size and the range of people concerned with them.[11] Secondly, the debate on corporate governance in practice extends beyond listed companies to analogous organizations, for example, public utilities, building societies,[12] NHS

---

[8]   For example S.M. Evers, 'The social role of business, tomorrow's company—inclusively ethical?' (1996) 5 *Business Ethics, a European Review* 76, reviewing the Royal Society of Arts report *Tomorrow's Company*.

[9]   See, for example, the consultation letter issued on 17 October 1996 by the Committee on Corporate Governance ('the Hampel Committee') which in Annex A specifically limits the remit of the committee to listed companies only. Para. (a) (ii) invites views as to whether the Cadbury Code should differentiate between companies by type of business or size. A Confederation of British Industry report published on 28 October 1996 and cited in *CCH Company Law News*, November 1996, 4, has called for a relaxation of certain corporate governance requirements for smaller quoted companies.

[10] The origins of the theme of a shift from ownership to control of the firm are traced in Farrar et al., *Farrar's Company Law* (Butterworths, 1991) pp. 9–10. See also J.E. Parkinson, *op. cit.* n.4, Chapter 2, 51 and S. Sheikh, *Corporate Social Responsibilities Law & Practice* (Cavendish, 1996) 27–36.

[11] See R.I. Tricker, *Corporate Governance*, Chapter 2 (Gower, 1984) 42 and J.E. Parkinson, *op. cit.*, 3–8.

[12] G. Cole, 'The Cadbury Committee Report — Implementation and Influence' in *Corporate Governance & Corporate Control* ed. S. Sheikh and W. Rees (Cavendish, 1995) 355 at 358.

trusts[13] and other institutions.[14] Great care should be taken in making such extensions. For example, it is doubtful that an NHS trust is really fulfilling the same purpose as a commercial company.

III.   WHAT SHORTCOMINGS DOES THE CORPORATE GOVERNANCE DEBATE REVEAL?

A lack of consensus as to the purpose of the company

a)   *The economic perspective.*
It is often said that the purpose of a company is the maximization of profit.[15] This statement, in fact, implies a behavioral theory which attempts to explain how decisions are actually taken in companies and to permit predictions to be made. It does not prescribe that there can be no other purpose for a company. Profit maximization has been the target of much of the criticism levelled at corporate

[13]   See, for example, C. Brophy, 'The NHS: Taking The Cadbury Report Seriously' (1995) *Solicitors Journal,* 324. The ethical tensions to which this gives rise have been explored by T. Sorell 'Ethics and the NHS reforms in the UK' (1996) 5, *Business Ethics* 196, E. Vallance 'Ethics in business and health' (1996) 5, *Business Ethics* 202 and H. Draper, 'Can Britain's NHS managers be business-like and should they adopt the values of business?' (1996) 5, *Business Ethics* 207.

[14]   See, for example, J. Dine, 'Corporate Governance, Cadbury and Friendly Societies' (1995) 1 *Web Journal of Current Legal Issues,* http://www.ncl.ac.uk/~nlawwww/; B. Harvey, 'The Governance of Co-operative Societies' in *Corporate Governance & Corporate Control, op. cit.,* 173.

[15]   See, for example, R.G. Lipsey, *Positive Economics* (Weidenfeld and Nicholson, 1989) 170–171 who states it formally as 'the desire to maximize profits is assumed to motivate all decisions taken within a firm and such decisions are uninfluenced by who takes them'. He notes two major criticisms, first that profit maximization is too crude an assumption about motivation and second that the firm's organizational structure must affect its decisions. He goes on to discuss various alternatives to the profit maximization theory. One is long-term profit maximization, i.e. that rational profit maximizing must take place over a realistic time horizon (273). Another is the maximization of managers' rather than shareholders' interests which may take the form of sales maximization to seek growth whilst aiming to make such minimum profits as will keep shareholders satisfied (274). This latter argument is explained as a 'principal-agent' problem arising from a conflict of interests between the shareholders as principal and managers as agent which can be solved by aligning the interests of managers to those of shareholders by appropriate incentives (275).

behaviour[16] and therefore the focus of attention for those seeking to reform corporate governance. Nonetheless, profit is a measure of efficiency of the use of assets, not least because to maximize profits costs must be minimized. A company which is inefficient will have difficulty in attracting further capital and may become liable to a takeover, in the case of a listed company, or risk insolvency. In any event it can be argued that it is not the profit maximization goal which needs reform but rather the legislative and other constraints on profit maximization.17 The aim of such reform would be to ensure that the maximization of profits coincides with the public interest. The reality is that there are already a large number of constraints in place, for example, in the form of employment legislation and so the question becomes one of whether the constraints are sufficient to satisfy current perceptions of the public interest.

An alternative approach to the purpose of the company, which can be traced to the US in the 1920s[18] is known as corporate social responsibility, which has been defined as 'the assumption of responsibilities by companies, whether voluntarily or by virtue of statute, in discharging socio-economic obligations in society'.[19] It embraces two main concepts.[20] The first is **corporate philanthropy**, whereby companies participate in society by engaging in social activism themselves. The second is the **trusteeship principle**, which views directors as trustees for those with differing interests in the company. The main arguments in favour of corporate philanthropy are responsible corporate citizenship[21] and enlightened self-interest.[22] In contrast to profit maximization, the goal is seen as profit optimization.[23] There are, however, some serious

[16] See, for example, S. Sheikh, *op. cit.* n.10, Chapter 2.

[17] J.E. Parkinson, *op. cit.* n.4, considers this question at length. He concludes that it is impossible to communicate through external legal controls all circumstances where it is desirable that profit seeking should be constrained (41–44). Furthermore, he argues that approaches based on management voluntarism are only likely to produce modest changes in company behaviour because of the absence of external stimulus whereas to increase the power of interest groups to shape company conduct seems capable of producing a more radical redirection of corporate conduct although there is room for doubt as to the magnitude of the likely effects (p. 346).

[18] See S. Sheikh, *op. cit.* n.10, Chapter 1, 9.

[19] *Ibid.*, 1.

[20] *Ibid.*, 15.

[21] *Ibid.*, 39.

[22] *Ibid.*, 48.

[23] *Ibid.*, 21. The term is used by S. Sheikh in contrast to profit maximization to connote the discharge of social responsibilities and obligations towards various potential claimants on the company. J.E. Parkinson, *op. cit.* n.4, 261,

objections to corporate social responsibility notwithstanding its seductive appeal. Friedman is well noted for arguing that 'the social responsibility of business is to increase its profits'.[24] In other words, successful companies are the best means of improving society.[25] Certainly, it can be argued that company directors are not qualified to attempt small-scale social engineering which is more democratically effected by central government through the tax system. Where company directors do get involved in corporate philanthropy it could easily become a route to social status for those conferring the largesse. At the end of the day, why should directors be allowed to give away money which does not belong to them but to the shareholders?[26]

b)   *The company law perspective.* Company law is seemingly silent on the rather abstract question of the purpose of the company. An impression of this can only be gained by considering the legal requirements for the company's constitution, the duties of management, the rules on distributions and the remedies available to protect shareholders and creditors. Even then the picture that emerges is less one of a statement of a positive purpose but rather a negative statement of what the purpose of a company is not to do. An interesting comparison is the approach taken by the American Law Institute which has recently completed a project to review the law on corporate governance. This has stated that:

. . . a [business] corporation should have as its objective the conduct of business activities with a view to enhancing corporate profit and shareholder gain . . . [e]ven if corporate profit and shareholder gain are not thereby enhanced, the corporation, in the conduct of its business . . . [m]ay take into account ethical considerations that are reasonably regarded as appropriate to the responsible

---

[23] *cont*
distinguishes between 'profit-sacrificing social responsibility' to indicate the voluntary sacrifice of profits, either by incurring additional costs or making transfers to non-shareholder groups and 'social responsibility' in the sense, for example, of increased sensitivity to the impact of the company's activities on third parties, without any necessary implication that a divergence from the profit goal is involved.

[24] The title of an article in *New York Times Magazine*, 13 September 1970.

[25] The theoretical basis for this is that a profit maximizing firm will allocate resources in the most efficient way.

[26] For a detailed review of the arguments against social activism by companies see J.E. Parkinson, *op. cit.* n.4, 337–344. See also S. Sheikh, *op. cit.* n.10, 22–27. An interesting illustration is provided by the case study on the 'Pennsylvania Act 36 of 1990' in R.A.G. Monks & N. Minow, *op. cit.* n.7, 39–40, which demonstrates the importance of retaining market confidence.

conduct of business . . . and [m]ay devote a reasonable amount of resources to public welfare, humanitarian, educational, and philanthropic purposes.'[27]

The constitution of a company must state its objects.[28] The legislation[29] appears to anticipate that this would be a short statement of the intended business activities[30] of the company. Instead, the result has been a very lengthy statement setting out both the objects of a company and the powers in support of those objects. The reason for this has been to attempt to avoid the dangers of the *ultra vires* rule applying. The effect of this rule at common law was that the courts would hold void any transaction between the company and another person which was *ultra vires* (literally beyond the powers of) the company and this was so whether or not the other person was aware of the irregularity.[31] Indeed this rule, notwithstanding its virtual abolition by statute,[32] still presents some dangers should a company wish to engage in corporate social responsibility.[33] One solution might be for a company to include an object in its constitution expressly permitting this.[34] No doubt the acid test of this approach would be whether shareholders, particularly institutional shareholders, would be prepared to approve such an object,

[27] See § 2.01 cited by R.A.G. Monks & N. Minow, *op. cit.*, 25. See also C.A. Riley for a recent UK analysis of this, 'The American Law Institute's Principles of Corporate Governance' (1995) 16 *The Company Lawyer*, 122.

[28] *Companies Act 1985*, s. 2 (1) (c).

[29] See *Table B, Companies (Tables A to F) Regulations 1985* SI 1985 No. 805 which uses as an illustration 'The company's objects are the carriage of passengers and goods in motor vehicles . . . and the doing of all such other things as are incidental or conducive to the attainment of that object.'

[30] Note the emphasis on activities. There is no assumption of any theory as to profit goals.

[31] See, for example, *Pennington's Company Law* (Butterworths, 1995), 15.

[32] See *Companies Act 1985*, s. 35 and also ss. 35A and B.

[33] See S. Sheikh, *op. cit.* n.10, 115–136 who argues that the statutory changes in the *Companies Act 1989* would allow companies to engage in corporate philanthropy subject to certain restrictions.

[34] See the dicta of Buckley L.J. in *Re Horsley and Weight Ltd* [1982] Ch. 442 at 450 which S. Sheikh, *op. cit.* n.10, interprets as sanctioning gratuitous distributions for philanthropic purposes if they are expressly stated in the objects clause. It seems that the company would be unlikely thereby to become a charity as its objects would not be exclusively charitable, see *Charities Act 1993*, ss. 96 (1) and 97 (1) and *CIR v. The Yorkshire Agricultural Society* (1927) 13 TC 58, although the interaction with charities law and practice would need careful consideration. The requirements of the Stock Exchange would also require consideration, see for example *Yellow Book Chapter 13*. See also notes 55 and 56.

and with what restrictions, and whether the disciplines of the market might frustrate it in any event.

The directors of a company must act in what they consider to be the interests of the company and not for any collateral purpose.[35] The extent to which a wider range of interests may properly be taken into account is very limited. In any event the duty is owed to the company and not to shareholders individually.[36] However, a broader approach to defining the objects of a company might go some way to resolving this. The statutory framework anticipates that a company will aim to make a profit for distribution to its shareholders.[37] The implications of dividend policy have been considered in the context of minority shareholders' remedies by Harman J. who has stated:

> It seems to me that it is important to remember that a company is simply a vehicle for carrying on a business for the benefit of all members . . . the position which I am sure all the Victorian judges and legislators, who first created companies from 1862 onwards, would have thought obvious . . . that one of the prime purposes of a company is as a vehicle to earn profits which should be distributed by way of dividend to the members of it.[38]

Nonetheless, although this recognizes the profit motive it does not preclude a company from having corporate social responsibility amongst its objects.

Quite clearly the prospect of a company pursuing objects other than profit maximization is one that could be of concern both to shareholders and to creditors. Shareholders would have the opportunity to consider the matter. Creditors would not. Whilst a company is a going concern and able to pay its creditors this should not normally present any difficulty. But if such an object of

[35] This general statement is based on the oft-cited dicta of Lord Greene MR in *Re Smith & Fawcett Ltd* [1942] Ch. 304. See also *Howard Smith Ltd v. Ampol Petroleum Ltd* [1974] AC 821.

[36] See *Percival v. Wright* [1902] 2 Ch. 421. Where a company is insolvent it seems that the interests of creditors intrude who become prospectively entitled through the mechanism of liquidation to displace the power of shareholders and directors to deal with the company's assets, see *West Mercia Safetywear v. Dodd* [1988] BCLC 250. The matters to which the directors of a company are to have regard include the interests of employees as well as the interests of members: *Companies Act 1985*, s. 309 but note this is owed to the company alone and is enforceable in the same way as any other fiduciary duty owed to a company by its directors.

[37] See *Companies Act 1985*, Part VIII (distribution of profits and assets).

[38] *Re a Company (No. 00370 of 1987) ex parte Glossop* [1988] BCLC 570 at 576.

corporate social responsibility was to be pursued otherwise it could deplete the assets available to creditors on liquidation of the company. It would be important to take into account the risk of creditors' remedies then applying.[39]

A lack of consensus as to the purpose of company law

Much as the purpose of the company is uncertain, there is also a lack of consensus as to what company law is for. Gower[40] has divided its functions into 'enabling'[41] and 'regulatory'.[42] However, how the balance is struck between these two functions depends on which model of incorporation[43] is adopted. There are those who believe that corporate status is a privilege conferred by the state (the 'legal privilege model')[44] and therefore it is for the state to decide on the level of corresponding duty owed.[45] There are those who believe that corporate status is a right and that the company is a nexus of private contracts (the 'freedom of contract model') which the state should facilitate without the need for many mandatory rules.[46] The relevance of this to the corporate governance debate is that those who subscribe to the 'freedom of contract model' are unlikely to see additional regulation as appropriate and are likely to want substantial corporate deregulation with the safeguard against abuse provided by strengthening the action of market forces.[47] Those who subscribe to the 'legal privilege model' are likely to seek additional regulation to stamp out abuse. It can be argued that additional regulation as a cure-all if continually pursued over decades may bring down the corporate edifice altogether.[48] Sealy wisely pointed out in 1984 that the risks of the company

[39] See S. Sheikh, *op. cit.* n.10, 133–135.

[40] L.C.B. Gower, *Principles of Modern Company Law,* 5th ed. (Sweet & Maxwell, 1992) 7.

[41] In the sense of empowering people to do what they could not otherwise achieve, i.e. the creation of a body with distinct corporate personality.

[42] In the sense of prescribing the conditions which have to be complied with to obtain incorporation and protect others from the inherent dangers.

[43] See Farrar *et al., op. cit.* n.10, 95–99 for a discussion of these.

[44] Alternatively referred to as the 'concession theory'.

[45] Although it can be argued that the conferment of limited liability only warrants the imposition of safeguards to prevent its abuse, i.e. creditor protection, and not general intervention and that therefore the true justification of a general right to state intervention lies with the concentration of power which is brought about by the existence of the company, see J.E. Parkinson *op. cit.* n.4 at 30.

[46] Sometimes referred to as 'contractarians'.

[47] An economic justification for this being that this will result in a reduction of transaction costs.

[48] The debate may well be more theoretical than real in terms of its application to the UK. Although it was carried out some time ago it is interesting to

were well known when the decision was taken to let it loose on the world without introducing elaborate, clumsy and costly procedures as safeguards.[49] The burden has grown immensely since 1984 with new company legislation,[50] separate insolvency legislation[51] and financial services legislation.[52] Nonetheless, the cynic might argue that it is since this mammoth increase in legislation that some of the major scandals have taken place.

The UK has in theory subscribed to the legal privilege model in the sense that corporations in the UK can only be created by the Crown or Parliament. Nonetheless, it has adopted a combination of approaches to company law. First, it has provided for both direct regulation of particular aspects of corporate life where there is a risk of abuse[53] and the disclosure of information to interested parties.[54] Secondly, it has established a limited menu of corporate models[55] and prescribed the boundaries in which these can be tailored to meet corporate needs.[56] These models can be criticized

[48] *cont*

note the conclusions of the Report *Burdens on Business* (HMSO, 1985) where company law requirements rated a low index for seriousness, close to fire regulations, consumer law or national insurance contributions whereas value added tax, employment protection and statistics scored very highly. A more recent survey reported in ACCA Research Report No. 42, *Alternative Company Structures for the Small Business* by A. Hicks, R. Drury and J. Smallcombe (Chartered Association of Certified Accountants, 1995) again identified value added tax as the most overwhelming complaint, see 21–22.

[49] L.S. Sealy, *Company Law and Commercial Reality*, (Butterworths, 1984), 12–13.

[50] Including the *Companies Act 1985*, the *Companies Consolidation (Consequential Provisions) Act 1985*, the *Company Directors Disqualification Act 1986* and the *Companies Act 1989*.

[51] Including the *Insolvency Act 1985*, shortly after replaced by the *Insolvency Act 1986*.

[52] Including the *Financial Services Act 1986*.

[53] See, for example, *Companies Act 1985*, Part X (enforcement of fair dealing by directors).

[54] See Farrar *et al.*, *op. cit.* n.10, Chapter 28.

[55] The overwhelming majority of companies are incorporated under the *Companies Act 1985*, although incorporation may still be achieved by other means, for example, by Royal Charter. The *Companies Act 1985* distinguishes between the registration of public companies and private companies limited by shares or by guarantee or without limited liability. In general terms, companies limited by guarantee may be appropriate for charitable or non-profitmaking purposes whereas companies witout limited liability may be appropriate to incorporate some professional partnerships.

[56] For example, by establishing *Table A The Companies (Tables A to F) Regulations 1985* SI 1985 No. 805, Sch., as a model form of Articles of Association for companies limited by shares, which a company has considerable freedom to adopt, modify or substitute with its own preferred form.

as old-fashioned, the most common model assuming a simple democratic system of shareholder supervision of directors supported by mainly financial reporting subject to independent audit. The concept underpinning the models for the company is that of contract.[57] Analysis of this contract has yielded some valuable insights. In particular, Drury[58] has argued that any analysis of the company contract must take into account the long duration and changing nature of the relationships involved[59] so that a 'relational approach'[60] is appropriate. On this basis, the company contract constitutes the framework of a long-term relationship and must be viewed in that context and the aim of the dispute resolution machinery contained in it must therefore be the preservation of the long-term relationships between the participants in the company.[61] Generally, there have been a number of serious criticisms levelled at UK company law in addition to those directed at its burden. Many are based on the substance of the law but, equally, many are based on the complexity of the statutory drafting and the fact that many important principles are not even incorporated within statute.[62] A question mark can also be raised as to precisely what values company law is based upon and should foster.[63]

Concern over corporate structure

The principal UK corporate model, the company limited by shares, has been so successful that its key features have substantially survived intact for nearly a century and a half, not merely in the UK but in a host of

[57] *Companies Act 1985*, s. 14 (effect of memorandum and articles).
[58] R.R. Drury 'The relative nature of a shareholder's right to enforce the company contract' (1986) 45 *Cambridge Law Journal* 219.
[59] *Ibid.* at 222.
[60] *Ibid.* at 224.
[61] *Ibid.* at 246.
[62] See, for example, A. Hutchinson, 'Looking for direct results' *Law Society Gazette*, 8 December 1993, 19; P. Morgan 'A cold climate for business law' *Law Society Gazette*, 8 December 1993, 3; L. Sealy 'Small company legislation' *Law Society Gazette*, 8 December 1993, 16; A. Hutchinson and I. Smedley 'The juggernaut comes to grief' *Law Society Gazette*, 17 February 1993, 21; S. Sheikh, 'UK company law reform: towards a 21st century corporate revolution' [1996] 4 *International Company and Commercial Law Review* 119.
[63] Interestingly, the Law Commission Consultation Paper No. 142 *Shareholder Remedies* completed on 31 July 1996 identified six 'guiding principles' for resolving the problems identified in that area, including sanctity of contract, freedom from unnecessary shareholder interference and efficiency and cost effectiveness. See further, C.A. Riley, 'The Law Commission Consultation Paper on Shareholder Remedies: Problems, Principles and Evidence' SPTL Workshop 13 December 1996.

other countries which have adopted similar models.[64] There are, however, a number of factors which have led to dissatisfaction with this corporate model. Firstly, the model has attempted to provide a substantially similar framework for all companies, from, say, a company owned by a husband and wife to operate a small business to a group of companies operating a substantial multinational business. Indeed, the pressure to change the model has been particularly strong in relation to both these extremes. Secondly, the relative economic progress of the UK compared with, say, Germany and Japan, has led to a reappraisal of this corporate model by comparison with the different models prevailing in those countries.[65] This has been inescapable in the UK because of its membership of the EC, given the objective of harmonization of company law envisaged in this. Thirdly, there has been a growing debate as to the relationship between a company and its stakeholders and whether and, if so, how the UK corporate model should be modified to recognize the interests of such stakeholders.

The problem of attempting to provide a substantially similar framework for all companies has been recognized. It has been tackled at the level of smaller companies by an increasing degree of deregulation, for example, in relation to the accounting and audit regimes as well as the introduction of an elective regime to, in effect, allow private companies to opt out of some of the more inconvenient provisions of company law. It has been tackled at the level of larger companies by the longstanding distinction between public and private companies whereby public companies are subject to a higher standard of regulation in specified areas and also by the application of higher standards to those companies whose shares are marketed to the public. In addition, much of the impetus towards the reform of corporate governance on a self-regulatory basis has been limited to such companies. It is not surprising therefore that this trend for the requirements for the two broad categories of companies to diverge has led to calls for a broader reappraisal of the corporate models and the legislation serving them.

The reappraisal of the corporate models by comparison with those prevailing in other countries calls for more detailed comment, particularly in the light of EC membership. The German model for major companies,

---

64 Typically, Commonwealth countries such as Canada, New Zealand and Australia but other models which were not greatly dissimilar developed independently, for example, in the US.

65 Perhaps ironically in the case of Japan because the two Japanese forms of corporate governance do not in principle differ very much from those of the public and private company of the UK, see R.I. Tricker *International Corporate Governance* (Prentice Hall, 1994), 3. What is very different is Japanese corporate culture and practice, see *op. cit.* 19–22. In particular, R.I. Tricker draws attention to high levels of unity throughout the company and decision-making by consensus. The German model will be considered below.

to look at one particularly influential European model, has developed along very different lines to that of the UK. Firstly, there has been a far higher level of shareholder supervision and, secondly, there has been greater employee representation. A high level of shareholder supervision has been achieved since 1870 by the adoption of a two-tier board structure comprising a supervisory board consisting of shareholder representatives to control the basic policy of the company and a management board, appointed by the supervisory board, to be responsible for managing the company's operations. Since the 1950s the management board has been required to consist of a minimum proportion of elected employee representatives reinforced by works councils.

The European Commission has favoured a two-tier model over the UK type 'unitary' board, where, arguably, a similar function has been performed by a distinction between executive and non-executive directors. Accordingly, in 1972 a draft Fifth Directive was proposed,[66] incorporating a two-tier structure and a choice of models for employee participation. The UK has consistently opposed the Fifth Directive notwithstanding a substantial revision in 1988[67] which would permit a unitary board with diluted provisions for employee representation. One other aspect of the proposal which the UK has opposed is that directors should be jointly and severally liable to make compensation for all damage sustained by the company as a result of breaches of duty by one or more of them.[68] The question of employee representation has, in some measure been effectively sidestepped by the adoption of the Works Council Directive[69] passed under the Maastricht Protocol on Social Policy Agreement from which the UK had opted out. Despite the opt-out the Works Council Directive had a substantial impact on UK multinational companies.[70] After the Labour Party Election victory in May 1997 the UK agreed to the social Protocol. The Works Council Directive will not have to be implemented in the UK for two years from the date when the Directive is extended to the UK.

[66] Proposal for a Fifth Directive on the structure and management of public limited liability companies and the powers and obligations of their organs O.J. 1972 C131/49.

[67] Amended proposal for a Fifth Directive on the structure of public limited liability companies and the powers and obligations of their organs, as set out in a DTI Consultative Document, January 1990.

[68] *Ibid.*, Article 14 (2).

[69] Council Directive on the establishment of a European Works Council or a procedure in Community-scale undertakings and Community-scale groups of undertakings for the purposes of informing and consulting employees O.J. 1994 L254/64.

[70] Industrial Relations Services, European Works Councils: Planning for the Directive (1995) cited *Financial Times* February 27 1995, cited in *Palmer's Company Law* at 16. 305. See also the *Collective Redundancies and Transfer of Undertakings (Protection of Employment) (Amendment) Regulations 1995.*

The final question that has been identified is whether and to what extent the UK corporate governance structure should attempt to recognize the interests of the various 'stakeholders' in a company. C.W.L. Hill and T.M. Jones take it to refer to groups of constituents who have a legitimate claim on the firm, based on the existence of an exchange relationship, and which include stockholders, creditors, managers, employees, customers, suppliers, local communities and the general public, each of which can be seen as supplying the firm with critical resources and therefore as expecting its interests to be satisfied in return.[71] A broader definition is that of R. Gray *et al.* who define it as 'any human agency that can be influenced by, or can itself influence, the activities of the organization in question'.[72] Their definition is also of interest in that they specifically go on to note that the groups include 'future generations'.

The significance of the use of the term 'stakeholder' has grown as it has entered the process of political debate, where it gained prominence when Tony Blair, Leader of the Labour Party, advocated a vision of the 'stakeholder economy' in a speech to the Singapore business community on 8 January 1996.[73] The scope of Tony Blair's vision was far wider than the company, aimed at ensuring that all citizens achieve a 'stake' in society generally. Applied to the company he saw the vision of the company 'as a community or partnership in which each employee has a stake, and where a company's responsibilities are more clearly delineated'. Significantly, he saw it as necessary 'to build a *relationship of trust* not just within a firm but within society'.[74] Other writers have stressed the link between economic success and the need for companies to build long-term relationships with stakeholders, noting that such relationships are more easily sustained in countries such as Germany and Japan where loyalty and trust are encouraged.[75] One important facet of the need for loyalty and trust to build long-term relationships is economic. One economic justification for the company is the reduction in transaction costs that the company results in. This argument is often used to support deregulation. It can further be argued that the need to build long-term relationships based on trust and loyalty is a necessary corollary to this, in so far as these will reduce the growing impact on transaction costs of short-term relationships which may require a higher degree of regulatory support and may be more prone to the costs of dispute resolution, for example, in the form of legal costs.

---

[71]   They trace the derivation of this term in, 'Stakeholder–agency theory' (1992) *Journal of Management Studies* 131 at 133.

[72]   *Accounting & Accountability* (Prentice-Hall, 1996) 45.

[73]   January 8 1996, see J. Plender, *A Stake in the Future, The Stakeholding Solution* (Nicholas Brealey, 1997) 12 for an extended quotation from the speech.

[74]   Emphasis added.

[75]   See, for example, a brief critique by C. Leadbetter and G. Mulgan, 'Stakeholding: Nice idea, shame about the reality', *The Observer* 6 October 1996; see also J. Plender, *op. cit.* n.73, Chapter 6.

It is important in addition to take into account the effect of voluntary measures to recognize the interests of other stakeholders which have been practised in the UK, some supported by fiscal incentives. Firstly, there are various forms of scheme to encourage commitment and long-term relationships with directors and/or employees by encouraging share ownership or profit-sharing. Secondly, there are various forms of scheme to provide customers with a voice. To a large extent these are driven by competitive pressures. In a very competitive market, companies will actively seek out the views of their customers, ranging from the use of customer questionnaires to seeking their participation in social auditing processes (see below) and will respond. In less competitive markets there may not be conferrable pressures and the solutions provided often involve a degree of Government regulation. There are clearly a number of ways in which stakeholder interests can be recognized in the context of corporate governance and these will be discussed as they arise later in this chapter.

Concern over high profile scandals

Many commentators have examined the various high profile corporate scandals which have affected UK companies in recent years.[76] These can be seen as evidence that something is profoundly wrong with UK corporate governance but this is not necessarily so. Quite apart from the fact that such scandals are not limited to the UK[77] and are not simply a recent phenomenon,[78] the difficulty with this approach is that it fails to consider the specific, and often unconnected, issues raised by the underlying conduct. Scandals can be the result of fraud or illegal activity, and no regulatory system has ever been able (or is likely) to prevent such activity. Major scandals can result from a relatively minor flaw in the regulatory system and may not require more than minor adjustments (many of which have already been put into place).[79] Indeed, there has been a major reform of legislation since the mid

[76] For a brief summary of those which led up to the establishment of the Cadbury Committee, see C. Boyd, 'Ethics and corporate governance: the issues raised by the Cadbury Report in the United Kingdom' (1996) 15 *Journal of Business Ethics* 167.

[77] See, for example, the problems which were experienced by the Sumitomo Corporation and the US operations of Daiwa Bank, J. Plender, *op. cit.*, 114.

[78] See, for example, *Re City Equitable Fire Insurance Co Ltd* [1925] Ch. 407 which concerned a company which had lost £1,200,000 partly due to the failure of certain investments but mainly due to the frauds of the chairman of directors.

[79] See, for example, J. Holland, 'Self-regulation and the financial aspects of corporate governance' [1996] *Journal of Business Law* 127 who examined the 'private' or 'behind the scenes' self-regulation process, the focal point of which he saw as the close co-operative relationship between financial institutions and their portfolio companies. He argues that the complexity and flexibility of this process suggests that any future legislative changes

1980s. The *Insolvency Act 1985*[80] made substantial improvements to both personal and corporate insolvency law and was followed by the *Company Directors Disqualification Act 1986*[81] and a revised insider dealing code in the *Criminal Justice Act 1993*.[82] The *Criminal Justice Act 1987* established the Serious Fraud Office to tackle City-style frauds with a multidisciplinary approach to the investigation and prosecution of large-scale fraud.[83] It is difficult to assess the success or failure overall of such measures. Clearly, they have not made high profile scandals a thing of the past.

There have also been attempts at self-regulatory reform. This is perhaps a reflection of doubts as to the efficacy of legislation to deal with such problems[84]

[79] cont
    should build on that process rather than be based on short-term reactions to highly public but relatively infrequent cases of error, fraud and criminality in the financial system (p. 163).

[80] Now replaced by the *Insolvency Act 1986*.

[81] The effectiveness of this legislation in practice has been called into question by a National Audit Office report of 20 October 1993, *The Insolvency Service Executive Agency: Company Director Disqualification*, see CCH Company News 15 November 1993. However, statistics published by the Insolvency Service on 20 February 1996 relating to directors' disqualification show considerable growth in the number of disqualification orders being sought and obtained (1145 actions taken in 1995 as against 747 in 1994 with 633 disqualification orders being made in 1995 as against 355 in 1994), see *CCH British Company Law & Practice* at 96-066.

[82] This has attracted considerable academic attention, in particular, the question as to whether criminal and/or civil sanctions are appropriate, a discussion supported not least by the disappointing level of effectiveness of criminal sanctions. See, for example, H. McVea, 'Fashioning a system of civil penalties for insider dealing: Sections 61 and 62 of the Financial Services Act 1986' [1996] *Journal of Business Law* 344 at 349–350.

[83] Although there have been criticisms of the Serious Fraud Office, both in relation to its effectiveness and its extensive powers, it has attracted some support, see Comment in 'When will we ever learn?' (1996) 17 *The Company Lawyer* 66 and 'Unsung Heroes?' (1996) 17 *The Company Lawyer* 130, the latter noting a 62.3% conviction rate since its establishment in 1988.

[84] See, for example, the London Society of Chartered Accountants Report, *Ethical Business in Britain, Recommendations for Improving Organisational Practice* (London Society of Chartered Accountants, 1996) at p. 4 has since taken the view that legislation and rules are not the solution. *Inter alia* it argues that structural changes in British society appear to have reduced the influence of many traditional forms of ethical control, that debate is required on how to replace or enhance those controls that may now be insufficient and that ethical outcomes can be managed in the same way as other valuable resources.

as much as a desire to avoid the necessity for further legislation.[85] The Cadbury Committee was established in effect by City institutions, rather than the Government. The reasons for setting up the Committee were expressed to be the perceived low level of confidence both in financial reporting and in the ability of auditors to provide the safeguards which the users of company reports sought and expected.[86] It stated that these concerns were heightened by some unexpected failures of major companies and by criticisms of the lack of effective board accountability for such matters as directors' pay.[87] Its stated basis was to be the principles of 'openness, integrity and accountability'.[88] The main way in which it sought to counter major scandals was to improve the working of the board of directors by issuing a Code of Practice (see above). Under the Code of Practice, no one individual should be able to dominate the board[89] and the positions of non-executive directors[90] and auditors[91] were strengthened to ensure an independent element.

Reactions to the Cadbury Report have been mixed. Research has shown that '. . . support for the *exercise* being carried out was overwhelming. Support for the detailed recommendations was much thinner on the ground'.[92] While some improvement is doubtless better than nothing, the criticisms levelled at the Report are very telling. The Code of Practice is seen as imprecise.[93] The language used makes it difficult to say precisely what standards have been set in some areas.[94] It is seen as toothless.[95] The

[85] See the *Cadbury Report* para. 3.6 which noted that if standards were not generally seen to be raised a greater reliance on regulation might be inevitable.

[86] *Ibid.*, para. 2.1.

[87] *Ibid.*, para. 2.2.

[88] *Ibid.*, para. 3.2.

[89] For example, see the *Cadbury Report*, Code of Practice, para. 1.2 which provides that there should be a clearly accepted division of responsibilities at the head of a company which will ensure a balance of power and authority such that no one individual has unfettered powers of decision.

[90] For example, see *ibid.*, para. 1.3, 2 and 4.3.

[91] *Ibid.*, para. 4.2–4.3.

[92] See J. Dine 'The governance of governance' (1994) 15 *The Company Lawyer* 73.

[93] Note the discussion of V. Finch 'Board performance and Cadbury on corporate governance' (1992) *Journal of Business Law* 581 at 584.

[94] For example, see the *Cadbury Report*, Code of Practice, para. 1.2 which states that 'where the chairman is also the chief executive, it is essential that there should be *a strong and independent element on the board* with a recognized senior member.' (Emphasis added). Conversely, it can be argued that imprecision can be the strength of such a code because it enables goals to be set of substance rather than of form, which therefore may be more difficult to evade.

[95] Note the discussion of C. Boyd 'Ethics and corporate governance: the issues raised by the Cadbury Report in the United Kingdom' (1996) 15 *Journal of Business Ethics* 167 at 172 who also notes against the credibility of the reforms the persistence of scandals in firms which apparently conform to some of the Cadbury norms, p. 174. See also V. Finch, *op. cit.*, at 584.

Listing Rules of the London Stock Exchange[96] require only that a company provide a statement in its annual report and accounts as to whether it has complied with the Code of Practice throughout the relevant accounting period and, if not, to specify particulars and reasons. It is also seen as impracticable.[97] There may simply not be enough suitable non-executive directors to provide independent scrutiny on boards.[98] Nonetheless, research indicates that the Code of Practice has made a substantial impact on corporate governance in the UK.[99] Unfortunately, it will be very difficult to ascertain whether it has achieved its objectives. Even a decline in high profile scandals will be no proof of this, given the wide range of factors which may also have a bearing.

Concern over directors' remuneration levels

There is international concern about both the absolute levels of, and the rate of growth in, the remuneration of directors of large companies. A US survey by Forbes Magazine of 800 leading US companies in 1991 revealed that during that year one chief executive officer received remuneration totalling US $75 million and that the average for a chief executive officer of such companies was US $1.8 million.[100] A survey by Graef Chrystal in 1991 showed that the average remuneration of a chief executive officer in the US had risen since 1974 from 35 times to 160 times that of an average industrial

---

[96]   Para. 12.43 (j).

[97]   Note the discussion of C. Boyd, *op. cit.* n.95, at 174–175.

[98]   Even if it was likely that the presence of non-executive directors would be effective, a concept which has been questioned, see for example H. Short, 'Non-executive directors, corporate governance and the Cadbury Report: a review of the issues and evidence' (1996) 4 *Corporate Governance* 123.

[99]   A monitoring subcommittee of the Cadbury Committee has issued a report on compliance with the Code of Best Practice (summarized in *CCH British Company Law & Practice* 96-022) based on a sample of 684 annual reports out of a potential sample of 710 companies reporting after 30 June 1993. In particular, it found that all companies contained a statement of full or limited compliance and only one failed to specify matters of non-compliance. In terms of substantive change, there was evidence, for example, of a very significant increase over the period in the disclosure of the existence of audit, nomination and remuneration committees of the board. Nonetheless A Belcher, 'Compliance with the Cadbury Code and the reporting of corporate governance' (1996) 17 *The Company Lawyer* 11 at 17, based on a sample of 106 companies, notes that directors are less forthcoming about the *effectiveness* of structures which, arguably, is the matter which most concerns shareholders. (Emphasis added).

[100] Cited by I.M. Ramsay in, 'Directors and officers' remuneration: the role of the law' (1993) *Journal of Business Law* 351 at 352.

worker. The survey revealed that in 1991 the ratio was 33 times in the UK, 21 times in Germany and 16 times in Japan.[101]

A recent article in *Management Today*[102] identified the performance-linked 'package' of one director as £5.2 million in 1993, £8 million in 1994 and £7.5 million in 1995. The Independent on Sunday has reported a survey on the remuneration of directors of the privatized water companies which calculates one 'annual package' as being worth in excess of £1 million.[103] A further survey by the Monks Partnership reported in August 1996 shows that the earnings of top executives of FT-SE 100 companies rose by more than twice the level of inflation in 1995.[104] It has been reported that 'the overwhelming majority of Britons think incomes have become too unequal'.[105] However, a totally different perspective can be provided by international comparison of pay and buying power which shows that directors and managers in the UK have the lowest gross salaries in Europe.[106]

One problem is that remuneration packages have grown notoriously complicated. There can be non-cash elements, such as a company car. There can be deferred and/or contingent elements, such as performance-related pay and share options. Both give rise to problems of valuation and therefore comparability. Nonetheless, the tax system manages to tackle this and perhaps too much is made of this aspect of the problem. More problematic in practice is ensuring that there is adequate disclosure of information to those interested in corporate remuneration. Company law has failed to achieve this adequately.[107] Once a remuneration package has

---

[101] Cited by I.M. Ramsay, *op. cit.* n.100, at 352. Obviously, care has to be taken in the interpretation of these statistics. For example, they could be used to argue that average industrial workers are underpaid; they may also reflect structural differences in the relevant employment markets, for example as to job security, job mobility and taxation.

[102] August 1996, 43.

[103] R. Dobson, S. Castle and A. Minton, 'How the polluters get paid' *Independent on Sunday*, 11 August 1996, 9. The figure includes salary, bonuses, other emoluments, pension fund contributions and share options.

[104] W. Lewis, 'Top executive pay increased at twice rate of inflation' *Financial Times*, 9 August 1996. The survey was based on information given in companies' annual reports as at 30 June 1996. The report also noted that nearly half of these executives are now entitled to participate in both share option and long-term incentive schemes.

[105] See D. Coyle 'British unite against unequal society', *The Independent*, 18 November 1996, citing the 13th Annual Survey of British Social Attitudes.

[106] R. Donkin *Financial Times*, 13 November 1996, citing a recent survey by ECA International, *Inter Country Executive Remuneration*.

[107] I.M. Ramsay 'Directors and officers' remuneration: the role of the law' (1993) *Journal of Business Law* 351 and C. Villiers, 'Executive pay: beyond control' (1995) 15 *Legal Studies* 260, have argued for improvements in

been appropriately valued and disclosed the question becomes whether a given level of remuneration is excessive or not. This is more difficult than it might seem, particularly given the tendency to an intuitive reaction in the face of the highest levels of remuneration. Ramsay[108] notes that empirical studies have generally found that there is a weak relationship between executive remuneration and company performance or, indeed, no relationship at all. Villiers[109] argues that it is impossible to conclude firmly that executive pay is excessive although suspicions are raised.

The general approach of company law in regulating directors' remuneration is to govern the procedures which must be followed as a precondition of a company awarding remuneration to its directors and the disclosure of such remuneration.[110] The overall effect of these procedures is that the shareholders have ultimate control over remuneration, but only in the sense that they can adopt such constitutional procedures as they see fit for it to be awarded[111] and the ability to remove directors if they see fit.[112] In practice, however, the constitutional procedures adopted tend to leave directors with substantial control over the remuneration process, within certain parameters laid down in statute. In principle, company law does provide limited remedies which can assist interested parties who may be affected by an award of excessive remuneration and even lead to the disqualification of the directors who approve an award which the company cannot afford. Generally, however, it is a longstanding principle of company law that the courts will not involve themselves in disputes over commercial decisions. The role that shareholders *could* play is, therefore, important. Inevitably attention has focused on institutional shareholders because of the

---

[107] *cont*

disclosure as a necessary element of establishing fair remuneration. This chapter later considers the self-regulatory measures that have been adopted for this purpose. C. Riley and D. Ryland 'Directors' remuneration: towards some principles of substantive and procedural review' in *Corporate Governance & Corporate Control, op. cit.* n.12, 181, argue that it is necessary to recreate within the company a process for determining directors' remuneration which mimics market exchanges because of the legitimacy conferred by market exchanges.

[108] *Op. cit.* n.107 at 353.

[109] *Op. cit.* n.107 at 282. The suspicions of the author are based on the size of directors' 'pay-offs,' above average rises and the growing size of the 'income gap'. The author believes, based on theories of distributive justice, that company law can establish criteria for fairness (at 281).

[110] See *inter alia Table A Companies (Tables A to F) Regulations 1985* SI No. 805, Reg.'s 82 to 84; *Companies Act 1985*, ss. 311 to 319 and Sch. 6.

[111] See *Companies Act 1985*, s. 9 in relation to changes to the Articles of Association.

[112] See *Companies Act 1985*, ss. 303–304 but note s. 303 (5) expressly preserves the right of a person so removed to compensation or damages payable as a consequence and s. 304 confers a right on the relevant director to protest against the removal.

size of their stakes and the ability to organize their response. Yet although there is evidence of a more vociferous stance, there is much less of its being translated into action. It has been estimated that institutional investors in the UK own between 65–75% of listed company shares in the UK yet UK institutions, it seems, have on occasions been outvoted by US institutional investors not because of the size of their shareholding but because they bothered to vote.[113]

The Cadbury Committee also attempted to tackle excessive directors' remuneration by giving further controls to shareholders and requiring improved disclosure.[114] These measures were ineffective to halt public disquiet and the Greenbury Study Group was set up by the Confederation of British Industry in January 1995[115] to identify good practice in determining directors' remuneration and prepare a code of practice for use by UK-listed companies. It reported in July 1995 and the Code of Practice adopted took a more stringent approach, requiring the establishment of non-executive director remuneration committees, increased disclosure, shareholder approval for all new, long-term incentive schemes and the banning of certain share option schemes. Aspects of the report have been supported by changes to the Stock Exchange Listing Rules and to the taxation system. The Institute of Directors has also produced its own guidelines for remuneration committees in recommending directors' remuneration which will also reinforce these measures.[116] One immediate impression is that the report has simply encouraged professional advisers to seek new ways to structure top executive incentive schemes which comply,[117] but it will be some time before the success of the measures can properly be evaluated. Further progress is afoot with the Hample Committee, which is examining a wide range of issues related to corporate governance.

Concern over corporate ethics

There is public unease as to the way in which companies are seen to act in the conduct of their businesses.[118] They are seen as willing to break

---

113   See C.A. Mallin 'The voting framework: a comparative study of voting behaviour of institutional investors in the US and the UK' (1996) 4 *Corporate Governance* 107 at 120.

114   The *Cadbury Report*, Code of Practice para. 3.

115   See P. Jeffcote and V. Walsh 'Directors' remuneration, the Greenbury Committee' *Practical Law for Companies* August 1995 p. 43 and 'Directors' remuneration — a report of a study group chaired by Sir Richard Greenbury' (1996) 4 *Corporate Governance* 24.

116   Summarized and considered by S. Sheikh in 'Curbing top pay bonanza' (1995) 16 *The Company Lawyer* 117.

117   See, for example, F. Jebb, 'New bones for top dogs' *Management Today*, August 1996, 56.

118   J. Plender, *op. cit.* n.73, 9 cites a MORI survey as having shown that 87% of people in Britain believe that large companies should have a wider responsibility to the community.

the law in pursuit of profit provided that the risks, weighed in the same way as other commercial risks, are acceptable. Legal regulation focuses on the specific nature of the conduct being regulated, for example, product liability or environmental liability. As a result it is fragmented, making it difficult to assess clearly what the law expects in the way of corporate conduct. Perhaps this is inevitable. There have been considerable legal difficulties as to how to apply criminal sanctions to corporations.[119] Both the approach and solution have been pragmatic but are arguably weakly underpinned conceptually. One problem is seen as the difficulty of attributing *mens rea* to a company, where decisions are rarely attributable to one person (whether a director or senior employee). There are also the difficulties of punishing a corporation appropriately. A rather cynical conclusion would be that criminal liability is not a live issue for corporate governance because no listed company is ever likely to be so simply organized as to permit identification through an individual with any wrongdoing by it. If a company breaks the civil law, then there is no corresponding difficulty, because there is no need to attribute *mens rea* to the company, and it can be sued, therefore, in the usual way.

It would be wrong to think that all business people are crooks or unprincipled on the basis of a few highly publicized cases. There is a growing interest in business ethics[120] (both at an academic and professional managerial level). For example, in 1986 the Institute of Business Ethics was launched, founded by the Christian Association of Business Executives.[121] There are an enormous number of ways in which companies attempt voluntarily to improve their ethical standards. Some of these are longstanding and largely ignored from the debate, such as the establishment of trade associations in particular industries, often as a voluntarily accepted external constraint. Others involve voluntarily attempting to change the ethical standards of a company from within. Companies, like all organizations, have values, whether they are articulated or not.[122] These values tend to be shaped at board level and are very

---

[119] For a wide-ranging consideration of the issues, see C. Wells, *Corporations and Criminal Responsibility* (Clarendon Press, 1993).

[120] There appears to be little consensus over the meaning of this term. K. Smith and P. Johnson, *Business Ethics & Business Behaviour* (International Thompson Business Press, 1996) cite P. V. Lewis, 'Defining business ethics: like nailing jello to a wall' (1985) 4 *Journal of Business Ethics* as noting that there are over 300 definitions available in the literature.

[121] See S. Kiaer, 'The Institute of Business Ethics — ten years' *Business Ethics, A European Review* (1996) 239.

[122] D.C. Robertson, 'Corporate instititionalisation of ethics in the United States and Great Britain' (1993) 12 *Journal of Business Ethics* 301 at 304 noting that 50.5% of a sample of 813 respondent UK companies had introduced written codes of ethics.

much the responsibility of the chairman or managing director.[123] Practical ways in which a company might try to change or reinforce its ethical standards are almost infinite. Techniques that have been adopted or considered include the use of codes of conduct,[124] social reporting,[125] social auditing[126] and the move towards corporate social responsibility, considered above. The important thing is that ethical standards are genuinely adopted by the company as a whole. When that can be achieved then it may provide an effective contribution to resolving the criticism levelled at corporate ethics. It may also have an influence, by example and interraction, on the wider business community and society generally.[127] Nonetheless, motives can be mixed for a company wishing to adopt such a stance. It may simply be an exercise in good public relations, influenced by investor and consumer preferences; it may simply be done out of a belief that it is the right way for a company to behave.[128] Whatever the motivation, the outcome is undoubtedly desirable.

[123] D.C. Robertson, *op. cit.*, at 305–306 found that in the UK the chairman/chief executive officer of 48.0% of respondent UK companies and the managing directors of 21.6% of such companies had primary responsibility for communicating company policies on business ethics and conduct.

[124] For a topical review of UK practice, see S. Bain, 'Coding for an Ethical Future' *CA Magazine*, August 1996 10.

[125] A range of terms are used with similar effect, including, for example, social responsibility accounting. The term has been defined by Gray *et al.*, *Corporate Social Reporting: Accounting & Accountability* (Prentice-Hall, 1987) 3 as 'the process of communicating the social and environmental effects of organizations' economic actions to particular interest groups within society and to society at large. As such, it involves extending the accountability of organizations (particularly companies), beyond the traditional role of providing a financial account to the owners of capital, in particular, shareholders. Such an extension is predicated upon the assumption that companies do have wider responsibilities than simply to make money for their shareholders.' cited by Gray *et al.*, *op. cit.*, 3.

[126] Gray *et al.*, *op. cit.* n.125, 272, note that 'defined broadly enough, social audits can encompass anything from *ad hoc* or more systematic analysis of specific and general issues of social accountability to investigative journalism.' This definition emphasizes the notion that many such audits involve an external appraisal of an organization without necessarily having its participation. Nonetheless, some organizations have voluntarily undergone a social audit, including Traidcraft and The Body Shop, with the active participation of the organization and stakeholders. See further, for example, *The Body Shop Values Report 1995* and *The Body Shop Approach to Ethical Auditing.*

[127] See Rt. Rev. R. Harries, 'the morality of good business' *Business Strategy Review* Spring 1993, 87 at 89.

[128] D.C. Robertson, *op. cit.* n.122, found that the most likely reason for UK companies to issue an ethics policy was growth (46.8% of responding companies) followed by motivation from the Board of Directors (36.4% of responding companies) 304–305.

One area that has attracted much attention is the development of ethical principles in an international context where ethical conduct has frequently come under scrutiny, particularly in relation to the role of multinational companies and groups. Attempts are being made to deal with this in the context of international law.[129] In addition the *Interfaith Declaration*[130] was released officially in 1994 including a code of ethics on international business behaviour for Christians, Muslims and Jews. It is based on four general principles (justice, mutual respect, stewardship and honesty) considered common to the three faiths and contains guidelines relating to 'business and political economy', 'the policies of a business' and 'the conduct of individuals at work'.

Finally, there is a growing movement towards ethical investment[131] and ethical consumerism. These are of considerable importance to the question of company ethics. Ethical investment offers an opportunity for large-scale shareholder involvement in encouraging ethical behaviour in companies, arguably a role that shareholders should play in any event. It is also an area in which Christian churches are very active and significant players. Nonetheless, it should not be assumed that there is a convergence in the aims of Christians and others concerned with ethical investment. In contrast, there is evidence of both convergence and divergence. One research project identified, for example, a marked divergence over alcohol but convergence over defence.[132] However, the ethical invest-ment movement has also revealed some inadequacies in corporate gov-ernance. Probably the most significant of these is the poor disclosure of information relevant to those seeking to make investment decisions on an ethical basis.[133] Ethical consumerism likewise offers an opportunity for large-scale influence in encouraging ethical business.

---

[129] See G. Ossman. 'The right and duties of transnational corporations under international economic law' [1996] 4 *International Company and Commercial Law Review* 139.

[130] For a brief review of the background to and substance of the *Interfaith Declaration*, including a copy of the Code of Ethics see S. Webley 'The Interfaith Declaration. Constructing a code of ethics for international business' (1996) 5 *Business Ethics, A European Review* 52. Clearly, the value of such a voluntary code lies in the extent to which it is adopted and adhered to.

[131] A subject considered in detail by R. Sparkes, *op. cit.*

[132] See R. Sparkes, *op. cit.* n.3, 7 citing a 1992 research project by C. Cowton.

[133] R. Sparkes, *op. cit.* n.3, 28, draws attention to the establishment of the Ethical Investment Research Service ('EIRIS') in 1983 by a group of churches to produce the information required to apply ethical criteria to investment, to identify alternative investments for ethical investors and to promote a wider debate on issues of corporate responsibility.

IV. SHOULD THERE BE A CHRISTIAN VISION FOR COPORATE GOVERNANCE?

It is perhaps a sad reflection on current perceptions as to the interaction between Christianity and business that it is necessary to include this section. It is submitted that there are three persuasive arguments supporting both the need for, and the existence of, a Christian vision for corporate governance. These are that Christian theology encompasses business; that Christian theology has been applied historically to business and finally that Christian theology has a unique role to play in the corporate governance debate.

Christian theology encompasses business

The Old Testament period was clearly a very extended one and accordingly it is inappropriate to make generalizations. The geographical setting of Palestine provided a setting in which trade was likely to develop and Israel came to participate actively in trading activities, based on agricultural and manufactured metal products. The Mosaic law was an entire social code, which did not make any distinction between social, business or personal morality. Its purpose can be said to have been twofold: to provide an ethical code and to distinguish Israel from the surrounding nations. The law was primarily orientated to an agricultural society[134] but also provided both general[135] and specific[136] rules in respect of trading activity. These rules are of interest insofar as they appear both to preclude profit maximization in business and to prescribe the ethical framework for a form of profit optimization.[137] The acquisition of wealth as a nation in the future was expressly anticipated and Israel was warned to remember that it was God

---

[134] See, for example, the rules on tithing which applied to grain, fruit, herd and flock (Leviticus 27:30–32).

[135] See, for example, the rules against stealing, lying and deception (Leviticus 19:11).

[136] See, for example, the rules against dishonest weights and measures (Leviticus 19:35) and delayed wage payments (Leviticus 19:13).

[137] See the rules above and Leviticus 19:9–10, which contains the following prohibition: 'When you reap the harvest of your land, do not reap to the very edges of your field or gather the gleanings of your harvest. Do not go over your vineyard a second time or pick up the grapes that have fallen. Leave them for the poor and the alien. I am the Lord your God.' The distinguishing feature from the contemporary debate is that there was no separation of ownership and control anticipated so that the owner would have been required to sacrifice his own profits and was not a manager sacrificing those of others. An example of the outworking of this law can be seen in Ruth 2:2. See also Deuteronomy 14:22–29 (tithes); Deuteronomy 15:1–11 (the year for cancelling debts) and Deuteronomy 15:12–18 (freeing servants).

who gave the ability to produce wealth and destruction would follow if Israel sought to assert that the wealth had been produced by its own power and strength.[138]

Much of the theological development of the Mosaic law took place through prophetic activity in a period when a shift in emphasis from agriculture to trade and manufacturing activities was causing social tensions of a comparable nature to those revealed by the corporate governance debate. This took place under the reign of Jeroboam II (c. 793–753 BC) described as a time of 'peace and prosperity'. Israel was called to repent or face judgement for its hypocrisy. In its prosperity conspicuous religious observance thrived[139] yet social justice was neglected. While some enjoyed an easy and opulent lifestyle[140] the poor were oppressed and the needy were crushed.[141] Accordingly, the prophetic perspective was that God would put an end to this; the rich would lose all that they had.[142] Nonetheless there is no reason to assume from this that business itself was seen as theologically wrong. In contrast, business activity could be praiseworthy, if conducted with hard work, generosity to the poor and general integrity.[143]

By the time of the origins of Christianity trade and commerce in Palestine were dominated by the Roman Empire and indigenous trading activities petty in scale. Jesus Christ and many of the early leaders of the Christian church were engaged in forms of trading.[144] They do not appear to have found any conceptual difficulty in this where it did not conflict with their vocations.[145] Much Christian theology is derived from illustrations taken from a commercial context.[146] Neither wealth

---

[138] Deuteronomy 8:17–20.

[139] Sacrifice, tithes, thankofferings and freewill offerings (Amos 4:4–5), religious feasts and assemblies (Amos 5:21) and songs and music (Amos 5:23).

[140] See Amos 5:11; 6:4–6.

[141] See Amos 4:1; 5:11; 5:12.

[142] See, for example, Amos 6:7. Indeed, Israel finally fell in 721 BC when a substantial number of Israelites were deported to Persia and Israel was repopulated by foreign colonists.

[143] See, for example, Proverbs 31:10–31 (the wife of noble character).

[144] Jesus Christ was a carpenter (Matthew 13:55), Paul was a tentmaker (Acts 18:3), Peter was a fisherman (Matthew 4:18), Matthew was a tax collector (Matthew 9:9).

[145] Paul, for example, continued to work to support his ministry, see 1 Thessalonians 2:9. Perhaps, in the light of this, care must be taken in the interpretation of what, if any, general principle is established by the precondition placed on one potential convert that he should sell everything he had and give it to the poor, see Mark 10:21.

[146] See, for example, Matthew 13:45–46 (a pearl merchant), Matthew 20:1–16 (a landowner's employment practices in a vineyard), Matthew 18:12–14 (farming), Matthew 7:24–27 (building works), Luke 16:1–14 (shrewd management).

nor poverty are idealized or demonized *per se*.[147] Instead, the focus of Christian theology is upon the effect of these on the attitudes of the individual and the effect that these attitudes have upon relationships with others and with God.[148] Of course, in analysing the theological development of the Christian Church and its application to business the eschatological element must also be taken into account. Whilst so many in the Early Church imminently expected the return of Christ, and were preoccupied with the immediate mission of the Church, it was unlikely that long-term questions as to business would have been high on the agenda, although Paul was at pains to stress the need to work and avoid idleness to correct any such tendency.[149]

Christian theology has been applied historically to business

Medieval society involved a culture pervaded by Christian values. Avarice[150] and usury,[151] arguably the foundations of the modern company if the true goal is profit maximization, were condemned. Trade was frowned upon by theologians even if its necessity was grudgingly

---

[147] Great care must be taken with the interpretation of a number of passages of the New Testament where in effect an attitudinal deficiency is indicated from the possession or seeking of wealth rather than wealth itself. In Luke 6:20–26 ('the Beatitudes') those present are commended in effect for choosing their poverty and the rich who are condemned appear to be those who have rejected their message. The 'rich fool' in Luke 12:13–21 is condemned for storing up possessions for a life of leisure when, of course, he cannot control how long he will live. The 'rich young man' in Matthew 19:16–30 clearly elicits some sympathy but was criticized for placing money before his Christian vocation. Similarly, in the well-known tale of Dives and Lazarus (Luke 16:19–31, Dives is condemned not for his wealth but because he lived in luxury while the beggar Lazarus was unable to eat even what fell from his table. Even Luke 18:25, where Jesus Christ is quoted as saying, 'It is easier for a camel to go through the eye of a needle than for a rich man to enter the kingdom of God' is balanced by Luke 18:27 with 'What is impossible with men is possible with God'. Paul makes the point clear in 1 Timothy 6:6–10 in the memorable phrase 'For the love of money is a root of all kinds of evil'.

[148] Ultimately, a Christian approach to relationships would lead to equality as no Christian would wish for another to be worse off than themselves, see Acts 4:32–35 and 2 Corinthians 8:13, 14.

[149] 2 Thessalonians 3:6–14.

[150] The significance of this term was that it represented a desire to accumulate money and/or possessions for their own sake.

[151] Although this term has now acquired the meaning of lending at excessive interest, it then extended to any lending for interest.

recognized.[152] Business organization mainly took place in simple fashion through guilds and organizations resembling the modern partnership.[153] Incorporation was permitted by Royal Charter but originally only rarely for business purposes.[154] The Reformation coincided with the move of society away from a feudal, status-based economy towards a trade-based economy based on consensual dealings. Some historians would link Protestantism and the rise of modern capitalism.[155] Trade was no longer disdained and moneylending was permitted within strict confines. Joint stock companies developed and by 1696 Parliament was obliged to regulate an embryonic market in their securities.[156] As is well known, all this came to an abrupt change with the South Sea Bubble, a major scandal involving the 'privatization' of the bulk of the National Debt to a joint stock company, The Company of Merchants of Great Britain Trading in the South Seas, which precipitated an unregulated boom in share dealings generally, and which collapsed in 1720. The result was the *1720 Bubble Act* which attempted to severely restrict the use of the corporate form without really making any attempt to recognize and regulate its use.[157]

The modern period of the company commenced in the Victorian era, a time of significant evangelical Christian influence.[158] First, incorporation by registration,[159] then limited liability[160] were introduced, culminating in the *Joint Stock Companies Act 1862*, arguably the first modern

[152] It is interesting to consider the arguments of M. Luther, 'Trade and Usury' in *Luther's Works*, Vol. 45 (Fortress Press, 1966) extract in R. Gill, *A Textbook of Christian Ethics* (T & T Clark, 1989). For a lively analysis of medieval practice on usury, see H. Pirenne, *Economic & Social History of Medieval Europe* (Routledge and Kegan Paul, 1936) 118–141.

[153] See Farrar *et al.*, *op. cit.*, 15–16.

[154] *Ibid.*, 16–17.

[155] The origins of this lie in what is referred to as 'the Weber thesis' which commenced with the publication by the German sociologist M. Weber of two articles entitled *The Protestant Ethic* and the *Spirit of Capitalism* (1904 and 1905). In the UK the later work of R.H. Tawney, an economic historian, *Religion and the Rise of Capitalism* (1926) is also well-known. M. Weber's work has been controversial. However, M. Weber did not argue that Protestantism caused capitalism, not least because capitalism can be seen to be older than Protestantism, but also because other factors can be seen to be important to the rise of capitalism. Rather his argument was that Calvinist theology created the psychological conditions, a new 'spirit of capitalism,' for the development of modern capitalism.

[156] See Farrar *et al.*, *op. cit.* n.10, 17.

[157] See Gower, *op. cit.* n.40, 24–28.

[158] See also T. Sutton, 'Christians as Law Reformers in the nineteenth and twentieth Centuries', above, 13–20.

[159] *Joint Stock Companies Act 1844.*

[160] *Limited Liability Act 1855.*

companies legislation in the UK. The introduction of modern companies proved to be controversial,[161] but a recent study by Garnett, 'Evangelicalism and business in mid-Victorian Britain'[162] shows that evangelical Christians generally did not oppose these changes and, indeed, many regarded them as beneficial.[163] Furthermore, in their relations with business, evangelical Christians were prepared to engage in constructive debate. This extended to developing a practical theology of business ethics. Evangelical Christians were concerned over a range of business practices, including overtrading,[164] consumer credit,[165] product adulteration,[166] poor accounting,[167] shareholder responsibility,[168] Sunday trading[169] and treatment of employees.[170] One interesting conclusion from Garnett's analysis is that legal structures were not regarded by evangelicals as sufficient to promote the active trust fundamental to business life.[171] A number of companies founded by evangelical Christians are still in existence today, for example, Thomas Cook.[172]

In the UK one of the more influential writers in the twentieth century has been the one-time Archbishop of Canterbury, William Temple, author of *Christianity & Social Order*.[173] It has been claimed that this book was 'one of the foundation piers of the Welfare State'.[174] Temple encompassed a wider range of social issues than the relationship between Christianity and business, including, for example, family welfare,[175] education[176] and personal freedom.[177] He argued strongly

---

[161]   See, for example, the comments of L.S. Sealy, *op. cit.* n.49, 12–13.

[162]   Part of a collection of papers published under the title *Evangelical Faith and Public Zeal, Evangelicals and Society in Britain 1780–1980* (SPCK, 1995) ed. J. Wolffe, 59.

[163]   J. Garnett, *op. cit.* n.162, 70.

[164]   *Ibid.*, 66.

[165]   *Ibid.*, 67.

[166]   *Ibid.*, 68.

[167]   *Ibid.*, 69.

[168]   *Ibid.*, 70.

[169]   *Ibid.*, 70–71.

[170]   *Ibid.*, 73.

[171]   *Ibid.*, 61.

[172]   *Ibid.*, 72. The Quaker roots of Cadbury's were recently discussed by N. Cope in, 'The Vogue for Looking Good' *Management Today*, October 1993, 69.

[173]   Originally published by Penguin 1942, reference made to Shepheard-Walwyn reprint 1987.

[174]   R. Preston, Introduction to *Christianity & Social Order*, *op. cit.* n.173, 6, citing D. Munby, *God and the Rich Society* (1960).

[175]   W. Temple, *op. cit.* n.173, 100.

[176]   *Ibid.*, 101.

[177]   *Ibid.*, 104.

for the right of the Christian church to be heard on political and economic issues and for personal engagement by Christians in the debates on these questions. In terms of business, he re-evaluated the abandonment of the prohibition of avarice and usury.[178] In setting out a social agenda, his key argument[179] was that although economic science was autonomous to explain, for example, the probable effect of economic reform, an economic system could be condemned if it offended natural law on moral grounds even if it was abundantly effective in material terms. One such moral ground could be that the system was a source of wrong personal relationships.

Another influential twentieth century theological development has been what is referred to as 'liberation theology'.[180] The roots of this are usually traced to the predominantly Roman Catholic churches of Latin America. The essential elements of liberation theology can be summarized as seeing the biblical accounts as a record of liberation, of Israel from Egypt in the Old Testament and of the poor and outcast by the gospel in the New Testament. Accordingly, God is seen as on the side of the poor and oppressed requiring social or political action by the believer in response. Liberation theologians have placed importance on Marxism as a form of analysis and have tended to be critical of capitalism.[181] There can be little doubt that liberation theology has been influential on some sections of the UK church notwithstanding criticisms that can be made of it on the basis of biblical hermeneutics and its approach to the nature of salvation.[182]

In popular Protestant evangelicalism there has been a retreat from interraction with business.[183] Certainly, there appears to be far greater demand, for example, for the production of books aimed at the Christian market concerned with matters of internal concern to the Christian community, such as personal piety, than for those critiquing business, economics or politics. Nonetheless, there is growing evidence of a reversal in this trend. Business has been addressed by, amongst others, the

---

[178]   *Ibid.*, 53–57.

[179]   *Ibid.*, 80–82.

[179]   *Ibid.*, 80–82.

[180]   See A.E. McGrath, *Christian Theology, An Introduction* (Blackwell, 1996) 105–107, which notes that the term in theory could be applied to any theology which is addressed to or deals with oppressive situations.

[181]   See further J.P. Miranda, *Marx and the Bible, A Critique of the Philosophy of Oppression* (SCM, 1977) esp. 250–255 and also J.M. Bonino, *Christians and Marxists, The Mutual Challenge to Revolution* (Hodder & Stoughton, 1976), esp. Chapter VI.

[182]   See A. McGrath, *op. cit.* n.180, 106–107.

[183]   See more generally D. Bebbington, 'The Decline and Resurgence of Evangelical Social Concern 1918–1980' in *Evangelical Faith and Public Zeal, Evangelicals and Society in Britain 1780–1980*, *op. cit.* n.162, 175.

Archbishop of Canterbury, George Carey,[184] John Stott[185] and Alan Storkey.[186] Furthermore, there are the activities of the Christian Association of Business Executives and the association of Christians with the ethical investment movement. There has been the establishment of a number of think-tank organizations, such as Christian Impact.[187] A new high quality Christian magazine, Ethos, has recently been set up aimed at the business community generally.[188]

There have also been further developments in Roman Catholicism since Pope Leo XIII's encyclical *Rerum Novarum* in 1891. Pope John Paul II issued the encyclical *Centesimus Annus* in 1991[189] to set out the foundations of a 'just economic order'. This encyclical is important to the debate on corporate governance because it is supportive of a market economy. The role of profits is supported as an indicator that a company's resources are being properly employed and that human needs are being satisfied. However, profitmaking

---

[184] See, for example, his address at the Confederation of British Industry service at Derby Cathedral, Sunday 10 May 1992, 'Industry: Burying its Talents?' included in *Sharing a Vision* (DLT, 1993) 46. He argues that the ultimate purpose of industry is to serve others by creating goods and services of use and value to meet their needs. It is not to make money for its own sake, profits for shareholders, or salaries and wages although these are necessary conditions for success.

[185] *Issues Facing Christians Today* (Marshall Pickering, 1984 and 1990). In Chapter 10 he considered the vexed question of industrial relations, identifying the problem as one of relationships. He identified the biblical principle of mutuality (mutual service based on mutual respect) based on justice. He proposed solutions based on the abolition of the management/worker distinction, increased participation in decision-making and profits and finally co-operation. In particular, he draws attention to the example provided by the profit-sharing scheme devised by the John Lewis Partnership.

[186] See *Transforming Economics* (SPCK, 1986). *Inter alia*, he argues for 'relational economics' where economic decision-making would take into account the effect on other people, see 72. Further, he evaluates the profit maximization theory and argues, firstly, that the guiding norm of the company should be service, not profit, in the sense of serving the wider public through the provision of goods and services and, secondly, that a company internally is a 'service unit' where the various parties (including consumers and the wider community) relate together in a framework of trust, respect and organic contribution. Accordingly, he argues for a form of board representation of both consumers and employees, see Chapter 7.

[187] Described in the *UK Christian Handbook 1996/7* (Christian Research, 1995) as 'relating biblical faith to every aspect of life through courses, seminars, consultations and publications'.

[188] Published by Ethos Communications Ltd, preview edition October 1996.

[189] For a helpful analysis and evaluation of *Centesimus Annus*, see S. Prakath Sethi and P. Steidlmeier, 'Religion's Moral Compass and a Just Economic Order: Reflections on Pope John Paul II's Centesimus Annus' (1993) 12 *Journal of Business Ethics* 901.

is not the sole purpose of a business, which should act as a community of persons endeavouring to satisfy the needs of the participants.

Christian theology has a unique role to play in the corporate governance debate

Christians see the world as God's creation[190] over which God has ultimate authority some of which God has delegated to mankind.[191] Companies bear a large part of the responsibility for how the world's resources are used. In a sense they have more real power over that than any government. Theologically, the Christian church is seen as struggling against the rulers, authorities and powers of 'this dark world' and spiritual forces of evil 'in the heavenly realms,'[192] reflecting the corruption of the use of God's authority in secular hands. Insofar as corporate governance is concerned with the exercise of authority and power in the corporate sphere, Christian theology will be concerned to see that such authority is exercised in accordance with Christian principles.

Christians see their role in society as participative and transformational rather than separative.[193] Christians are shareholders in companies;[194] Christians are company officers, company employees and company advisers; Christians are consumers of goods and services offered by companies; Christians are debtors and creditors of companies; Christians live in an environment affected by companies. They are, to use a current phrase, 'stakeholders'in corporate society.

Christian action has invariably sprung from concern for justice and love for the victims of injustice.[195] Christians are affronted by what is

[190]   See Genesis 1:1–2:2. For the theological development of this principle see for example Job 38–41 and Romans 1:18–20. See also D. Harte, 'A Christian Approach to Environmental Law?' above, 60 *et seq.*

[191]   Generally, therefore, Christian theology takes the view that political authority is legitimate, see, for example, Romans 13:1–7 and 1 Timothy 2:1–3. See also D. Bonhoeffer, *Ethics* (SCM Press, 1978), as well as other forms of authority, see Ephesians 5:22–6:9 and Colossians 3:18–4:1. Although Governments may effectively establish the external constraints upon such activity by regulation they generally find that they have little control over the generation of wealth or the activities of multinational companies and groups.

[192]   Ephesians 6:10–12.

[193]   See, for example, Matthew 5:13 and John 17:15.

[194]   According to R. Sparkes, *op. cit.* n.3, 168 the churches in the UK have in total about £4 billion of funds subject to some degree of ethical management. It would, of course, be difficult to estimate the value of shareholdings held by, or on behalf of, individual Christians.

[195]   The word justice is used in Christian theology with a wide range of meanings. The Christian concept of justice is considered briefly in the next section. See also T. Sutton 'Christians as Law Reformers in the Nineteenth and Twentieth Centuries', above p.7 *et seq.*, and J. Rivers 'A Bill of Rights for the United Kingdom?', above p.32 *et seq.*

happening with UK corporate governance. Directors of some listed companies and similar bodies are well remunerated by any standards. Generally in society it is becoming more common for employees to work longer hours entailing more stress for less pay and less security, often on short-term contracts. Spouses suffer; children suffer.[196]

Finally, Christian theology can introduce into the debate a framework of absolute values and principles, which will be considered below. It would be easy otherwise for the corporate governance debate to take on a utilitarian perspective.

V.   ON WHAT PRINCIPLES SHOULD A CHRISTIAN VISION FOR CORPORATE GOVERNANCE BE BASED?

To develop a Christian vision for corporate governance it is essential to first distill those principles on which it is based. This is a difficult task and it can be argued that it is conceptually misfounded.[197] Certainly many Christians would take the view that Christianity does not have an ethical theology as such and that Christianity is about the grace of God in opening up the way to a personal relationship with him through the death and resurrection of Jesus Christ. On that supposition, Christian ethics flow from that relationship and cannot be imposed on others outside of it. The author disagrees with that viewpoint. Firstly, it is submitted that Christian theology contains a coherent and rational set of ethical principles which

[196]   For a general consideration of the impact of employment changes in a relational context, see S. Dex, 'Employment and caring in households' and G. Cox, 'Fiscal and welfare policy: why families lose out', both in *Building a Relational Society, New Priorities for Public Policy*, ed. N. Baker (Arena, 1996).

[197]   See, for example, G.J. Rossouw, 'Where have all the Christians gone?' 13 *Journal of Business Ethics* (1994) 557. He argues against isolating Christian concepts, such as vocation, stewardship and justice from their original context of the reality revealed by God which gives them meaning or alternatively creating moral principles or guidelines from de-contextualized parts of Scripture which thereby become legalistic and lifeless. Instead he argues that Christianity provides a comprehensive understanding of reality which must first be accepted. These arguments have considerable force and this chapter has adopted a similar approach based on principles seen as appropriate to the corporate governance debate as covered in this chapter. L. Christenson *A Charismatic Approach to Social Action* (Lakeland, 1974) goes further, arguing that it is impossible to apply the standard of the Gospel to society at large as it can only be lived through the power of the Holy Spirit (106) and that the world can and will only translate the Gospel into a new law (p. 107). J.M. Bonino, *op. cit.* n.181, 96–97 argues that Scripture contains no abstract ethics but that love, justice and freedom are always embodied in concrete *relationships*, for example, justice to the poor. Emphasis added.

can be justified and which are applicable outside of a faith context provided that the principles which are derived retain their contextual character. Secondly, it is submitted that in a democratic society there is no question of the imposition of these ethical principles which must gain acceptance on their own merits in the ideological marketplace.

Nonetheless, it is also clear that Christian theology does not provide a detailed political programme applicable for all times and all places. Temple distinguished between the role of the church corporately which should frame principles but not policies and the separate political responsibility of Christian individuals.[198] C.S. Lewis said that when Christianity tells you to feed the hungry it does not give you lessons in cookery.[199] It does not provide a detailed political programme for applying to a particular society at a particular moment. Nor is it intended to replace the ordinary human arts and sciences. What this chapter will set out below is a distillation of principles seen as applicable to the corporate governance debate based on a biblical analysis of the nature and purpose of humanity which will form the basis for a Christian vision for corporate governance.

The nature of humanity

a)   *People are inherently unethical.* Christian theology presupposes that people are inherently unethical because of the doctrine of original sin. Questions of high profile scandals, excessive directors' remuneration and corporate ethics do not, therefore, come as a surprise from a Christian perspective. It is likely, therefore, that a Christian perspective on non-legal methods of developing ethics will be cynical and tend to favour a system of legal regulation backed by appropriate sanctions. It is also likely to be cynical on claims to ethicality made by companies or those connected with them. Are they just a marketing ploy? A Christian will also be cynical as to the source of values. Are they relativistic? Are they based on New Age principles? Do they denigrate the uniqueness of man?

b)   *People are of value.* Christian theology presupposes that people are of value, notwithstanding their inherently unethical nature, because they were originally created in the image of God.[200] A Christian perspective on corporate governance will therefore see economics as a servant of mankind rather than his master. An economic analysis or system which results in the devaluing of man to, say, a mere factor of production will be seen as inappropriate and in need of

---

[198] W. Temple, *op. cit.* n.173, Chapter 2.

[199] See *Mere Christianity* (Fontana, 1976) Chapter 3, 75. He was clearly suspicious that Christianity might be used to find support for partisan viewpoints (79).

[200] See Genesis 1:26–27 and also A. McGrath, *op. cit.* n.180, 369–370. A term used to establish the original uprightness and dignity of human nature.

revision. Furthermore, the recognition that all mankind has been created by God in God's image requires this to be reflected in the quality of relationships between people, a theme which is developed below in the context of how long-term relationships may be built. In addition, this principle provides the Christian foundation for the rejection of exploitation and improper discrimination in favour of consultative and participative processes.

The purpose of humanity

a)   *People are intended to live in relationship with God and each other.* Christian theology sees the purpose of people as to live in relationship with God and each other.[201] The centrality of the importance of those relationships is seen in the doctrine of redemption where God is seen in Jesus Christ suffering crucifixion to enable humanity to be reconciled first with God and then with each other.[202] A Christian perspective on corporate governance will therefore be one which would incorporate ethical principles which would strengthen the relationships on which a company is based. The importance of relationships to society is a theme which has been powerfully taken up by Schluter and the Relationships Foundation.[203] He argues that society has a foundation of relationships whose quality and effectiveness determine social well-being, society's 'relational base',[204] but that British politics often appears to arrive at solutions which are primarily economic and not relational.[205] He suggests that the goal of public policy should be the rebuilding of the relational base of the country.[206] The importance

---

[201]   Matthew 22:37–40 (the greatest commandment) presupposes this aim.

[202]   2 Corinthians 5:14–19.

[203]   Considerable work has been, and is being, done by M. Schluter and the Relationships Foundation founded and directed by him on how decisions in public life impact on individual and group relationships. See, further, M. Schluter, '*Building a Relational Society, New Priorities for Public Policy*', ed. N. Baker (Arena, 1996) Chapter 1, 3.

[204]   M. Schluter, *op. cit.* n.203, 8.

[205]   *Ibid.*, 12.

[206]   *Ibid.*, 13. This theme is explored in two chapters which are relevant to this chapter. J. Monks, 'Stakeholders in the workplace (121) considers the question of whether it is still possible to build long-term relationships between workers and employers and explores a 'stakeholder' model of corporate governance (131–132). C. Mather, 'Developing corporate responsibility' (135) argues that the health of the relational base is critical to the success of any enterprise (136) and explores this by reference to both how companies relate to their societal base and also their internal network of relationships (137). This approach provides a useful tool of analysis in assessing much of the corporate governance debate. Many of

of the need for companies to establish long-term relationships, with all stakeholders, founded on loyalty and trust has already been identified in this chapter. It is important, therefore, in developing this theme in this chapter to identify how Christian ethical principles indicate that relationships in a corporate context may be strengthened or damaged.

Central to the building of relationships is the Christian doctrine of love. So much Christian teaching surrounds this principle that it would be impossible to attempt more than a cursory consideration of it here. What follows will be based upon perhaps the best known exposition of the term by Paul.[207] Firstly, it can be seen that love is a matter of substance, not form. Accordingly, the focus is not on the nature of the act but on the motivation. In the context of the corporate governance debate, this is a useful reminder that profit-sacrificing social responsibility or profit optimization in isolation are not adequate, unless corporate culture is also affected. Secondly, it can be seen that love requires transparency. Accordingly, truth is commended whereas boasting, pride and self-seeking are condemned. Thirdly, love requires a positive culture to be adopted, involving kindness, protection, trust and hope. In terms of corporate culture, this indicates a need to move away from legal notions of how obligations are discharged, which may engender a culture where minimal legal compliance is all that is required, to a service culture where the aim is to ensure the satisfaction of the other party. Finally, love is inconsistent with an adversarial culture, involving patience, slowness to anger, keeping no record of wrongs and perseverance. This is particularly significant to the corporate governance debate because it points to some of the essential principles required to move from short-term to long-term relationships. For a relationship to become long-term it must contain a self-correcting mechanism which anticipates the possibility of factors arising which could lead to the breach of that relationship and enables these to be

[206] *cont*

the shortcomings which have been revealed in this debate can be seen to result from a breakdown in the relational base of the company and it is strongly arguable therefore that to be effective the measures taken in response must be those which will bring reconciliation into that relational base and strengthen it. For a fictional account of industry showing the need to value relationships, see D. Lodge *Nice Work* (Penguin, 1988).

[207] 1 Corinthians 13 generally. In particular, vs. 3–7: 'If I give all I possess to the poor . . . but have not love, I gain nothing. Love is patient, love is kind. It does not envy, it does not boast, it is not proud. It is not rude, it is not self-seeking, it is not easily angered, it keeps no record of wrongs. Love does not delight in evil but rejoices with the truth. It always protects, always trusts, always hopes, always perseveres.'

resolved so that the relationship is continued. The approach based on love is one which recognizes that problems will arise but that this should not form the basis for the termination of the relationship. Furthermore, it becomes unlikely that litigation will be an appropriate vehicle for redress because this may be totally destructive of any relationship.

There are clearly a number of objections to these principles which can be anticipated. They are, like all universal principles, general in nature and therefore require further consideration in the context of how they could be applied in a commercial setting. They may seem naïve and perhaps fail to adequately recognize the unethical tendency of mankind, a principle identified above. For this reason it is accepted that regulation and mechanisms for redress must remain. Nonetheless, it is submitted that these principles are an essential framework for establishing a Christian vision for corporate governance.

b) *People are trustees and managers of God's creation.* Christian theology sees the purpose of mankind to be responsible for God's creation. The basis of this is the doctrine of creation which culminated in God's blessing of mankind, followed by the commandment 'be fruitful and increase in number, fill the earth and subdue it. Rule over . . . [the animal kingdom]. . . .'[208] This can be summed up in the notions of trusteeship, in the sense that mankind does not enjoy absolute rights of ownership over creation, and management, in the sense that mankind possesses an active role in relation to the creation. The concept is often traditionally summed up by the use of the term 'stewardship' but this has not been adopted here as it is a term less frequently encountered in everyday usage. There are a number of important implications which flow from this.

Firstly, the world is intended to be sufficient for mankind's needs and therefore there should be no justification for poverty or starvation. Nonetheless, the consequences of mankind's sinfulness are that a livelihood may only be had by hard work.[209] Notwithstanding this, it is clear that God's ideal for mankind was that there should be more than bare subsistence. After Israel received the Ten Commandments it was promised that obedience would enable them to 'prosper'.[210] When Israel was promised a land to possess, it was to be a land 'flowing with milk and honey'.[211] Similarly, the

---

[208] Genesis 1:28. This clearly has relevance to the environmental responsibilities of companies, see further D. Harte 'A Christian Approach to Environmental Law?' above, 00 *et seq.*

[209] Genesis 3:17–19.

[210] Deuteronomy 5:33.

[211] See, for example, Deuteronomy 8:7–9.

New Testament recognizes this principle.[212] This must not be confused with the mistaken notion of the prosperity gospel[213] which argues that if Christian principles are followed then material success *will* necessarily follow. This is to confuse the working of secular and spiritual principles. It is also the mistake of many of those who try to argue for the ethical company.[214] The rationale for a Christian vision is to do what is right not what is more successful, although it is to be anticipated that in the normal course of things doing what is right will be more successful as it is part of God's natural ordering of things.

Secondly, there arises the principle of accountability, a principle which should manifest itself in generosity. God has given freely to mankind[215] and therefore mankind should give freely in return. Mankind does not have an absolute title to the earth and its resources. They are held from God, and mankind is accountable to God for their use. The notion of trusteeship and managerial status challenges any view that humanity is the master of its own destiny and accountable to no-one but itself. Christian theology acknowledges that there will always be the poor.[216] However, it does not accept this with a degree of fatalism. Instead, it sees it as providing an opportunity for the wealthy to give generously and as a result set themselves free from the tyranny of wealth.

c) *People should receive and deliver justice.* The concept of justice[217] is at the heart of Christian theology and forms a central theme of God's dealings with mankind and mankind's dealings with itself. Firstly,

---

[211] See, for example, Deuteronomy 8:7–9.

[212] Mark 6:30–44 (feeding of the five thousand) where there was a surplus, John 2:1–11 (turning of water into wine) where the wine was of superior quality, Philippians 4:10–13 (contentment in plenty or in want). Note also the careful emphasis in the teaching on worry in Luke 12:31.

[213] Described by the Rt. Rev. R. Harries, 'The morality of good business', *Business Strategy Review*, Spring 1993, 91 as '. . . the vulgar and dangerous doctrine that if only we put our trust in the Lord we will automatically prosper in material terms'.

[214] Nonetheless, Smythe, Dorward and Reback, *Corporate Reputation: Managing the New Strategic Asset* (Century, 1993) is cited by R. Sparkes, *op. cit.* n.3, 225 as showing that a survey of the top 500 of America's corporations showed that two-thirds listed in 1956 have disappeared and that only 29 of the biggest 100 were still there a working life later. He noted the author's conclusions that the survivors were companies with a strong moral core.

[215] A theme echoed in God's gift of his son, Christ, to suffer crucifixion for the sake of mankind, in the New Testament.

[216] See Deuteronomy 15:11; compare Matthew 26:11.

[217] Jurisprudential and philosophical interpretations of this term are outside the scope of this chapter, which is limited to an application of biblical norms to the corporate governance debate.

justice is an attribute of God's own character, closely associated with the absolute rectitude of the moral standards with which he acts. God is seen, therefore, as known by his justice,[218] loving justice[219] and having justice as the foundations of his throne.[220] Secondly, justice is an expectation of those with power to make decisions affecting others, which is particularly important in the case of rulers[221] and judges[222] but also mankind generally.[223] Thirdly, if mankind's decision-making leads to injustice then God may be called upon to intervene to provide justice.[224] True justice can be perverted, for example by the use of wealth,[225] or denied.[226] Those who are aliens,[227] those who are oppressed[228] and those who are poor[229] are especially vulnerable to this. Even when so-called justice is meted out by the courts in accordance with the law,[230] God's standards of justice may be offended. These propositions clearly have wide social implications since the moral standards that God has set out themselves have social implications. They also have eschatological implications.

These principles have the following relevance to the corporate governance debate. The decision-making processes of both companies, and their stakeholders, must be governed with justice and therefore have reference to an absolute moral framework. The outworking of this has largely been considered in the context of relationships in the company, above. However, given the unethical nature of mankind, combined with the ability of companies to accumulate wealth, and therefore in a sense power, which may be used in an oppressive manner, it is important that there is strong legal regulation to prevent the abuse of corporate power. Much the same applies to the power that particular stakeholder groups may possess, and so it is important that a balance is achieved between them.

[218] See Psalm 9:16.
[219] See Psalm 11:7.
[220] See Psalm 89:14.
[221] See Proverbs 29:4.
[222] See Amos 5:15.
[223] See Micah 6:8.
[224] See Psalm 140:12.
[225] See 1 Samuel 8:3.
[226] See Proverbs 18:5.
[227] See Malachi 3:5, where this is categorized as attracting God's judgment alongside such matters as sorcery, adultery, perjury and defrauding labourers of wages.
[228] See Amos 2:7.
[229] See Amos 5:12.
[230] See Amos 6:12

VI. WHAT IS THE CHRISTIAN VISION FOR CORPORATE GOVERNANCE?

This chapter has now considered the shortcomings revealed by the corporate governance debate, argued for the validity of a Christian perspective on this and attempted to establish the principles on which a Christian vision for corporate governance should be based. This section will outline the possible form a Christian vision for corporate governance might take. The term 'stakeholder'has been used unashamedly throughout this section because, it is submitted, it best reflects the way in which the various groups concerned with the company should be regarded from a Christian perspective.

A Christian vision for the company

This paper has identified that there is a lack of consensus, both in economic terms and in legal terms as to the purpose of the company. The following propositions are submitted as the basis of a Christian vision for the company:

a) *That the role of the company forms part of an integrated Christian vision for society as a whole.* One of the insights that the study of corporate governance has provided has been to move away from a narrow focus on the traditional model of the company as a separate legal person run by its officers to a wider and inclusive focus on the company as comprising groups of stakeholders, extending to local communities and the general public. This insight is important to developing a Christian vision for corporate governance because it emphasizes that the company is truly a part of society and not separate from it. The recognition of the interaction between the company and society is important when considering how to evaluate the shortcomings which the corporate governance debate has revealed. Companies, seen as part of society, should substantially at least reflect the values of the society of which they are part and so a critique of corporate values may well lead to a critique of the values of society as a whole. Some of the shortcomings revealed by the corporate governance debate may provide evidence that corporate values are out of step in some areas with those of society but may equally simply indicate a society which is less than happy with its own values. For example, it is questionable that the public outcry over excessive directors' remuneration reflects a society which eschews materialism when there is abundant evidence to the contrary. It may simply reflect an intuitive sense of injustice. A Christian vision for corporate governance should not be seen as in any way separate from a Christian vision for society as a whole and is incapable of fulfilment in isolation. Christian theology recognizes no distinction between business and personal ethics. Equally, Christians need to capture a vision for corporate governance. It is not merely an important secular debate but one which raises important issues of a spiritual nature. How the churches respond will be an important indicator of how they see their relationship with society more generally. Christians must be able to put forward solutions that are grounded in sound research. Corporate governance presents complex problems, particularly where ethics arise, and Christians must develop an appropriate response. There is much scope for multidisciplinary co-operation between academics researching in law, business and theology. Christians should work to seek to implement reform. They should engage with the secular debates for law reform; they should use their influence as stakeholders within the system so that their votes are exercised, through their pension plans and through their purchasing power. They should engage with others with similar objectives though they must be careful of being led by secular trends, for example, in relation to ethical investment, where there may be inconsistencies with Christian principles. Christians should develop a greater role in education and training for ethical corporate governance. Christians have established management consultancies and participate in business conferences. Christian companies, owned by and managed by Christians, have in the past made a major impact by their example. More new companies set up with the same vision are needed.

b) *That the true purpose of the company is to serve the needs of society as a whole.* One of the profound questions being asked as part of the corporate governance debate is what the purpose of the company really is, or ought to be. The traditional model of the company has resulted in a narrow focus upon the return provided to the providers of finance, whether in terms of the distribution of profits to shareholders or in terms of the payment of capital/interest to secured lenders, with the substantial advantages that such security can confer. Christian theology has long taken the view that the purpose of the company, or indeed any form of business organization, is to meet the needs of society for goods and services whilst meeting the needs of those that provide them. This recognizes the need for profit but places the focus on the benefit to society as a whole. This also recognizes a democratic imperative, that it would be absurd for an artificial creation of society, the company, to be permitted to survive and thrive whilst not meeting the needs of society. One problem that this presents at present is that there is little or no incentive to recognize wider objectives than profit maximization. This is not least because of the present form of financial reporting and auditing which is almost exclusively geared to financial measures of performance. To refocus the purpose of the company and those responsible for its affairs requires a change to wider forms of accountability that focus on a broader understanding of the objectives of the company.

The example of those companies which have voluntarily adopted social reporting and auditing is a useful one in attempting to formulate a new model. These approaches may also suggest an answer to the question as to how to achieve wider stakeholder involvement in the corporate structure. The anticipated response is that it would only represent an additional cost to a company and furthermore not be information of any value to shareholders. This assumes that investment decisions are motivated towards short-term profits only and there is growing evidence to refute this, not least the move towards ethical investment. This also assumes that the wider information disclosed would not have any financial implications. This may be incorrect if wider information throws light on, say, ethical matters which have a bearing on a company's long-term prospects.

c)   *That the goal of each company should be profit-sacrificing social responsibility/ profit optimization and not profit maximization.* One further question which the corporate governance debate has highlighted has been whether the goal of a company should be profit maximization or some other goal. This paper has identified that profit maximization is essentially a behavioural theory. It can certainly be argued that it has also become, in effect, a slogan, used to justify corporate profit-seeking devoid of an ethical context. The legitimacy of profit maximization is seen as being that it should lead to wealth maximization in society as a whole. However, this chapter has also identified that although company *law* does not expressly set any particular goal for the company in terms of profit maximization, a combination of principles may effectively achieve this result by limiting the scope for non-profit-maximizing behaviour. Christian theology does not support the goal of profit maximization. Firstly, profit maximization may well equate with avarice, or greed, which is condemned because of the attitude towards others which it engenders, and is not regarded as legitimized by wealth maximization. Secondly, the principle of giving runs through both the Old Testament and the New Testament, commended both because of the beneficial effect on the recipient, the poor, but equally, because of the beneficial effect on the giver. Accordingly, Christian theology would support any move to substitute as the goal of the company that of profit-sacrificing social responsibility or profit optimization. One obstacle must be overcome, however. That is the reasonable argument that any degree of corporate social responsibility which affects profits or involves corporate philanthropy is, in effect, theft from the shareholders, or, in the UK context, a tax on pensioners, whose pension funds depend on institutional corporate investment. It could equally be seen as potentially diminishing the availability of funds for payment of employee remuneration, potentially jeopardizing the payment of creditors and potentially leading to higher prices for consumers. Firstly, there is no question of compulsion, which would frustrate the purpose of the suggestion and turn it into another form of taxation. Secondly, decisions on this must be taken with the involvement of all the stakeholders in a company and not merely by its directors, as this chapter has identified earlier. Thirdly, the sums involved would not necessarily have any material impact on the position of stakeholders, for example, on dividend levels in the context of a large company (an argument which has been used to defend high levels of directors' remuneration).

A Christian vision for company law

This chapter has identified that there is a lack of consensus as to both the purpose and values of company law but also the need to consider the way in which other legal requirements impact upon corporate behaviour. This chapter has also looked at the considerable range of measures being undertaken on a self-regulatory or voluntary basis. The Christian vision for company law set out below is based on the need for the law to play a role. That is not to say that self-regulatory or voluntary measures are regarded as of no value. They have a significant effect in enabling innovation, flexibility in changing circumstances and an improvement in standards. It is inevitable that some companies will seek higher standards than others. In considering the role of law this chapter is considering what should be the minimum mandatory standards for all companies.

The following propositions are submitted as a basis of a Christian vision for company law:

a) *That the nature of mankind is such that effective legal regulation of the activities of the company is required.* Amongst the shortcomings revealed by the corporate governance debate is the perception that the legal regulation of companies and their directors is insufficient to protect those who are affected and that this has been manifested in high-profile scandals, excessive directors' remuneration and poor corporate ethics generally. As this chapter has identified, all these are complex issues. Accordingly, a cautious approach must be adopted in attempting to arrive at a solution. Firstly, it has been seen that the legal regulation of the business activities of companies is fragmented, with only a small proportion being contained in the companies' legislation, the rest being contained, for example, in environmental or other legislation designed to protect a wide range of interests. Such legislation is often designed to regulate the activities not simply of companies but other businesses and organizations. Accordingly, it would seem reasonable to assume that the adequacy of such regulation or otherwise is not a problem specific to companies. What may well be more problematic is the effectiveness of certain types of sanction in a corporate context, for example, criminal sanctions. Secondly, the debate on company law has resulted in few calls for additional regulation, in fact, the converse. It is widely believed that much of the regulatory function of company law amounts to using a sledgehammer to crack a nut. In addition, there is a growing proliferation of voluntary measures, often taking the form of codes of conduct. From a Christian perspective, this chapter has identified the principle that mankind is inherently unethical and therefore legal constraints are normally to be preferred over voluntary constraints. Furthermore, if a clear vision for company law can be identified, it may be possible to avoid additional regulation and provide a simpler regulatory framework.

b) *That the role of company law in establishing the values necessary to build long-term relationships should be recognized and reviewed.* One of the problems identified has been the need to build the foundations for long-term relationships into corporate governance, both at a secular level and also from the basis of Christian theology. The question arises as to whether company law provides an adequate foundation in terms of values, despite the volume and complexity of regulation. Company law is, of course, based upon values, even if they are generally obscured. At the risk of gross oversimplification, these values often involve a balancing exercise between competing principles, for example, sanctity of contract as against the role of regulation; democratic decision-making by a majority as against the protection of a minority. Such values have some support in Christian principle. One strength of the contract model is the assumption that the law should enforce agreements freely entered into, which is supported by the Christian principle of justice. The contract model also necessitates and supports one or more *relationships*; this is not the quintessential purpose of property rights, and, for example, the implications of the categorization of a share as personal property merits further examination. Similarly the notion of democracy is supported by Christian principles, not least, because of the way it reflects the value of mankind. Nonetheless, questions can and should be raised as to whether these apparent values are supported by Christian principles at a deeper level. What is found in company law is democracy measured by reference to wealth, in the sense of the proportion of shares held. The position of a majority shareholder, therefore, has the potential not to be democratic but oppressive instead. There is a need to test such values carefully and to consider whether Christian principles, for example, as to the value of long-term relationships can be incorporated or substituted.

A Christian vision for corporate structure

This chapter has identified a lack of consensus as to corporate structure firstly as to the growing divergence between the appropriateness of the classical form of corporate structure for larger and smaller companies and, secondly, the growing pressures for a wider recognition of other stakeholders, in terms of employee participation deriving from EC harmonization and more generally deriving from notions of corporate social responsibility. The following propositions are submitted as the basis of a Christian vision for corporate structure:

a) *That corporate structure should encourage the development of long-term relationships between the stakeholders in the company.* A Christian perspective on shareholding, directorship, employment and other dealings with a company sees the status as relationship-based, whatever the legal form, because of the high value placed on mankind. The acquisition of a share in a company is accordingly not merely regarded as the acquisition of property but the commencement of a relationship both with other shareholders and the directors, on the basis of the current model. The acceptance of a directorship is regarded as a crucial matter, because the directors of a company are the focus of relationships with all other interests, again, on the basis of the current model. The position of employees and others will very much depend on the particular circumstances but the relationship may well be weak, certainly in terms of a voice in the company. Once it has been recognized that participation in a company represents the creation of a relationship, rather than, for example, simply a property interest, then one threshold question which must be addressed from a Christian perspective is whether it is appropriate to enter a particular relationship at all. Some relationships, of course, are more voluntary than others. Potential shareholders often have considerable freedom of choice whereas a potential employee may not. Commitment to a relationship should involve a moral dimension greater than the likely financial return. The corporate governance debate has identified that one problem in corporate governance may be poor relationships between the stakeholders in the company and the need to improve these relationships on a long-term basis. It is possible that short-term relationships not built on trust and loyalty may involve higher transaction costs, for example, the legal costs of dispute-resolution. This chapter has identified above that the key to building long-term relationships is the Christian concept of love. In this context, this must involve genuine motivation and not mere form, transparency, the adoption of a positive culture, based on service, and the rejection of an adversarial culture. It is immediately clear that these may not be objectives which can simply be achieved by the adoption of regulation backed by appropriate sanctions. A more fundamental approach is required. It is submitted that this might be achieved by the removal of the barriers which exist in a company to effective relationships.

b) *The structure of the company must be reformed so that it no longer exists for the principal benefit of the shareholders alone.* Under UK company law shareholders enjoy powers which are disproportionate to their contribution. For example, they have the power to wind up a company, to control the composition of the board of directors, to change its constitution, as well as the principal supervisory role. Notwithstanding this, many shareholders' only contribution to a company is the purchase of shares and receipt of dividends. The role of institutional investors must also come under scrutiny. The question, therefore, becomes one of whether other groups should have greater involvement in the company and, if so, how might this be achieved. From a Christian perspective it is desirable that the mutual value of those involved in a company be recognized, whether by consultation or participation. There has been considerable controversy over the involvement of employees. There are a number of potential ways by which this might be achieved. Employees might participate at an operational level, ranging from schemes for consultation to board membership. Alternatively, or in addition, employees might be encouraged to become shareholders, either individually or collectively. The former possibility is relatively straightforward to legislate for, the latter is more likely to be (and is) encouraged either by employer benevolence or fiscal incentives. The former is more likely to give rise to conflicts of interest and confidentiality whereby the employee director may have difficulty choosing between loyalty to the company and fellow employees. From a Christian perspective it is also desirable that long-term relationships are built up with others with whom there are business dealings. As in the case of employees there are strong arguments against board involvement. Similarly, shareholding may be encouraged although it might be argued against this that the cost would outweigh the voice achieved, especially in dealings with large companies. A case may also be made for the involvement of the community on behalf of wider social and environmental interests.

The present UK corporate model is however unsuitable for the purpose of increasing democratic participation in the company with its sharp division between shareholders and directors, and the perception of an ineffective shareholder voice. One solution to this would be the creation of a supervisory committee of shareholders to exercise a more effective role than the company in general meeting is capable of doing. In fact, this leads to a model rather similar to the two-tier board structure originally sought as part of EC harmonization which the UK has so consistently rejected at least prior to the Labour election victory in 1997. This would be particularly effective if the composition of shareholders was to represent employee and other interests to a greater extent, and in fact an increase in shareholder voice might provide an incentive for this. This is particularly important as the Christian basis for adopting this approach is to ensure that long-term relationships are built by removing the barriers to these. It is not to replace the dominance of one stakeholder group with that of another. Organizations orientated to producer/community needs may well provide a poor and expensive service. The goal of the company must remain the service of society as a whole.

c) *That corporate structure should ensure that all stakeholders receive a return which adequately reflects their contribution to the company.* Concern over directors' remuneration levels has been one of the most prominent features of the corporate governance debate and certainly one of the issues to attract regular headline news coverage. It is also one which raises substantial issues of principle from a Christian perspective. Firstly, Christianity recognizes the inherently unethical nature of mankind such that it is thoroughly to be expected that if there are inadequate controls over directors' remuneration then it is likely that directors would take advantage of the situation and also resist any change. Secondly, it raises the question of the value of mankind. To say that in the UK a director is entitled on average to 33 times the wage of the average industrial worker as noted earlier, recognizes such a differential as to devalue the contribution of the latter. Thirdly, it raises the question of relationships. Such a differential in remuneration places in jeopardy the relationship between directors and employees because, as this chapter has identified, self-seeking is inconsistent with the positive culture required for building relationships. Fourthly, such unjustified differentials in remuneration contravene the notion of mankind's trusteeship and management of creation because it represents an attempt to take an unjustified proportion of a creation intended for the benefit of mankind generally. Finally, there is the question of justice. This chapter has identified that Christian theology does not condemn wealth in itself but rather the attitudes that it can engender, such as hard-heartedness towards the poor extending even to outright exploitation. In so far as these may result in injustice they are of concern to God. The principle from a Christian perspective is that each of the stakeholders concerned with a company is entitled to a just return for their services. This chapter has identified the difficulties that have been encountered in attempting to solve this problem and that the general approach that has been adopted, in the case of directors' remuneration, has been to encourage greater disclosure and the involvement of remuneration committees composed of non-executive directors. There are reservations as to whether such measures are likely to succeed. Perhaps the suggestion most likely to succeed would be if it were possible to recreate market forces with the legitimacy they confer. It has been suggested above that there are good reasons from a Christian perspective to enhance

democratic participation in the company in any event and it is
suggested that these measures themselves may enable the creation
of an effective control over directors' remuneration, as these might
bring to bear the views of a wider range of interests, less likely to
be sympathetic to arguments for higher remuneration.

VII. HOW CAN LAW REFORM HELP THE REALIZATION OF THIS VISION?

It is quite possible that some of the Christian vision for corporate
governance set out above could be achieved without the need for
substantial law reform. Improvements in corporate governance have
already been made by voluntary and self-regulatory means. Yet the
process is slow and may not succeed in satisfying public demands for
reform, particularly over matters such as directors' remuneration which
have reached levels widely regarded as unacceptable and which are not
likely to fall. It would be inappropriate in this chapter to attempt detailed
proposals for law reform. Instead, it will seek to set out briefly what the
objectives of law reform might be, based on the Christian vision for
corporate governance set out above.

The reform of corporate governance must be part of a wider reform
of UK law aimed at restoring Christian foundations to UK society.
Some of the problems which afflict corporate governance, for example,
self-seeking materialism, are endemic to a society which no longer
shares a common Christian set of values. The focus of reform needs to
be the framework of corporate governance applicable to listed companies because they form such an important part of that society. The
principal method adopted is to attempt to reduce the legal barriers
between effective relationships in the company. In terms of company
law, the focus of law reform should be on the identification and
evaluation of the values which do and should underpin it, prior to more
detailed reform.

Firstly, company law should redefine the purpose of a company
(perhaps along the lines of the proposals of the American Law Institute
mentioned earlier) so that the focus is on the benefit to society. This is a
difficult task because company law does not at present focus on abstract
concepts and this would need to be reflected by a variety of changes in
terms of directors' powers and duties and shareholder and creditor
protection. Such changes would need to permit and require the directors
to take into account a wider range of interests than those of the company
as a separate legal entity. They should also permit philanthropy by the
company, subject to an appropriate framework for this to be regulated
by law to protect against abuse and provide suitable shareholder supervision. These changes would be supported by expanding the financial
reporting and audit requirements to encompass a range of non-financial

matters relevant to assessing how the company was satisfying its obligations to society generally. These would need to be carefully designed to ensure comparability between companies and objectivity. Some types of information would lend themselves naturally to this, for example, details of regulatory breaches and their effect; others would be more difficult to assess, for example, the culture of employment relations.

Secondly, company law should redefine the structure of a company so that barriers to effective relationships are reduced by encouraging greater participation by shareholders in the supervision of management. The present structure with its division between the roles and responsibilities of board and shareholders has proven to be unsatisfactory in practice for this purpose, not least because of the unsuitability of the general meeting for shareholders to exercise their powers but also the role played by institutional shareholders. There is much merit in the development of a supervisory committee of shareholder representatives to scrutinize the board rather than for scrutiny to be provided by non-executive directors. For example, only negotiations between shareholder representatives and the board over remuneration are likely to replicate the operations of an open market. Clearly, such a proposal bears considerable resemblance to the EC two-tier board structure and there may be merit to revisiting that. In terms of encouraging mutual supervision of directors there is much to be said for the partnership model of joint and several liability, in the case of directors for breaches of duty rather than for liabilities generally. Clearly, again, this bears resemblance to EC proposals. Equally, the role of institutional shareholders should be examined to reduce the barriers to effective relationships between the beneficiaries and those who invest funds on their behalf.

Thirdly company law, combined with other legal measures, should further aim to remove barriers to effective relationships by aiming to encourage shareholding amongst a wider range of stakeholder groups. There are already a range of schemes to encourage employee share ownership involving fiscal incentives. The increased shareholder voice that a revised corporate structure might provide may also serve to encourage this for other groups.

These measures should additionally aim to facilitate long-term relationships within the company structure. There may be some merit in a re-examination of the consequences of categorizing a share as personal property with the non-relational connotations that ownership conveys. There is also much to be said for a re-evaluation of the role of the contractual basis for the company and whether this might be remodelled to provide greater support for long-term relationships. Measures could be taken to discourage short-term passive shareholding, which is again non-relational in nature, possibly by a combination of fiscal measures and by imposing an obligation to vote at general meetings.

VIII.   CONCLUSIONS

The debate on corporate governance should be welcomed by Christians. Issues that it raises, such as the purpose of the company, how companies should be regulated and structured, corporate scandals and ethics, are issues that Christians have been attempting to address for some time. Christians have to date been divided as to how to apply Christian theology to the company, some condemning capitalism outright as founded on a profit motivation equating to greed, and others desiring a reformed capitalism with others preferring to concentrate on other issues. The approach adopted in this chapter has been to argue that Christian theology is capable of being applied so as to reform the company.

The debate on corporate governance raises a real possibility of the goal of the company being reformed to the wider service of the community with a greater democratic mandate and supervision by the community. This reform might go some way towards resolving concerns over corporate scandals, directors' remuneration and corporate ethics. A growing number of companies are transforming themselves in this direction voluntarily and the law should help this.

Perhaps in a hundred years or so the debate on corporate governance will be as redundant as past debates over the ethics of slavery, the use of child chimney sweeps, discrimination and so on. All of these debates have turned around the same essential question: profit or principle? Principle has invariably won over profit eventually. Corporate governance unfortunately presents more difficult issues to resolve; it cannot simply be dealt with by the abolition of a particular form of conduct but rather by the changing of more complex patterns of behaviour. Against reform is pitted the fear of economic disaster. However, those who have prophesied economic disaster in the past have been proven wrong time and time again. Perhaps from a Christian perspective the exercise will be disappointing. New problems may well arise which will require a response because of the inherently imperfect nature of humanity. A Christian perspective therefore would see the only real answer as being for society to return to God through a personal relationship with Jesus Christ, the outworking of that in the lives of all those involved and the ultimate creation of a new heaven and new earth.